D1372722

The Experimental Impulse in George Meredith's Fiction

The Experimental Impulse in George Meredith's Fiction

Richard C. Stevenson

Lewisburg
Bucknell University Press

Associated University Presses
2010 Eastpark Boulevard
Cranbury, NJ 08512

I wish to acknowledge permission granted to use revised material from the following:

"Comedy, Tragedy, and the Spirit of Critical Intelligence in *Richard Feverel*," by Richard C. Stevenson, from *Harvard English Studies* 6: 205–222, edited by Jerome Hamilton Buckley. Copyright © 1975 by the President and Fellows of Harvard College.

"George Meredith: 1828–1909" and *"The Ordeal of Richard Feverel* by George Meredith," by Richard C. Stevenson, copyright © 1998 from *Encyclopedia of The Novel,* edited by Paul Schellinger, 934–35; 964–65. Reproduced by permission of Routledge/Taylor & Francis Books, Inc.

"Innovations of Comic Method in George Meredith's *Evan Harrington*," by Richard C. Stevenson, from *Texas Studies in Literature and Language* 15: 313–314. Copyright © 1973 by the University of Texas Press. All rights reserved.

"Laetitia Dale and the Comic Spirit in *The Egoist*," by Richard C. Stevenson, from *Nineteenth-Century Fiction* 26: 406–18. Copyright © 1972 UC Press, Journals Division.

"Lord Ormont and His Aminta and *The Amazing Marriage*," by Barbara Hardy, from *Meredith Now: Some Critical Essays,* edited by Ian Fletcher, 296–97. Reproduced by permission of Thomson Publishing Services. Copyright © 1971.

The paper used in this publication meets the requirements of the American National Standard for Permanence of Paper for Printed Library Materials Z39.48-1984.

Library of Congress Cataloging-in-Publication Data

Stevenson, Richard C., 1939–
    The experimental impulse in George Meredith's fiction / Richard C. Stevenson.
        p. cm.
    Includes bibliographical references and index.
    ISBN 0-8387-5575-5 (alk. paper)
        1. Meredith, George, 1828–1909—Technique.   2. Experimental fiction, English—History and criticism.   3. Fiction—Technique.   I. Title.
    PR5017.T4S74   2004
    823'.8—dc22   2004002994

PRINTED IN THE UNITED STATES OF AMERICA

For Laura Jane

Contents

Acknowledgments

I FEEL A STRONG SENSE OF GRATITUDE TO MY EARLIEST MENTORS IN LIT-erary studies—in particular, Jerome Hamilton Buckley, Robert Kiely, Richard Poirier, and Edgar Rosenberg—all of whom continue to exert a distinct influence on how I read a text. I am also grateful to colleagues in the Department of English at the University of Oregon for generous support and encouragement over the years I was working on this book. First among these is Donald Taylor, who was good enough to read the earliest version of the manuscript in its entirety and to offer helpful and timely advice that allowed me to continue the project with renewed energy and purpose. Later in the process Paul Peppis, Ian Duncan, and Dick Stein all provided useful commentary on various parts of the manuscript, aiding me in moving it beyond the beta stage. And along the way Karen Ford, Harry Wonham, John Gage, and Warren Ginsberg all contributed to a belief in the project while also providing a sense of intellectual community that was truly gratifying and sustaining. Graduate student Joan Herman worked on the bibliography at just the point help was needed, and I am much indebted to my students at the University of Oregon, past and present, for their contributions to my thinking about the art of fiction.

I want to acknowledge the support of the National Endowment for the Humanities and the University of Oregon Center for the Study of Women in Society for financial aid in the earlier stages of this project, and I am also most grateful to Christine Retz, managing editor, and Elizabeth Ricciardelli, production editor, at Associated University Presses for their patient and skillful help in seeing this book through its final stages. Copyeditor Pat Lichen did a wonderful job in clarifying several stylistic issues.

I have long been fascinated by George Meredith's uneasy presence in Victorian letters, and consequently this study sometimes borrows or produces echoes from material I have previously published on the subject, some of it recent, some not so recent. I am indebted to *Encyclopedia of the Novel, Harvard English Studies,*

9

Nineteenth-Century Fiction, and *Texas Studies in Literature and Language* for permission to use revised material from essays published under their copyright. In addition, I am grateful to the publishers of *Meredith Now: Some Critical Essays* for permission to use an extended quotation from an essay by Barbara Hardy in my chapter on *Lord Ormont and His Aminta.*

Finally, I want to extend my warm thanks to Linda Rose and Eldon Haines for their extraordinary friendship and persistent support of this project, to Beth Duncan for expressing such a strong interest in it, and, most of all, to my wife Laura, without whose love, resilience, and ability to attend to matters non-Meredithian this book would never have been completed.

The Experimental Impulse
in George Meredith's
Fiction

Introduction

[The Ordeal of Richard Feverel] goes on so so. Everything I do is an Experiment, and till it's done, I never know whether 'tis worth a farthing.

George Meredith to Eyre Crowe, 4 January 1858[1]

IN THIS BOOK I ARGUE THAT GEORGE MEREDITH AS A WRITER OF VICTORian fiction is most important and interesting for us today in the way he wrote against—or beyond—convention, convention taken to mean novelistic tradition as well as that compendium of attitudes and values we associate with Victorian culture. The French critic Abel Chevalley, writing in *Le Roman anglais de notre temps* in 1921, produces a useful early twentieth-century perspective of Meredith's position in relation to Victorian convention by comparing him, when still in the first decade of his publishing career, with his mid-century contemporaries. Musing on the fact that both *The Ordeal of Richard Feverel* and *Adam Bede* were published in 1859, Chevalley notes that

> Nothing is more deceptive than dates. . . . Dickens and Thackeray, the Brontës and George Eliot, all were locked in a debate with their age [while] Meredith had already gone beyond it. English novelists between 1840 and 1870 were all struggling with the compromises and conventions of Victorian civilization. Meredith had prematurely escaped from all that. On the subjects of the economic and moral life, the relations of the sexes, the conditions of marriage, even the meaning of human existence, he had . . . gone ahead by at least fifty years.[2]

My focus in this study will be on those novels that most clearly illuminate the experimental and transgressive impulse in Meredith, as seen in his treatment of controversial contemporary themes—like those mentioned by Chevalley—in his departures from conventions of genre, and in his innovations with narrative technique and the representation of consciousness. These are novels that had a profoundly stimulating effect on many of those canonical writers we now associate with the first wave of modernism

13

in the English novel. James, and then Woolf, Forster, Lawrence, Conrad, Ford, and Joyce, to varying degrees, all saw Meredith as an influence to be reckoned with, for better or worse, in their own novelistic experiments.

Virginia Woolf's assessment of Meredith's impact on her generation[3] is of particular interest for our purposes because she, like Chevalley, so clearly recognized his role not only as a questioner but also as a disrupter of tradition, along with all the liabilities that such a role involves. In "The Novels of George Meredith," an essay first published on the centenary of his birth (1928), she takes his extraordinary first novel, *The Ordeal of Richard Feverel*, as primary evidence that Meredith was writing against novelistic convention: "He has been, it is plain, at great pains to destroy the conventional form of the novel. He makes no attempt to preserve the sober reality of Trollope and Jane Austen; he has destroyed all the usual staircases by which we have learnt to climb."

What Woolf is particularly interested in here is technique— Meredith's jettisoning of many of the traditional narrative strategies that had become the staples of nineteenth-century realism, with its stylistic immersion in quotidian detail and implied provision of a simulacrum of the "actual" world. This sacrifice of "the usual staircases," what Woolf also calls Meredith's "defiance of the ordinary,"[4] contributes to much of what is both fascinating and, at times, maddening about his work:

> [I]f fiction had remained what it was to Jane Austen and Trollope, fiction would by this time be dead. Thus Meredith deserves our gratitude and excites our interest as a great innovator. Many of our doubts about him and much of our inability to frame any definite opinion of his work comes from the fact that it is experimental and thus contains elements that do not fuse harmoniously. . . . We must not expect the perfect quietude of a traditional style nor the triumphs of a patient and pedestrian psychology.[5]

The experimental impulse Woolf describes in Meredith found expression in a variety of ways, both thematic and technical, and his escape from the quietude of traditional narrative style is an attribute all of his readers will recognize at once. This is a style that involves "lyrical intensity"[6]—at times anticipating Woolf herself— along with the kind of self-consciousness and artifice often associated with modernist work. But it is also wise to keep in mind that "modernist" is not necessarily synonymous with "twentieth-century." As Richard Poirier has aptly noted, "features thought to be unique to twentieth-century literary modernism are to be found, often with corresponding evidences of cultural disenchantment, nearly everywhere in English literature."[7] The experimental and questioning impulse I am describing in Meredith is as much an innovative state of mind—that we find, say, in Sterne's narrative play with Lockean notions of duration or Radcliffe's reinvocation of romance as a narrative genre[8]—as it is an anticipatory leap into the twentieth century, as Chevalley claims. In fact, from a political perspective one can argue, as Neil Roberts has done, that Meredith "was the precursor of a modernism that never happened in [Britain]—a liberal, socially committed modernism."[9]

No matter how we may situate "modernism," however, our encounters with the experimental, transgressive, and re-evaluative qualities associated with the term are inescapable in Meredith's narratives. I am suggesting qualities here that both include and extend well beyond the attributes that Suzanne Keen has associated with what she calls "narrative annexes" in Victorian fiction—constructions whereby novelists briefly move "the plot-line across a boundary. . . . [to] challenge both cultural and literary norms." Keen is careful to situate such tactics as both forward- and backward-looking:

> Victorian annexes simultaneously anticipate the fragmentation associated with modern fiction, and resemble the flexible worldmaking of prose fiction before the novel. . . . Narrative annexes are sites of Victorian novelists' negotiation with the conventional, and as such they reveal not only the effort to employ alternative representational strategies, but also the subjects that instigate that effort.[10]

Keen's criteria for narrative annexes—brief alterations in genre and setting linked with depictions of literal transgressions of boundaries that in turn produce a significant impact upon the kernal plot—are characteristics we find repeatedly in Meredith's fiction. But herein also lies a strategic difference between Meredith and other nineteenth-century novelists—like Charlotte Brontë, Dickens, Disraeli, Hardy, Kingsley, and Trollope—on whom Keen focuses her attention: Meredith tends to extend his transgressive tactics well beyond the brief annexed moments of "renovation" Keen analyzes so tellingly. Moreover, as we shall see, he complements boundary crossings in genre and setting with a variety of other narrative strategies, many of which have a distinctive norm-challenging "modernist" quality. At the same time, Keen's reminders that Victorian novels are "a blend of old and new techniques" and that the "effort to write a truly modern book . . . may lead to the reinvention of the method of earlier novelists,"[11] like the cautionary remarks of Richard Poirier and others, are useful to bear in mind as we proceed.

There are, then, a number of specific qualities in Meredith's fiction that prompt me to view him as experimental[12] and, with the above qualifications, as having in some very significant ways a "modernist" sensibility. We find such qualities in the self-reflexive and artificial style I have already mentioned, in the dialogic narrative interaction of playful and competing voices that suggest a corresponding distrust of such abstractions as truth and identity, in the depiction of a disintegrating subject (Richard Feverel, Richmond Roy, Willoughby Patterne, Victor Radnor, and Lord Fleetwood[13] all come to mind as increasingly unstable Meredithian personalities), in what Lyn Pykett has called a "late nineteenth-century discourse of rupture,"[14] in his use of the city, especially in *Richard Feverel*, *The Adventures of Harry Richmond*, and *One of Our Conquerors*, as a setting for disorientation and loss, and, late in his career, in a rendering of characters' thoughts that suggests the simultaneity of past, present, and future we associate with stream of consciousness writing.

We can see the "cultural disenchantment" and questioning impulse of a modernist sensibility in Meredith's instinctive distrust of traditional generic boundaries (a distrust extending, as I have already suggested, well beyond the limited generic boundary-crossing Suzanne Keen associates with the Victorian "annex"), in his repeated and increasingly radical questioning of proper roles for women in marriage and society,[15] and in his running critique of the endemic sentimental egoism he saw everywhere cloaking the presumptions of Victorian patriarchy. Directly connected with these concerns is Meredith's fascination with and questioning of the Victorian construction of relations between parents and children, especially fathers and sons and, late in his career, fathers and daughters.

Finally, and crucially, I will argue that his invocation of an ethic of "common sense" is the traditionalist basis to Meredith's experimental impulse, underlying everything from his feminism to his rejection of the limitations of genre. Such a traditional base is a clear indication that Meredith looks backward as well as forward—which in itself may be viewed as a signifier of a modernist sensibility. As Astradur Eysteinsson has argued, "some influential modernists, despite breaking with prevalent literary traditions, were deeply involved in 'salvaging' fragments of the past."[16] Meredith's "salvaging" of a traditional standard of common sense is a hallmark of his writing from the beginning to the end of his career.

Because the many unsettling, disruptive elements in Meredith are linked in complicated and interesting ways, my approach to his transitional—and strategic—position in the history of the English novel will be as comprehensive as possible. Issues of gender, narrative strategies, the Meredithian touchstone of common sense, the preoccupation with generic boundaries—all these will be important to developing an understanding of his innovative genius. Questions of genre, for example, have been a central concern of Meredith's audience from the beginning of his novelistic career. When he is recognized at all today by the reading public, Meredith is typically regarded as the premier Victorian theorist of comedy and, somewhat more hazily, as the—or at least a—premier creator of Victorian comic fiction. This reputation is partly due to his famous treatment of the comic spirit in *An Essay on Comedy* (1877), partly due to the fact that *The Egoist: A Comedy in Narrative* (1879) is his most famous novel, and partly due to Joseph Warren Beach's classic interpretation, *The Comic Spirit in George Meredith* (1911), that appeared just two years after Meredith's death. Beach, following what he saw as an apparent invitation in the *Essay*, contended that the comic spirit provides the "chief distinction" of Meredith's novels. Using this key, he argued that we can adopt the *Essay*, in which the comic spirit is brilliantly analyzed, as a handbook to the novels.

But one way in which the experimental Meredith is so interesting is the manner in which he resists, extends beyond, and deconstructs the very categories he himself helps to provide. This is a quality that Beach's approach, along with a substantial body of Meredith criticism that followed Beach, tends to miss. Meredith's own impatience with the restrictions of comedy becomes clear in the simple fact that only two of his novels—*The Egoist* and *Evan Harrington* (1861)—really fit the definition of comic structure implied by the *Essay*. Mohammad Shaheen is right when he observes that Beach's book "forces an interpretation which applies only to one stage of Meredith's development."[17] Nevertheless, I will argue that the *Essay is* extremely valuable for understanding Meredith, though not in the way Beach implies. Underlying the theory of comedy laid out in the *Essay* is an ethic of "common sense" that, as I have already suggested, will provide us with a traditionalist framework useful for understanding Meredith's experimental fiction, no matter what generic direction it may take.

Meredith's self-conscious stylistic exuberance is another innovative aspect of his work that will be a preoccupation in this study. To begin, one might state the problem of style in terms of the traditional approach to Meredith—as a corollary to the problem of comedy: does he develop a style in his fiction that can at all consistently by his own definitions be called "comic," even in the one novel he designated as a "A Comedy in Narrative"? Do the capering imps and sententious narrative commentary in *The Egoist* contribute to the sane disinterestedness that Meredith identifies with the comic spirit, or do these elements embody precisely the kind of ridicule that drives "into the quivering sensibilities" and is distinguished from the true comic by Meredith in the *Essay*?[18] In other words, does Meredith follow his own "rules" or does he delight in a dialogic questioning of rules even as he appears to be expounding them?

Beyond this kind of question, it seems to me to be of great importance in considering Meredith to combine "critical" and "scholarly" roles, to be willing, in the case of style, to discriminate between what is rhetorically effective and what is rhetorically troublesome—and to try to see why. Like D. H. Lawrence, whom he anticipates in some interesting ways, Meredith is capable of extraordinary flights of descriptive and analytical prose—a style Virginia Woolf characterizes as an "intermittent brilliancy" that is "Meredith's characteristic excellence."[19] But also like Lawrence, his style can be extremely uneven, given to turgidity, opacity, and grotesque pomposity that will drive even the most sympathetic reader to distraction. As Joseph Moses has noted, "If criticism is to reach through to Meredith, it must fix its scrutiny on the often discomfiting features that characterize him: the archness, the density and strain of language, the elaborate self-consciousness, the insistent philosophizing, the disjunction in story and character, the manifest artificiality."[20] Moses goes on to quote David Howard's astute comment: "We must remember that Meredith is the most irritating novelist of the nineteenth century, and if we ignore that capacity to irritate we are inventing a safe Meredith to argue about."[21]

To gloss over Meredith's stylistic idiosyncrasies, then, is to ignore a major part of the experience of reading him—and also to miss important clues to the nature of his experimentation and related problems like the generic one I have raised above. Much of the difficulty encountered late in *Richard Feverel*, for example, may not be the result of Meredith's gratuitously obtruding tragedy upon an essentially comic situation, as many critics have argued, but just the reverse—that he takes an increasingly serious situation which has grown quite plausibly out of the preceding circumstances, and then disrupts its somber tone by intruding from time to time with the comic style of the earlier part of the novel. Or, to suggest a positive reading of an even more controversial novel, one may examine the highly idiosyncratic—and more than occasionally irritating— style of *One of Our Conquerors* and discover that, rather than being a continuous piece of stylistic self-indulgence, the extravagant and tortuous rhetoric often provides astonishingly direct access to the anguished psychological states of central characters who appear comic only when viewed from the outside, while Meredith's development of interiority suggests something much closer to tragic awareness. One preoccupation in what follows, then, will be Meredith's difficult style as a key to questions of genre, structure, characterization, and theme, and as an essential means to arriving at a balanced assessment of the experimental impulse in his work.

Also directly connected with stylistic and generic innovation in Meredith is a quality that has come under increasing critical scrutiny in recent years, especially through the illuminating work of Donald Stone, David McWhirter, Susan Payne, and Neil Roberts[22]—Meredithian dialogism. Virginia Woolf, who remains one of Meredith's most brilliant readers, can provide us with a useful, pre-Bakhtinian starting point to this productive line of analysis. In commenting on *Richard Feverel*, she notes that "[t]he style is extremely uneven. Now he twists himself into iron knots; now he lies flat as a pancake. He seems to be of two minds as to his intention. Ironic comment alternates with long-winded narrative. He vacillates from one attitude to another. Indeed, the whole fabric seems to rock a little insecurely. . . .—what an odd conglomeration it is!" Woolf wishes to emphasize here "that the writer is a novice at his task,"[23] and Meredith's later attempts at revision of *Richard Feverel* suggest that he would at times have agreed. But another, more interesting point also emerges in her commentary—the observation that there is an interplay of more than one voice in the novel: "ironic comment alternates with long-winded narrative." Such interplay is evident all through *Richard Feverel* and is still present in quite another way at the end of Meredith's novelistic career in *The Amazing Marriage* (1895), where two narrators frame events in entirely different styles and perspectives, satirizing and undermining one another as they compete for the reader's attention and produce a decided sense of indeterminacy.

This characteristic interplay in Meredith's narrative can be linked directly to the impulse to "become more free and flexible" that Mikhail Bakhtin associates with the novel as genre—that is, the experimental and questioning quality so evident in Meredith's fiction can be seen as a manifestation of precisely the tendency Bakhtin associates with the dialogic imagination. This "novelization" process occurs for Bakhtin when language becomes

> dialogized, permeated with laughter, irony, humor, elements of self-parody and finally—this is the most important thing—the novel inserts . . . an indeterminacy, a certain semantic openendedness, a living contact with unfinished, still-evolving contemporary reality (the openended present).[24]

The countervailing narrative voices in *Richard Feverel* give an excellent example of just such a dialogic impulse, one that propels the narrative away from any kind of generic unity to a dizzying mixture of satire, comedy, romance, and, finally, tragedy. Or, as another way to make the same point, one could say that Meredith seems sometimes to delight in disrupting our conventional notions of how a novel should be constructed, of whether or not traditional plotting or a sustained narrative tone, for example, are even necessary. In this first novel, then, we find "a certain semantic openendedness" with a vengeance, a lack of conventional ordering that acts as an innovative hallmark at the beginning of Meredith's career.

Still another area of major innovation in Meredith is found in his treatment of gender issues, most readily seen in the role of the heroine in his work. Susan Morgan directs our attention to this element when she suggests that "the place to look for Meredith's significance . . . is in [his] presentation of women."[25] What particularly interests me in the Meredithian presentation of women is that one sees again and again how principal feminine figures in his fiction tend to possess—or to be in the process of acquiring—the com-mon-sensical qualities he associates with the comic spirit in the *Essay*, while central male figures most often do *not* have these qualities. It is, in fact, in their relations with women that the male characters are repeatedly shown to be most prone to the artificial conduct and egotistical insensibility that are prime Meredithian targets, a pattern we can see being worked out in double measure in some of Meredith's explorations of father-son relationships.

Again, *Richard Feverel* provides a ready example. Early in the novel, the heroine, Lucy Desborough, introduces a delicacy of comic intelligence into the narrative that acts to highlight per-verted masculine thinking, first of Sir Austin Feverel, and then of his son, Richard. Yet Lucy's role in the face of this father-son enact-ment of benighted male prerogative also returns us directly to the interesting question of generic distinctions in Meredith: her fate, in spite of various references early- and mid-narrative to the novel as "comedy," is radically different from that of the common-sensi-cal heroine of stage comedy whom Meredith apotheosizes in the *Essay*, the woman whose sane and ordered view of the world finally triumphs. One must also account for the fact that Lucy's sane view does *not* triumph, that she suffers a pathetic, wasteful death that would seem to make critical discussion of comedy at the novel's end inappropriate.[26] Lucy, then, along with other characters who suffer under similar tragic circumstances—Clare Forey, Dahlia Fleming, and Nataly Dreighton all come to mind[27]—simply cannot be adequately discussed as part of a Meredithian comic scheme. Rather, the question is whether she and her destruction can be seen as part of a coherent pattern that is in some way more com-prehensive than what is implied by the comic spirit and limiting notions of Meredith as "comic novelist."

As I have indicated, my examination of these and related ques-tions about the experimental Meredith will center on his invocation of a principle of "common sense"—or what I shall also refer to as the spirit of critical intelligence.[28] It seems to me that one can in-deed discover a coherence in Meredith, a coherence to be found in this rationalist spirit rather than in any attempt to classify the extraordinary range of his novelistic experiments under the rubric of comedy. What often holds Meredith's work together is a consis-tent attitude towards the self-defeating actions of men and women, whether those actions lead to the "laughter of the mind" described in the *Essay*, to a world of impossible romance, in the direction of

tragedy, or, as is sometimes the case, in all of these directions. For
Meredith, it is betrayals of common sense, lapses into sentimental
egoism—that isolating, monological compound of self-delusion,
vanity, and hypocrisy treated extensively in the *Essay*—that account for human absurdity as well as for much of human suffering.
The tension that develops between Meredithian common sense
and this sentimental egoism, I will argue, is in one way or another
at the center of all of his fiction.

What we have, then, is an orientation, both forward- and backward-looking, that is essential to understanding Meredith's art:
while he refers back to rational norms we associate with classicism
and the eighteenth century, he also invokes these traditional values
as the basis for his radical critique of—and departure from—what
he saw as regressive or merely trendy in Victorian art and society.
The experimental and questioning instinct I find so interesting in
Meredith is inseparable from this strong rationalist bias.

But another point is equally important, and that is Meredith's
recognition of the limitations of the intellectual component. From
the beginning of his career he insisted upon the necessity for harmonious balance within the triad of "blood and brain and spirit."[29]
The characterization of Sir Austin Feverel suggests at once Meredith's keen sense of the extreme dangers of a purely rationalist androcentric position. Instead, the term common sense, as he uses it,
suggests a union of intellectual *and* emotional intelligence[30] combined with a Goethean openness to the many-sidedness of life.

Historical context is also essential to understanding the Meredithian experimental impulse: as he began his writing career in the
1850s, he was running exactly counter to an increasingly strong
popular impulse to associate matters of emotion with "women's
writing"; it is worth remembering that Coventry Patmore, that
quintessential perpetrator of separate spheres, began publishing
The Angel in the House in 1854, three years after the appearance
of Meredith's first volume of poetry and the year before the publication of *The Shaving of Shagpat.*

What I have said in this introduction could be taken as an indication that in this study I will be privileging the authorial consciousness, seeing Meredithian texts in direct relation to a consistent
Meredith as their point of origin. But I also want to argue another
side of this issue: Meredith, always nervously intellectual and self-
regarding, leaves us texts, to use Hillis Miller's term, full of "hidden
energy" that at times suggests that the novels are at war with them-

selves; to put this a different way, one could say that Meredith's dialogic impulse sometimes seems out of control. Thus in what follows I will examine not only essential Meredithian attitudes that persist from the beginning to the end of his career, but also a range of revealing tensions and inconsistencies in his style that may suggest at times a lack of clear unified or authoritative authorial consciousness, a kind of creative dissonance that can also be read as a strategic marker to Meredith's experimental impulse—what Miller calls "the anomalous within the work of an author, those features which do not fit."[31] Overall, the focus of this study will be on the ways in which Meredith transmuted his analysis of rational-humane and irrational-inhumane behavior into a fictional world that is remarkable for its innovative questioning and transgression of traditional boundaries, its psychological insights, and its celebration of a liberating dialogism, all of which helped to move the English novel into a new phase we now associate with the great writers of modernist fiction.

I

An Essay on Comedy: Theorizing Tradition and Innovation

1

GEORGE MEREDITH'S PRONOUNCEMENTS ON THE NATURE OF COMEDY, as I have suggested, can be both a help and a hindrance to understanding the experimental impulse in his fiction. Since the early part of the twentieth century, when Joseph Warren Beach proclaimed in his enthusiastic study of the comic spirit in Meredith that "no writer since Ben Jonson has given plainer advertisement of what he was about,"[1] many readers, finding Meredith not at all plain, have turned to the famous *An Essay on Comedy* (1877) for guidance. The *Essay*, along with the cryptic "Prelude" to *The Egoist* (1879) and passages on comedy in a number of the poems, does indeed provide a number of important critical touchstones useful in assessing the novels. A point often overlooked, however, is that only one of Meredith's own works—*The Egoist*—is ever referred to in these extra-fictional commentaries on comedy, and then only indirectly in the "Prelude." The "Prelude" confirms what is already evident from the subtitle and the novel itself: in *The Egoist,* Meredith experiments with creating a "Comedy in Narrative" in many ways close in spirit to the comedy of manners brilliantly analyzed in the *Essay*.

When one reads a novel like *The Egoist* or *Evan Harrington* (1860) that appears to fall more or less neatly within the generic limits of the *Essay*, then, the critical predisposition to view the Meredithian world as essentially comic may be illuminating, even essential, to one's understanding of that world.[2] But when one moves on to other novels in the canon this predisposition may *create* problems of interpretation rather than solve them. Expectations may be raised, based on assumptions about the nature of

24

comedy and other extrinsic evidence, that may limit—even severely limit—our ability to observe Meredith's characteristic impulse to write against the constraints of genre and novelistic
convention.

The hero of *The Tragic Comedians* (1880), for example, is described by one critic as being "handed over to the Comic Muse"[3]
because he falls short of the "nobleness" required of the tragic hero
in Meredith's 1887 poem "The Two Masks." It is certainly true that
there are comic aspects to the character and history of Sigismund
Alvan, the hero—that would seem to be a part of Meredith's point.
But to imply that such a history can be dealt with adequately under
the aegis of the "Comic Muse" is to narrow the range of the novel
unnecessarily, to miss Meredith's experimentation with a border-
line area that moves from comedy to tragedy. What the narrator
does suggest about Alvan's career, based upon the life of the brilliant German Social Democrat Ferdinand Lassalle, is summed up
at the work's end, after the protagonist has died in a duel: "The
characters of the hosts of men are of the simple order of the comic;
not many are of a stature and a complexity calling for the junction
of the two Muses to name them" (15:200). The meaning here
seems clear: a simple generic distinction does not suit the "complexity" of Meredith's rendering of the world of Alvan and his fiancée Clotilde, and hence the novel's title.[4]

Much of the same may be said about the narrative of Richard and
Lucy in *The Ordeal of Richard Feverel* (1859), a novel whose critical history provides a classic example of the determination of readers to recast and conventionalize Meredith's experimentation by
attempting to view his work through a comic lens. Joseph Warren
Beach solved the difficulty of the more somber elements in the
novel by dividing it into two parts: the tragedy of Richard and Lucy
and the comedy of Sir Austin and his System. Beach then proceeded, logically enough, to devote his discussion of comedy to the
latter. Subsequent critics have seen the fallacy in this selective approach and have recognized and dealt with the noncomic elements
in the novel.[5] But repeatedly many of these same critics have returned to Beach's basic premise—*Richard Feverel* is or ought to be
essentially comic—and have treated the novel as comedy manqué.
A review of commentary on *Richard Feverel* since Meredith's death
shows this idea reasserting itself again and again as critics have insisted on reading Meredith's challenges to the boundaries of genre
as, quite simply, a tactical error—a breaking of immutable generic

rules. J. B. Priestly, writing in 1926, said that *"Richard Feverel* is presented as a comedy, and has a tragic ending thrust upon it, quite arbitrarily."[6] Joseph C. Landis, thirty years later, argued that the failure of many of Meredith's novels is due to their "violation of [Meredith's] comic formula and the resulting forced mating of incompatible elements destructive of the aesthetic unity of the work[s]." *Richard Feverel*, we are told, "is marred by a similar distortion of the formula": "the suffering of the major figures in the novel . . . [is] a violation of aesthetic propriety."[7] John W. Morris a few years later made essentially the same point: "Richard's suffering destroys the previously established comic decorum of the work."[8] I. M. Williams began his 1967 essay on *Richard Feverel* by defining Richard as a comic hero but ends with the observation that he is "more than comic": "the reader is forced to feel a sympathy which takes him too close to the character to leave him free at the end of the novel to make the objective estimate which is necessary to the author's comic purpose."[9]

And the wish to view *Richard Feverel* as comedy or comedy manqué has persisted. Roger Henkle, in *Comedy and Culture* (1980), cites *Richard Feverel* and *The Egoist* as "Meredith's major comic novels,"[10] while Richard Keller Simon in *The Labyrinth of the Comic* (1985) provides a convenient summary of the mono-generic approach to *Richard Feverel*, echoing at once Priestly and, in quite a different way, Samuel Johnson: the novel "appears primarily as a comedy gone bad or a comedy with a tragic ending yoked by violence onto it."[11]

What strikes me as problematic in all such readings of *Richard Feverel* is that they tend to transfer notions of decorum derived from stage comedy intact to the novel without adequate recognition of the fact that the novel is a radically different—and more flexible—form of literary art. Even more to the point, the mono-generic approach misses what I am arguing to be an essential element of Meredith's genius—his purposeful playfulness in the face of the constraints of traditional form. But where, then, does the *Essay*, which if anything is a compendium of the constraints of comic form, fit into this view of an innovative, experimental Meredith? The most direct answer to such a question is that the *Essay* is primarily a discourse on the theater, not a generic theory of fiction. "The narrow field, or enclosed square" (23:44–45) Meredith describes as the province of the comic dramatist is not necessarily the province of the novelist. Robert Martin puts the point more bluntly

in his "Notes Toward a Comic Fiction": "Meredith the novelist for-
tunately knew too much to put up with the postulations of Meredith the critic. . . . His own novels . . . are uninhibited by a tedious
worry about what category they should fit into,"[12] or, as Daniel
Smirlock has succinctly suggested, "Meredith treats the comic perspective as suspect. . . . The world of *Richard Feverel* [is] a world
that resists human attempts to structure and fix it."[13]

Robert Scholes and Robert Kellogg in *The Nature of Narrative*
provide a useful historical overview of the process, so evident in
Meredith, that Bakhtin has called the "novelization of other
genres": "The decorum of separate tragic and comic formulations
had given way by the nineteenth century to a powerful new impulse
[in novelists] to find a common vehicle which would unite the neo-
classical realism of social type and the romantic realism of unique
individuality. The novel's great virtue lay in finding a way to combine the tragic concern for the individual with the comic concern
for society."[14] Or, as Joseph Moses has put it more recently, "the
novel . . . may be seen as one attempt to transcend [the] artificial
confinement [imposed by] . . . the classical separation of modes."[15]
And Gillian Beer, in commenting upon the Morris essay, notes that
to treat such experiments with multi-generic techniques as a
breach of comic decorum can

> flatten and resolve precisely what is energetic and equivocal in Mere-
> dith's handling of plot. Like Thackeray in *Vanity Fair*, Meredith is not
> just repeating well-known literary forms, nor even composing variations
> on them; he invokes them as emblems, as possible but limited ways of
> looking at his world. He discards them as his characters move into ex-
> periences not within the compass of, say, Menander's comedy. He
> counterpoints literary patterns against life.[16]

Donald Stone, arguing that Meredith is the most Bakhtinian of
nineteenth-century English novelists, puts the point this way:
"Other genres respond to the rules laid down for stabilized forms,
but the novel flaunts its instability; it thrives on the rejection of
rules."[17] And Neil Roberts, in his extended Bakhtinian reading of
Meredith, notes that "generic models—often competing models
within a text, such as the novel of education and New Comedy in
Richard Feverel, Romance and Bildungsroman in *Harry Richmond*, Molièrean comedy and the Richardsonian novel in *The Egoist*—are not taken for granted but exposed to the reader's scrutiny,

and to questioning."[18] It is just such a reader that Fredric Jameson has in mind when he argues in *The Political Unconscious* that "*all* generic categories, even the most time-hallowed and traditional, are ultimately to be understood (or 'estranged') as mere ad hoc, experimental constructs, devised for a specific textual occasion and abandoned like so much scaffolding when the analysis has done its work. . . . Genre criticism thereby recovers its freedom and opens up a new space for the creative construction of experimental entities. . . ."[19] The aim of this study is to read Meredithian texts precisely as such "experimental entities," to appreciate the innovative habits of mind that make Meredith a frequent rule breaker, one who questions, deconstructs, and transgresses conventions such as those of genre in one text, only to return to embrace them in another, when it suits his purposes.

As I have noted in the Introduction, however, it is not my purpose to claim that experimentation with genre in Meredith's fiction makes the *Essay* and his other commentaries on comedy irrelevant to the noncomic portions of his work. Quite the contrary, I find the *Essay* to be of first importance to understanding Meredith, especially in his development of a prevailing attitude that lies behind genre or "literary pattern," an attitude central to the comic spirit and at the same time antecedent to it in all of his art. It is this principle that, for purposes of convenience, I call the spirit of critical intelligence in Meredith. This is the same primary critical spirit that Ramon Fernandez had in mind when, in his 1926 essay, "The Message of Meredith," he noted that "Meredith . . . soon convinces us that the exercise of intelligence is indispensable, not only for the full comprehension, but also for the perfect realization of life, that one lives more intensely and better in proportion to one's being more lucid."[20]

This premium on lucidity, on seeing life clearly, steadily, and whole, is equally characteristic of tragic and comic art and, as I have already suggested, a far more reliable basis for assessment of Meredith's fictional experimentation than are the generic distinctions that have so preoccupied many of his critics. But to observe Meredith's typical dramatization of a struggle between critical intelligence or "common sense" and self-ignorance is not to imply, of course, that Meredith is always lucid or common-sensical—far from it. Some of the most interesting moments in his fiction are those points at which we become aware of him undermining and veering away from his own rational standards; it is also at such mo-

ments, however, that we can see even more clearly how an awareness of Meredith's notions of common sense are useful as a
touchstone to understanding his work.

2

For Meredith, Molière represented the quintessence of the
"school of stately comedy" (23:9), and as such he provides an illuminating standard by which to examine Meredith's notions of
"clear reason," first as they coincide with Molière's tactics within
the boundaries of comedy, and then as they contrast when Meredith moves, as he so often does, beyond these limits.

Meredith's 1877 lecture, "On the Idea of Comedy and the Uses
of the Comic Spirit"—or *An Essay on Comedy,* as it was called
when published—marked the first time he had set down, in a form
separate from the novels themselves, an extended treatment of his
views on such issues as rational values, comedy, social conventions,
male sentimentalism, and the role of women in society. His primary aim was to present by degrees a view that equated the comic
spirit, not with the humor and outright laughter that had domi-
nated comic writing for over a century, but with rational analysis of
behavior. As Robert Martin has pointed out in *The Triumph of Wit,*
"Rather than a piece of original speculation, the *Essay* may be seen
as the culmination of the attempt to rid Victorian writing of the in-
cubus of sentimental humour."[21] If there were to be laughter, it was
to be "thoughtful laughter"—turning on what Martin terms
"wit"—with the stress on the ability of the spectator to see the relevance of the laughter to his own conduct. The comic spirit was to
be above all a reforming force, one that would induce the individual
to develop a sharpened vision of himself and others and thereby
would lead to a more humane and civilized society. James Gindin
puts the point succinctly: "The aim of comedy, according to the
Essay, is socially prescriptive, reforming the individual vagary or
egoism and assuming that a collection of individual reforms would
beneficially alter the society as a whole."[22] And within the work itself this reformative process would presumably be a major factor in
producing the "new society" Northrop Frye sees crystalizing
around the hero of New Comedy.[23]

In the *Essay,* when Meredith wishes to illustrate clarity and
steadiness of vision, he turns repeatedly to Molière: "The source of

his wit is clear reason: it is a fountain of that soil; and it springs to vindicate reason, common sense, rightness and justice" (23:17). A convenient summation of Molière's views on the relation between comedy and rationality is found in the anonymous "Lettre sur la comédie de L'Imposteur," an essay that provides some interesting and strategic correspondences between the theoretical position of Molière and that of Meredith in the *Essay*. The "Lettre" appeared in 1667 in defense of *Tartuffe*, which had been banned as a result of pressure exerted on Louis XIV by church conservatives. The authorship of the pamphlet has been the subject of some critical dispute, but it may quite possibly have been written by Molière himself.[24] In any case, the second part of the "Lettre" contains a useful analysis of his theory of comedy, one which, along with the rest of the pamphlet, became a standard appendix in editions of Molière and would have been readily available to Meredith. According to this analysis, the source of the ridiculous is to be found in any departure from sound sense: "The ridiculous is therefore the external and perceptible form that nature's providence has associated with all that is unreasonable in order to make us perceive it and compel us to fly from it. To recognize this ridiculousness, one must recognize the good sense (*la raison*) which is its opposite, and see what characterizes such good sense. The character of good sense is found, finally, in that which is harmonious and suitable (*la convenance*)."[25] For Molière, then, "good sense" (*la raison*) is a loaded term—"understanding, perceptiveness, sensitivity, balance,"[26] as one critic has defined it—a term very close to Meredith's use of "common sense."

The argument of the "Lettre" continues: if "good sense" (*la raison*) is manifested in harmony and fitness (*la convenance*), then "the ridiculous consists in some disharmony or unsuitableness (*la disconvenance*) and it follows that all delusion, artifice, hypocrisy, and dissimulation, all contradictory appearances originating from the same principle, are essentially ridiculous."[27] And in the familiar peroration of Meredith's *Essay*, it is this same idea of "*disconvenance*," an essential incongruity resulting from one's dishonesty to others and to oneself, that is seen as the true subject of the "unsolicitous observation" of the comic spirit:

> Whenever they wax out of proportion, overblown, affected, pretentious, bombastical, hypocritical, pedantic, fantastically delicate; whenever [the Comic Spirit] sees them self-deceived or hoodwinked, given to run

riot in idolatries, drifting into vanities, congregating in absurdities, planning short-sightedly, plotting dementedly; whenever they are at variance with their professions, and violate the unwritten but perceptible laws binding them in consideration one to another; whenever they offend sound reason, fair justice; are false in humility or mined with conceit, individually, or in the bulk—the Spirit overhead will look humanely malign and cast an oblique light on them, followed by volleys of silvery laughter. (23:47)

In short, both Molière and Meredith place the highest premium on common sense and the knowledge of self and society that the term implies; both, in turn, see a departure from this norm as a self-betrayal into absurd conduct, conduct signaled by the incongruity of men "at variance with their professions." The similarity of these views is not surprising: Molière and Meredith are alike in their sympathy with the classical tradition that stresses reason and moderation. It could be argued, in fact, that the offhand remark put in the mouth of Socrates by Plato in the *Philebus*—that the comic or ridiculous originates in self-ignorance[28]—provides us with the rationalist basis for the views of both writers.

One can also see ample evidence of the popularity of common sense philosophy in eighteenth-century British writers like Shaftesbury and Thomas Reid, who may well have had some influence, directly or indirectly, on Meredith, at least in the notion of common sense as referring to natural, instinctive shared beliefs of rational beings. What is interesting about Meredith, of course, is how often his notions of what was common-sensical, especially in regard to the role of women in society, placed him, not within a Victorian community of shared belief but distinctly ahead of it. For our purposes, however, what is finally most important here is what becomes of the theory in practice—what may be revealed by looking at Meredith and Molière as practitioners, respectively, of narrative and dramatic art.

3

There is one aspect of Molière's technique that is of particular interest to an examination of the rationalist basis to Meredith's fiction: this is Molière's use of the *raisonneur*, or spokesman for common sense. Cléante in *Tartuffe*, Chrysalde in *L'École des femmes*,

Philinte in *Le Misanthrope*, Ariste in *L'École des maris*[29]—all of these characters play roughly similar roles in that they dramatize a moderate and sane point of view in contrast to the antics of men of deformed reason such as Orgon and Arnolphe. The *raisonneur* is also a familiar figure in Meredith's fiction—Austin Wentworth in *Richard Feverel*, Merthyr Powys in *Sandra Belloni* (1864), Gower Woodseer in *The Amazing Marriage* (1895), Vernon Whitford in *The Egoist*, to name a few. Besides their reasonableness, however, these figures share another trait: they are all more or less uniformly predictable and dull. The obvious reason for this is that in both Meredith and Molière, the real artistic and moral interest is found less in the rational men than in the figure who is *déraisonnable*, who illustrates a violation of the "unwritten but perceptible laws binding us in consideration one to another," and who shows where that violation leads. Roger Henkle notes in *Comedy and Culture*, "it is often the connivers, the perpetrators of far-fetched hoaxes, the would-be empire builders who attract us through their vitality. There is something splendid in self-centered human intelligence."[30] It is these same figures, as J. B. Priestly has put it, who "are so much more vital and arresting than the characters who are right."[31] Yet the man who is "right" is also present for a clear purpose: he helps to keep our eyes set clearly on the norm that is being violated. Molière's *raisonneurs*, according to W. G. Moore, "ensure symmetry and roundness of comic presentation. Excess is the more distinguishable if its opposite is exhibited at the same time. Sense shows up nonsense, sobriety offsets bad temper. To insist that one should be 'sage avec sobriété' is a piece of rather flat moralizing unless and until it is put in contrast to a man doing the precise opposite."[32]

But this stress on the rational, especially with the distinctly androcentric spin given the term by critics like Priestly and Moore, can raise an interesting question: does the central role of a rational norm in a writer make him or her vulnerable to the critique recent feminist theory has made of claims to objectivity? Put most succinctly, this critique, in the words of Susan Bordo, sees the post-Cartesian "flight to objectivity" as a "flight from the feminine."[33] In answer, I will be at pains to show throughout this study that Meredith's own feminism does much to counteract concerns that his notions of critical intelligence may be an expression of a patriarchal undermining of women's difference—especially since he so often links rational thinking and behavior with his central women characters in contrast to the wrongheaded and often misogynic behavior of his central male characters.[34]

As I pointed out in the Introduction, Meredith is a writer who, on the one hand, looks back to classical, seventeenth- and eighteenth-century norms of reason and common sense and, on the other, instinctively questions contemporary social and artistic conventions—on the basis of common sense—in ways that look forward to attitudes and techniques we now tend to associate with twentieth-century modernism. Thus I am not making a claim that Meredith's work fits a late-twentieth-/early-twenty-first-century definition of feminist writing; what I do claim is that as a nineteenth-century feminist and literary innovator, his experiments in fiction can teach us much about the transition from a Victorian to a modernist sensibility.

David McWhirter[35] can be helpful in dealing with some of these issues. For one thing, he reminds us of Judith Wilt's remarks "on the little-noted fact that in both *The Egoist* and the *Essay on Comedy*, the 'Comic Spirit,' gendered male, is gradually transformed into a feminine 'Comic Muse.'"[36] And he notes further that "the 'Alpine survey' of the Comic Spirit images the possibility of a perspective reflecting . . . a truly *common* sense, a 'common voice' . . . of men and women. What comedy's distance discerns, however, is not monological unity, but polyphonic wholeness."[37]

To limit discussion of the *raisonneur* in Meredith and Molière to the rational male figures, as Priestly and Moore tend to do, is a failure to discern just such polyphony—a gendered polyphony inherent in the strategic role played by the *raisonneuse*[38] in both writers. Not surprisingly, the role of the *raisonneuse* is an aspect of comedy on which Meredith places great emphasis in the *Essay*. Already intimated at the opening in the comic poet's antipathy to "marked social inequality of the sexes," the central importance of the position of women in "true Comedy" receives increasing emphasis as Meredith's discussion goes on:

> Comedy is the fountain of good sense, not the less perfectly sound on account of the sparkle: and Comedy lifts women to a station offering them free play for their wit, as they usually show it, when they have it, on the side of sound sense. The higher the Comedy, the more prominent the part they enjoy in it. (23:14)

As McWhirter notes in commenting on this passage, "the *Essay*'s insistence that a critique of society's gender assumptions constitutes a necessary element in the best comic writing has never been sufficiently stressed."[39]

Comedy, then, not only portrays women of innate refinement and wit; it "lifts" them to a position of freedom where they may display and act on their natural intelligence. And for Meredith, Célimène of *Le Misanthrope* is the epitome of the comic heroine whose wit is "on the side of sound sense": "Célimène is a woman's mind in movement, armed with an ungovernable wit; with perspicacious clear eyes for the world, and a very distinct knowledge that she belongs to the world, and is most at home in it. She is attracted to Alceste by her esteem for his honesty; she cannot avoid seeing where the good sense of the man is diseased. . . . He is only passively comic. Célimène is the active spirit" (23:21–22).

When we turn from Philinte to Célimène, or from Cléante to Dorine in *Tartuffe*, we find sound sense characterized in a manner that is clearly "vital and arresting." Almost invariably in the *Essay*, Meredith's search for positive examples of the spirit of critical intelligence leads to a woman. In the one native drama he is willing to discuss in the same breath with Molière—Congreve's *Way of the World*—"Millamant overshadows Mirabel, the sprightliest male figure of English Comedy" (23:14). Mrs. Millamant, provided the lifting effect of comedy, may give full exercise to the sanity and common sense that are the quintessence of the comic spirit.

But, suggests Meredith, such a woman as Mrs. Millamant might be objected to as "heartless" and therefore not an exemplum of comic sensibility after all. The objection, however, is that of the sentimentalist and demonstrates the attitude Meredith saw as most antipathetic to a humane, clear-eyed vision of the world: sentimentalism—or "feverish emotionalism"—is directly linked with man's assumption of spiritual superiority over woman:

> Is it not preferable to be the pretty idiot, the passive beauty, the adorable bundle of caprices, very feminine, very sympathetic, of romantic and sentimental fiction? Our women are taught to think so. The Agnès of the *École des femmes* should be a lesson for men. The heroines of Comedy are like women of the world, not necessarily heartless from being clear-sighted: they seem so to the sentimentally reared only for the reason that they use their wits, and are not wandering vessels crying for a captain or pilot. Comedy is an exhibition of their battle with men, and that of men with them. (23:14–15)

Clear-sightedness and a strong sense of spiritual equality are the two great attributes that mark the comic heroine and provide her

with resources for her battle with men—the same battle that is repeatedly the subject of Meredith's novels.

This battle does not take place in a vacuum, however. In the
Essay, Meredith shows a lively consciousness of the essential relation between a work of literary art and the society that it depicts.
And the greater the sense of mutual respect between the sexes in
that society, the more likely should be the flourishing of the high
comedy that he envisions: "Where women are on the road to an
equal footing with men, in attainments and in liberty—in what they
have won for themselves, and what has been granted to them by a
fair civilization—there, and only waiting to be transplanted from
life to the stage, or the novel, or the poem, pure Comedy flourishes"
(23:31–32).

The problem, of course, is where to find examples of such a "fair
civilization" in the real world—and thus Meredith's difficulty in
providing more than a handful of examples of "pure comedy" and,
with those examples, his implied idealizing of the status of women
in later seventeenth-century France. He counters this idealized vision with its more familiar converse: "where the sexes are sepa-
rated, men and women grow, as the Portuguese call it, *affaimados*
of one another, famine-stricken; and all the tragic elements are on
stage" (23:29). Meredith is speaking here of the theater of Spain,
but it was the same, if more subtle, separation of the sexes in Victorian England—and its attendant sentimentalism and male arrogance—that acted as a major source of somber elements in his own
fiction. In fact, as David McWhirter has pointed out, for Meredith
"the most crucial quality of the comic perspective lies in its acknowledged status as an as yet unrealized possibility [that] . . . does
not and cannot exist within the current construction of bourgeois
society." And it is precisely this tension between a comic vision of
"genuine dialogue of men and women"—"a dialogic consensus"[40]
(to use McWhirter's adaptation of Bakhtin)—and Meredith's highly
critical view of his own androcentric world that accounts for a basic
Meredithian paradox: a "comic novelist," most of whose experiments in fiction cannot begin to be adequately understood within
the confines of traditional notions of comedy.

4

The role of the Victorian heroine for Meredith was necessarily
more complicated and perilous than that of the Molièrean figures

he used as paradigms of the comic heroine—characters with extraordinary self-possession who emanate an air of spiritual and intellectual equality from the outset. These common-sensical women tend to arrive on stage equipped for battle, their intellect fully formed: Célimène's "perspicacious clear eyes for the world" are at work from the moment of her first appearance. Although Noorna bin Noorka in *The Shaving of Shagpat* (1856) is an important exception, such is generally not the case with Meredith's women. Typically, the heroine of a Meredith novel must undergo a painful re-education in order to overcome her inherited views of self-effacement; it is only through innate intelligence and a developing ability to see things as they are and as they should be that she may eventually assume a role in relation to her male counterpart approaching that of Célimène to Alceste. This process of education—education leading away from the sentimental and uncritical notions of the world and men that most of Meredith's women initially hold—is experienced by such levelheaded figures as the Princess Ottilia in *The Adventures of Harry Richmond* (1871), Aminta Farrell in *Lord Ormont and His Aminta* (1894), and Carinthia Jane Kirby in *The Amazing Marriage* (1895). In each of these novels the heroine comes to act as a rational foil to the irrational excesses of, respectively, Harry Richmond, Ormont, and Fleetwood. In *The Egoist* this pattern is repeated no less than three times, and in each case Sir Willoughby Patterne's arrogance and utter lack of rational perspective are highlighted by a woman's discovery of her own intelligence. By the time the Egoist has joined his hand with Laetitia Dale's at the novel's end, he has met his match in a wife who is to become not only resident *raisonneuse* at Patterne Hall, but also Willoughby's sole chance—and a slim one at that—of salvation from his love of self.

Although the process by which Constantia Durham, Clara Middleton, and Laetitia Dale gain their wisdom is depicted as a painful one, *The Egoist* remains a "Comedy in Narrative" as Meredith seems to have intended. More typical of the range of his fiction is *Richard Feverel*—more typical because in it he tries to go in so many directions at once: elements of burlesque, comedy, romance, and tragedy are all important in this extraordinarily innovative and ambitious first full-length novel. Here one can see the artistic impulses that led to more somber works like *Rhoda Fleming* (1865), *The Tragic Comedians*, and *One of Our Conquerors* (1891), as well as to comic narratives like *Evan Harrington* and *The Egoist*. The novel's heroine, Lucy Desborough, is a spiritual sister to Molière's *raisonneuses* in that her intuitive common sense illuminates the distorted reason of the male Feverels; she is quite unlike these women in Molière, however, in that she must suffer anguish and finally death in her futile efforts to transform the promptings of her intelligence into action. The part played by Lucy—and by Richard's cousin, Clare Forey, whose fate prefigures Lucy's—helps to demonstrate not only the comic implications of the role of common sense in Meredith's fiction, but also the potentially tragic result when reason is flouted for too long.

As we proceed to Meredith's first great exercise of innovative genius in *Richard Feverel*, a side glance at his very first fictional offering, the curious "Arabian Entertainment," *The Shaving of Shagpat* (1855), will be useful. *Shagpat* is above all else an experimental fiction and in that sense sets the direction of Meredith's career as novelist. In this whimsical romance, the young Meredith plays with themes—issues of feminism, male sentimentalism, initiation into the moral life, grandiose aspiration—that were to preoccupy him throughout his career, but in the appealingly escapist style of *The Thousand and One Nights*, a book that became available in English in Edward William Lane's translation when Meredith was twelve, becoming his favorite reading in early adolescence. *Shagpat*, then, was in part Meredith's homage to this early literary love, but one can also clearly see the influence of Molière in a Célimène figure who acts as an agent of common sense more unambiguously than anywhere else in Meredith's subsequent fiction. Noorna bin Noorka perceives at once where the good sense of her beleaguered and distractible barber hero, Shibli Bagarag, is diseased; with timely advice and admonition she is able to spur him on, finally, to "Mastering the Event," which involves the epic task of shaving the extraordinarily hairy (and self-signifying) Shagpat. Shibli himself is prototypal of the Meredithian hero, well-intentioned but self-indulgent, lacking in the discipline and self-discernment that marks the fully developed Meredithian heroine.

But as I have indicated, the great difference between *Shagpat* and what was to follow was that as an "Arabian" romance, it permitted Meredith to experiment with serious contemporary themes in a setting that did not require a contemporary tone or resolution. This distinction is of considerable importance, because for Meredith the pressures inherent in the darker nineteenth-century European context of the later fiction were repeatedly to make excursions beyond the limits of comedy and romance a moral necessity.

2

The Ordeal of Richard Feverel: Challenges to Patriarchy and the Boundaries of Genre

I<small>N</small> *THE ORDEAL OF RICHARD FEVEREL*, THE EXOTIC FOREIGN SETTINGS OF *The Shaving of Shagpat* and *Farina, a Legend of Cologne*, an excursion into burlesque sentimental romance that appeared in 1857, have been replaced by an ancestral mansion "in a certain Western County folding Thames" (11),[1] but Meredith clearly continues in a mode, at once playful and serious, that is reminiscent of his earlier experimental narratives. He is again intent on exploring male arrogance and self-delusion, but this time embodied in a psychological study of a father-son relationship that puts problems of patriarchy—literal and figurative—at the center of the text. This is one of several interrelated issues that I find especially intriguing about *Richard Feverel* as transgressive fiction—its scathing critique of Victorian patriarchy and gender relations played out in a context, after an oddly burlesque opening, that increasingly insists on a rigorous standard of psychological analysis. A linked issue of fundamental interest is the formal one I have already touched on—the manner in which Meredith plays, sometimes almost obsessively, with conventional notions of genre and associated literary language in ways that question, disrupt, and extend our sense of traditional novelistic boundaries and decorum as he shows that the comedy of patriarchy may well develop into its tragic counterpart. Still another significant issue, however, is that all the while he is conducting his narrative experiments, Meredith also frequently employs a style full of tensions, awkwardnesses, and apparent contradictions that provide, as we shall see, a revealing metacommentary of their own. To revert to the words of Virginia Woolf, "What an odd conglomeration it is!"[2]

In *Shagpat* and *Farina* there appear to be self-imposed limits as to where the text will go with its uses of burlesque language appropriate to the exploits of the sword-wielding barber-as-hero, Shibli Bagarag, or the invention of Eau de Cologne, but hardly a style that could depict the tragic circumstances that end *Richard Feverel*. But, of course, precisely the same point may be made about *Richard Feverel* on the basis of its first chapters. The tone is considerably more urbane and sententious than that of *Shagpat* or *Farina*, but the predominant note is still broadly satirical: the inhabitants of Raynham Abbey, like the oddities who inhabit Meredith's father-in-law's *Nightmare Abbey,* are presented in a blend of parodic styles that would seem to prepare us for anything but tragedy.[3] The pointed references to Sir Austin's "Pilgrim's Scrip" on the opening page provide an ironic commentary on the action much as do the pithy rhymes interspersed in the narratives of *Shagpat* and *Farina*. Almost the first aphorism quoted—" 'Life is a tedious process of learning we are Fools' " (9)—makes fun of Sir Austin not only because he is a fool, but because he never learns he is one. At the novel's end we see him still trapped within the aphoristic monologue with which he begins.

Just as satiric in effect as the Aphorist's complacent pronouncements is the liberal sprinkling of mock heroic epithets referring to him in the early pages—the Sage, England's Christian La Rochefoucauld, Gamaliel, Solomon, and the unhappy Griffin. Most important of all in striking the opening burlesque note is the "Court" formed about the baronet by the swarm of idolatrous women come down to Raynham to do battle with his misogynic views, a situation with clear affinities to the amusing chapter in *Shagpat* in which Shibli Bagarag is enraptured by the attention of a circle of apparently adoring women in the Palace of Aklis. Meredith sets up the scene as Menippean satire, stressing eccentricities in the manner of Dickens and Peacock. But the strain becomes more and more evident, and suggests the difficulties he would have encountered in sustaining this arch style for five hundred pages: "But he had written a book; he had made himself an object: Miss Blewins was in the field; the lean, the long-nosed, the accomplished, the literary: . . . Lady Blandish was in the field; the fairest sweetest sensible widow ever seen, a dead shot with her eyes, when she used them: . . . All these female harriers were in the field prepared to give chase to the Griffin" (12).

Much of the unevenness of *Richard Feverel* originates in what Meredith himself later recognized as a false start. By making "an object" of Sir Austin, and Lady Blandish as well, he set severe limitations on the reader's expectations and then, in what was to become a characteristically Meredithian gesture, proceeded to ignore

the limitations altogether: both Sir Austin and Lady Blandish become increasingly human, psychologically complex studies in subjectivity as the novel progresses. We are far better off for Meredith's
impetuosity—there was certainly no great need for a three-volume
Nightmare Abbey—but his entry into subject matter inappropriate
to Menippean satire did not always mean a departure from the
early satirical style. This, in fact, is one of the most revealing and
recurrent problems posed by the stylistic experimentation in this
novel—the Peacockian note continues to be heard at odd places
throughout.

A telling early example is found in the description of Richard's
seventh birthday. Sir Austin is described as spending the day in
nervous anticipation of some form of unpleasant event, another
manifestation of what he considers to be the curse on the family
by "Mrs. Malediction"—the feminine form is all-important—or the
Ordeal of the Feverels. When such an event does occur it is actu-
ally quite serious and involves the loss of a leg on the part of Richard's uncle Algernon, a gentleman of the Guards whose particular
eccentricity is a fanaticism for cricket. But the whole incident is
carried off as opera buffa and leaves one with an odd sense of incongruity between the flamboyant style and the rather somber subject:

> His Uncle Algernon was still in, batting gloriously: his elegant figure
> and fine legs deservedly admired by the ladies. A shot from Bursley's
> terrible-swift bowler took him on the forward thigh, and he was seen
> limping towards the tents with considerable lack of grace, and a rue-
> fully-animated expression. Dr. Clifford of Lobourne was present, and
> perused the bruise. He had him conveyed immediately to the house,
> where, towards night, it was debated whether there was to be a leg less
> in the family, as was soon the case. (29)
> "Said I not, Something would happen?" remarked Sir Austin, not al-
> together dissatisfied.
> "Oh, confound Mrs. Malediction!" . . . cried the poor one-legged
> Guardsman. (29)

When Meredith revised the novel for a new edition in 1875, he
condensed the first four chapters into one, deleting, among much
else, the feminine court at Raynham and most of the description
of Algernon's misfortune—including "perused the bruise." But, as
most readers have agreed, the result is less satisfactory than the
original. The revision appears to have been made without great

care, since a considerable amount of pertinent information is left out, and the incidents that survive, like Algernon's accident, are condensed without losing their essential incongruity of tone. Meredith made a further attempt to give the novel stylistic unity in the 1896 Deluxe Edition when he cut and simplified some of the more exaggerated language in later parts of the text.[4] But these changes could not alter the real problem: the stylistic incongruities were symptoms of Meredith's wish to write a new form of novel combined with his uncertainty about exactly what that form was or how to go about achieving it. In spite of certain infelicities that are symptomatic of this innovative impulse, then, I wish to argue that *Richard Feverel* has very substantial significance as ground-breaking experimental fiction. I don't think Donald Stone overstates the case when he suggests that, "published in the year of the *Origin of Species* and *On Liberty*, Meredith's novel created a revolution of its own, even if the full effects were not felt for many years afterward. In many respects the modern English novel, with its psychological intricacies and subjective language, begins with *The Ordeal of Richard Feverel*."[5]

2

The great thematic difference between the fiction Meredith had already written and *Richard Feverel* was that in the latter he wished to take an initially comic situation—based again on male egoism and self-ignorance—and develop by degrees what he saw as its tragic implications. As we have seen, the initial situation proved so tempting to his playful and satirical instincts that he allowed these instincts to control the style of the opening chapters. Brilliant as it is, then, *Richard Feverel* remains an apprenticeship novel in which Meredith was working his way out of the burlesque mode of *Shagpat* and *Farina* toward a more flexible style that could embody his maturing vision of a fictional world made up of psychological complexities that produce an amalgam of comic, romantic, and tragic elements.

What Meredith produces in his portrait of Sir Austin Feverel is quite literally a psychological critique and parody of the patriarchal claim to objectivity: the father, posturing as "Scientific Humanist," is intent, not on dispassionate, methodical, or humane thinking, but rather on an elaborate scheme of retribution that he himself cannot fully recognize. Abandoned by his wife after the birth of their son, he has proceeded to sublimate his extreme sense of damaged self-esteem into a scientific "System," ostensibly to protect Richard from the dangers of a similar ordeal. In a letter written just after the publication of the novel, Meredith noted succinctly that the System "had its origin not so much in [Sir Austin's] love for his son, as in wrath at his wife, and so carried its own Nemesis. . . . [N]o System of the sort succeeds with human nature, unless the originator has conceived it purely independent of personal passion. This was Sir Austin's way of wreaking his revenge."[6]

For Meredith, the possibility of escape from any "personal passion" was highly questionable. And in his satirical portrait of Sir Austin's "science," he anticipates in some important ways the modernist/postmodernist distrust of claims to objectivity—what Thomas Nagel has called "the view from nowhere." David McWhirter has discussed Nagel's analysis of objectivity claims in relation to *The Egoist*, but his discussion of the later novel may also be seen to have interesting implications for the case of Sir Austin: "Meredith, like Nagel, believes that the 'pursuit of objectivity' is a natural human endeavor, but that it 'cannot completely subordinate the personal standpoint and its prereflective motives'—that any 'view from nowhere,' in other words, 'includes irreducibly subjective elements.'" As McWhirter goes on to point out, recent feminist treatments of objectivity claims make a similar point, but go further—in a way that can also illuminate Meredith's treatment of Sir Austin's misogyny: "Feminist theory and practice have tended to distrust . . . objectivity claims, not only because 'views from nowhere' so frequently turn out, upon closer examination, to be versions of a male gaze, but also because the very drive for distance and abstraction has increasingly been seen as a male-gendered epistemological strategy that is deeply implicated in androcentric culture's suppression of women's difference."[7] Meredith's presentation of Sir Austin provides a precise dramatization of this process, and extends it with an instructive corollary: the patriarch's way of knowing the world is to suppress women's difference in a manner that is ultimately self-destructive—for son as well as father.

In spite of all its trappings of inscrutable omniscience, then, the System is founded on "personal passion" and acts as a constant reminder of Sir Austin's betrayal of his own intelligence, especially in his attempt to deify mind through denial of the presence of emotion—a clear perversion of Meredithian common sense. As William

Buckler has summed up the case, "[t]he System, having grown out of a mad self-deceit and unrelenting wrath, is implacable: it will not permit the natural affection and paternal love of Sir Austin to grant forgiveness to his son after he has deceived him; and it has so imbued the systematized youth with abstract principles and sentimentality that he cannot fight his father's egoism until all is lost."[8] A product of the System, the "young Experiment" becomes a comic figure much in the manner of his father, equally prone to his own romantic brand of vanity, egoism, and monologism. He is presented to us with many of the same tricks of style as is Sir Austin; in the first half of the novel, for example, his various exploits are referred to as acts in a comedy, though this practice ends, significantly, when he links his fate irrevocably with Lucy Desborough's in the chapter entitled "The Last Act of a Comedy."

Richard's most important similarity to his father is his tendency, in his relations with women, to lose his grasp on what common sense he has. The repetition of the characteristic is shown to be no accident. Sir Austin, in his efforts to shield Richard from the threats of Eve and the "Apple Disease," effectively makes his son an idealizer of femininity; due to his cloistered upbringing, then, Richard is shown to be free from any practical experience with women—or women's difference. This in itself might be innocuous enough—the process does not seem much different from the custom of packing boys off to boarding school at the first sign of adolescence—except for the part this inexperience plays when Richard later leaps into the role of lover, husband, and rescuer of fallen women all at once. Before he has had a chance to reach any kind of understanding of gender differences or of himself, he is forced to make decisions that are literally matters of life and death. The fact that he is so poorly prepared for these roles turns the story away from comedy and in the direction of tragedy.

It is not too much to say, as Walter Wright has done, that Richard's entire career consists in his preoccupation with women.[9] The novel is full of female figures who play important roles in his development, first as a comic and then as a potentially tragic hero. These figures fall into two rough categories—those with whom Richard has romantic relationships and those who attempt to assume a maternal role towards him. The first group consists of Clare Forey, Lucy Desborough, Bella Mount, and Lady Judith Felle, though "romantic" takes on a different meaning in each case, and Bella and Lady Judith also have strong maternal feelings toward Richard. The second group is comprised of Lady Blandish, Mrs. Doria Forey, Mrs. Berry, and the shadowy figure of Richard's mother, Lady Feverel. As part of their maternal attentions to Richard, these older women all stand in opposition to Sir Austin's System. In the case of Mary Feverel, the opposition lies in the fact that Sir Austin has in effect divorced her and subsequently "wedded the System," which is premised on her physical and spiritual banishment. All of these women are important to understanding Meredith's experimentation with feminist themes and the styles that convey them, but in the discussion that follows I will concentrate on the three feminine figures most directly involved with the novel's problematic transition from comedy to tragedy—Clare, Lucy, and Lady Blandish.

3

Richard's cousin Clare is the first of these to attract our full attention. Her role provides a good example of Meredith's often effective structuring in this novel, a sign of the unity of conception that develops in *Richard Feverel* once one is past the difficulties of the opening. The episode in which Clare is introduced—Richard's fourteenth birthday—is a curious and important one. As is hinted at the time, and as becomes clear later, the family ghost Clare thinks she has seen as she waits for Richard is in fact Lady Feverel, briefly returned from banishment to catch a birthday glimpse of her son. Clare's impression of the apparition suggests that she is a reader of gothic romance, and at the same time provides a striking representation of Lady Feverel's psychological state—"the Ghost of a lady, dressed in deep mourning, a scar on her forehead, and a bloody handkerchief at her breast, frightful to behold!" (64).

Meredith's linking of these two melancholy figures takes on significance as the novel progresses. Both seek a more natural and direct relationship with Richard, which they are never permitted to enjoy—the closest either gets to him that night is to hear him shout for his dinner—and both are to become the objects of his well-intentioned but inept efforts at salvation later on. Both are treated as outcasts from Raynham Abbey—Clare is soon dismissed by Sir Austin on the ground that her worshipful attitude toward Richard is a threat to the System—and both are made to suffer in silence ordeals just as trying as those endured, with considerable commentary and clamor, by Richard and Sir Austin. In these last respects the experiences of the two women—Clare's in particular—foreshadow and prepare for the trials that lie ahead for Lucy.

In her relations with Richard, Clare seems at first Lucy's direct opposite. Richard falls in love with Lucy instantly and ignores Clare, whom he sees every day; Lucy becomes the constant subject of Richard's thoughts, while Clare's departure from Raynham produces barely a ripple. But one of Meredith's innovative narrative tactics here is to produce conventional romantic patterns of this sort and at the same time to undercut them with ironies that show, finally, a larger and more revealing pattern. One is tempted by Meredith's narrative emphasis to forget that the first place Richard and Lucy meet is not on the banks of the river as Ferdinand and Miranda, but in the prosaic living room of Farmer Blaize, where Richard treats her—or rather, ignores her—with the same rudeness he shows toward Clare. This apparently harmless adolescent insensibility is a sign of the same egoism that later, grown to enormous proportions, allows him to ignore Lucy's pleas and pursue a duel to vindicate, not her honor, but his own: like father, like son. The novel has its intensely romantic moments—the meeting of Richard and Lucy by the river is the most familiar example—but the larger pattern that emerges is clearly a rejection of a romantic sensibility that does not incorporate the moderating influence of critical intelligence, that is, a balance of passion with self-knowledge and dialogic openness to the voices of others. What is striking about this lesson is that Lucy and Clare, as well as Richard, must pay so dearly for his self-indulgent excesses—violation of common sense in this novel leads directly from comedy to tragedy. Richard's recognition of the destructive role he plays in Clare's life and in Lucy's comes too late in both cases.

Immediately before the "Ferdinand and Miranda" chapter, Meredith introduces one of his sharpest touches of irony in his use of Clare to highlight the difficulties to be implicit in Richard's relations with Lucy. Richard's mind has been set afire by the sight of Sir Austin kissing the hand of Lady Blandish: "There was, then, some end in existence, something to live for! to kiss a woman's hand, and die!" (123). Full of sighs, Richard rows unwittingly toward his meeting with Lucy, but, once again, it is easy to forget that it is his friend Ralph Morton whom he meets first. Ralph, also undergoing romantic raptures, has already fastened on Clare as the personification of consummate womanhood. When he leaves a letter with Richard for delivery to Clare, Richard experiences a sudden awakening:

> For the first time it struck him that his cousin Clare was a very charming creature: . . . What business, pray, had Ralph to write to her? Did she not belong to him, Richard Feverel? He read the words again and again: Clare Doria Forey. Why, Clare was the name he liked best: nay, he loved it. Doria, too: she shared his own name with him. Away went his heart, not at a canter now, at a gallop, as one who sights the quarry. He felt too weak to pull. Clare Doria Forey—oh, perfect melody! Sliding with the tide, he heard it fluting in the bosom of the hills. (127)

Delightfully comic as this passage is, it is at the same time foreboding: the arrogant possessiveness of Richard's humorless romanticism is a manifestation of the same male egoism that brings about the novel's tragic conclusion. In addition, after the Shagpatian uncertainty of the opening chapters, this section and what follows show the rapid gains Meredith had made in developing and controlling a style suitable for effectively embodying his extraordinary blend of comedy, romantic lyricism, and incipient tragedy. In particular, the outbursts of narrated monologue[10] display a developing technique he was to use to great effect throughout his career. This is not to say, however, that by this point Meredith had solved his stylistic problems; as we shall see later, "Ferdinand and Miranda" is by no means free of the kind of erratic rhetorical effects that continued to mar Meredith's work to the very end of his career.

The only true confrontation between Richard and Clare occurs in a scene shortly before her wedding to John Todhunter, the amiable and brainless elder suitor of Mrs. Doria who has graciously consented to shift his attentions from mother to daughter once Richard's unavailability has become clear. The scene marks Richard's final effort to dissuade Mrs. Doria and Clare from pursuing the marriage and is important because it brings together and clarifies many of the themes already established in the novel. The phrase used by Mrs. Doria to describe the marital scheme is "common sense," and thus her egotistical manipulations are categorized as still another perversion of the spirit of critical intelligence in the novel. In spite of her limitations, however, she is still shown to have enough sense to attack Sir Austin's System, but this is largely because it frustrates her own machinations: "His System, and his conduct generally, were denounced to him [by his sister], without analysis" (356). When Richard attempts to interfere with the wedding, in the scene under consideration, Mrs. Doria's response follows the same tack; characteristically, she is made to say more than she can understand: " 'Really,' Mrs. Doria said to her intimates, 'that boy's education acts like a disease on him. He cannot regard anything sensibly. He is for ever in some mad excess of his fancy, and what he will come to at last Heaven only knows! I sincerely pray that Austin will be able to bear it' " (360).

Richard's education, like Clare's, has had as its object the very perverted "sensibleness" that he repudiates here and in his marriage to Lucy. By acting in a "mad excess of fancy," however, he rebels against Mrs. Doria's limited meaning of "common sense" while at the same time failing to grasp its possible larger meanings. His appeals to Clare to refuse Todhunter are passionate and founded on a just revulsion; at the same time, Richard acts out of profound ignorance of Clare's feelings and of the ultimate effect his words may have on her. As is evidenced by the repetition of the first-person pronoun, he is thinking primarily of himself:

> "I tell you it's an infamy, Clare! It's a miserable sin! I tell you, if I had done such a thing I would not live an hour after it. . . ." He burst into tears.
> "Dear Richard," said Clare, "you will make me very unhappy."
> "That one of my blood should be so debased!" he cried, brushing angrily at his face. "Unhappy! I beg you to feel for yourself, Clare. But I suppose," and he said it scornfully, "girls don't feel this sort of shame." (359)

That Clare does feel shame becomes clear to Richard only after her suicide. It is then that her diary and the second ring on her finger tell him what he has been unable to perceive before. The experience fills Richard with contrition, but Meredith had no interest in providing an escape from the tragic pattern he had so carefully constructed: Richard does not respond to Clare's death by recognizing the web of egoism that entangles him. Rather, he experiences sorrow and then, true to character, continues headlong on the disastrous path he has by this time chosen.

It is Richard's aunt, Mrs. Doria, whom Meredith shows gaining some tragic understanding from the loss. Like Jane Austen's Mrs. Bennet, "the business of her life" (115) has been the marriage of her daughter; without Clare, Mrs. Doria is able to look with some disinterest to the welfare of others: " 'Richard,' she said, 'the worst is over for me. I have no one to love but you, dear. We have all been fighting against God, and this . . . Richard! you will come with me, and be united to your wife, and spare my brother what I suffer.'" Richard, who has just emerged from his liaison with Mrs. Mount, is incapable of recognizing what is now genuine and humane common sense on Mrs. Doria's part. Instead, he strikes a pseudo-Byronic pose which, by this late point in the novel, epitomizes his melodramatic conception of heroic behavior:

> "I cannot go with you to my wife, because I am not worthy to touch her hand, and were I to go, I should do this to silence my self-contempt. Go you to her, and when she asks of me, say I have a death upon my head that—No! say that I am abroad, seeking for that which shall cleanse me. If I find it I shall come to claim her. If not, God help us all!"
> She had no force to contest his solemn words, or stay him, and he went forth. (446)

It is just this mode of theatrical solemnity—echoed here by the wonderfully ironical pomposity of the narrator's final sentence—translated into action that brings about the novel's tragic conclusion. As for Mrs. Doria, she has reached the impasse typical of a number of women in this novel: she finally sees clearly but does not have the means to contest the destructive effects of sentimental male egoism.

4

When Lucy Desborough is first described on the banks of the river just before the opening of the "Ferdinand and Miranda" chapter, she is a "daughter of Earth," one of Meredith's natural women. Like many of the heroines who were to follow (Ottilia, René, Clara, Aminta, and Carinthia are all most at home in natural settings), Lucy is in perfect harmony with her surroundings in this scene and at peace with herself. Identified with Earth, she is the possessor of a unified personality, a balanced embodiment of Meredith's triad of blood, brain, and spirit. True common sense for Meredith involved this same synthesis of human powers, the control and interdependence of emotion, intellect, and the spiritual he depicted in "The Woods of Westermain":

Blood and brain and spirit, three
(Say the deepest gnomes of Earth),
Join for true felicity.
Are they parted, then expect
Some one sailing will be wrecked:
Separate hunting are they sped,
Scan the morsel coveted.
Earth that Triad is: she hides
Joy from him who that divides;
Showers it when the three are one
Glassing her in union.[11]

These lines act as a gloss not only on Lucy's unified emotional intelligence but on its opposites as well—as seen in the increasingly fragmented male figures who wield patriarchal authority at Raynham Abbey and Belthorpe Farm.

In addition to directing us forward in Meredith's work, Lucy also directs us back—to Noorna bin Noorka. Lucy shares Noorna's instinctive good sense but, without her magic, the situation becomes quite the reverse of that found in the land of Shagpat. And where Shibli Bagarag characteristically turns to Noorna for guidance in moments of crisis, the last thing Richard's education has prepared him for is to listen to a woman's voice. Meredith shows him at various points in a state of self-imposed monological ignorance, turning from the good council of Lucy as well as that of Lady Blandish, Mrs. Berry, Mrs. Doria, and, ironically, Bella Mount.

A significant feature of Lucy's personality, one that recalls Noorna and has obvious affinities with the comic spirit, is her sense of humor. The laughter in the novel before Lucy's appearance has an unhealthy, unpleasant edge to it—Adrian Harley's cynical asides and Richard's and Ripton's raucous guffaws at the expense of Farmer Blaize, for example. As for Sir Austin, "he was cognizant of the total absence of the humorous in himself." This comment is followed by a statement that could well have been included in the *Essay*: "For a good wind of laughter [would have] . . . relieved him of much of the blight of self-deception, and . . . given a healthier view of our atmosphere of life: but he had it not" (204).

On the other hand, Lucy, to whom Sir Austin "would have thrown . . . the handkerchief for his son" (129) had he been given the opportunity, is healthiness personified. Practically her first reaction to Richard in the "Ferdinand and Miranda" chapter is to laugh at his excessive sentimental behavior. After he has leaped into the water to retrieve her lost book, he emerges to claim, "in all sincerity," that he does not feel wet:

> [H]er blue eyes lightened laughter out of the half-closed lids.
> "I cannot help it," she said, her mouth opening, and sounding harmonious bells of laughter in his ears. "Pardon me, won't you?"
> His face took the same soft smiling curves in admiration of her.
> "Not to feel that you have been in the water, the very moment after!" she musically interjected, seeing she was excused.
> "It's true," he said; and his own gravity then touched him to join a duet with her, which made them no longer feel strangers, and did the work of a month of intimacy. (132–33)

Developing what was to become one of the major critical premises of the *Essay*, the passage effectively dramatizes the dialogical contagiousness of Lucy's goodnatured humor and how it allows Richard to see himself as she does. The scene shows not only that she has common sense but that he, were it not for the System lurking at Raynham, would be quite capable of benefiting from her insight. Nothing could be more remote from Richard's later theatricality at the time of Clare's death.

But to stop here would be to ignore an aspect of the experimental Meredith that is at once extremely irritating and utterly characteristic. In the next sentence the narrative's rhetorical control falters. Problems of style similar to those I have discussed in the novel's first chapters reappear—problems strategically important because they directly affect our responses to Richard and Lucy: "Better than sentiment Laughter opens the breast to Love; opens the whole breast to his full quiver, instead of a corner here and there for a solitary arrow. Hail the occasion propitious, O ye British young! and laugh, and treat Love as an honest God, and dabble not with the spiritual rouge" (133). What began well turns to stylistic disaster. In later years, as we have seen, Meredith showed some awareness of the difficulty. A letter written in 1873 bears this note in the margin: "I opened a volume of Richard Fev the other day, and had a sharp distaste. The lumpy style is offensive."[12] This passage was evidently not the one he had come upon, since it went virtually untouched in the 1875 and 1896 revisions.[13]

The problem here is more than one of "lumpiness," however, although that term is not inappropriate, especially for the narrative expostulation to British youth. The real difficulty lies in the curious blend of styles: the heightened language is reminiscent of that used to burlesque Sir Austin in the opening chapters, and at the same time it appears to contain a genuine outburst of romantic enthusiasm. The result is that we are left in doubt about how to take the narrator's meaning, and this same confusion is encountered at one point or another in all of the romantic scenes involving Richard and Lucy. The pompous address seems to ask us to assume an Adrian-like nonchalance towards the young lovers, while the point being made is clearly one to which we are intended to give our unqualified assent—that honest love and laughter, epitomized in Lucy, are natural counterparts, opposed to Richard's earlier sentimentalism. In the previous scene, in which irony effectively undercuts his humorless romantic effusions over Clare, Richard was all possessiveness and arrogance; here, to serve Lucy he is willing to risk anything, including his sense of dignity. But the dramatic effect of this transformation is blunted—if not lost—by the Carlylean verbal play which tends to repel rather than enlist our sympathies.[14] There is no sense here—as there is in the passages I discussed earlier—of an implied author directing us to balance the narrator's pompous tone against a larger clarifying vision of the action. Instead, we have an instance of what Jacques Derrida describes as the "supplement" produced by *"différance"*—that is, "the opposition or tension . . . between what a text 'declares' and what it 'describes'"—a supplement that leads, in this case, to our uneasy sense of narrative out of control.[15]

Despite sporadic excesses of this sort, however, Meredith is quite capable of exerting firm control over his poetical style in this section. And when he does we feel the magic of Richard's and Lucy's attraction for one another most powerfully and directly:

> If these two were Ferdinand and Miranda, Sir Austin was not Prospero, and was not present, or their fates might have been different.
> So they stood a moment, changing eyes, and then Miranda spoke, and they came down to earth, feeling no less in heaven.
> She spoke to thank him for his aid. She used quite common simple words; and used them, no doubt, to express a common simple meaning; but to him she was uttering magic, casting spells, and the effect they had on him was manifested in the incoherence of his replies, which were too foolish to be chronicled. (130)

The experimental impulse in Meredith can also cast spells, or lead to stylistic incoherence, and this was to be the pattern throughout the rest of his career.

5

The freedom and enchantment of the early scenes in nature, when Lucy's instinctive intelligence is ascendant, give way as the novel progresses to an increasing sense of constriction as Richard's single-minded egotism gains control. By the time Richard hustles her into Mrs. Berry's house, Lucy is no longer Miranda, but "a captive borne to the sacrifice" (248). Richard, in removing Lucy from the arbitrary authority of Farmer Blaize and Sir Austin, places her, "like a dutiful slave" (260), under his own equally implacable brand of patriarchal authority. Her good sense directs her to the more reasonable course—" 'Your father may be brought to consent by and by, and then—Oh! if you take me home now' " (261). But Richard's rebellion against the creator of the System in no way frees him from the wrongheaded presumptions fostered by the System itself. His sentimental and self-pitying arguments—" 'Would you have me lost? . . . I have staked all I have on you' " (260)—act as a thin veil to his position of power: any resistance on Lucy's part is made to appear as a repudiation of her fidelity. Under this pressure, she is shown by the end of this chapter to slide into a state of sentimental passivity: "Sweet to shut out Wisdom; accept total blindness, and be led by him" (261). Janet Horowitz Murray, in commenting upon this passage, suggests that such "passivity is no less culpable than heroic aggression to Meredith's unvictorian mind. Lucy commits one of the central sins of the novel by closing her eyes to Wisdom . . . ; her willingness to suffer is no more admirable than Clare's and has the same result."[16] And Gary Handwerk takes essentially the same position in regard to Lucy, arguing that she "fails Richard" through her "nonoppositional, yielding nature. . . . Her inarticulate inability to do more than sense crimps her influence."[17] It is also important to see, however, that by "The Last Scene" (473 f.) Lucy has returned to a much more assertive and clearheaded role, but by this time it is too late to change the course of events.

As we examine the transition from comedy to tragedy taking place in this flawed but nevertheless remarkable first novel, it should be clear that I have no wish to suggest that we are in the presence of an exemplum of "organic unity." However, I do want to argue that the generic transition is consistent and well prepared for. As various commentators have shown,[18] there are a number of structural, symbolical, and rhetorical devices used by Meredith from the beginning to undercut the novel's comic tone and to fore-shadow its outcome. The role of Clare, which I have already dis-cussed, the recurring image of the cypress, the elaborate role played by the infallible System, parallels to the Agamemnon/Iphi-genia myth, the narrator's foreboding comments, and the motif of knight errantry are all examples.

This last is especially important in tracing the development of Richard's potential for his tragic role as instigator of the duel with Mountfalcon, which in turn leads to Lucy's death. Early and late in the novel, Richard's chivalric posturing acts as an index of his ego-tism and self-ignorance, for Meredith primary sins against common sense. Richard is shown at the outset to be an essentially well-intentioned young man whose character and education progres-sively combine to produce grand visions and disastrous actions. Meredith does not condemn the visions themselves—the liberation of Italy, for example, was one of his own enthusiasms—but rather Richard's Mrs. Jellyby-like neglect of the responsibilities closest to him. Like Stendhal's Fabrice del Dongo, to whom he shows some striking resemblances, Richard confuses adopting the style and dreams of a romantic hero with heroic action itself.

Or one might go further and suggest that Meredith is bent on bringing traditional notions of the "heroic" into question, a point that could also be effectively argued in *Beauchamp's Career*. In Richard's case, what we see is a wholly artificial standard of con-duct that stands in contrast to his instinctive gallantry and humor in the early nature scenes with Lucy. As U. C. Knoepflmacher has said in his discussion of the novel's ending, "by falling back on his notions of heroism and honor, [Richard] escapes the harder task of reconciling himself to his own faults. . . . He shows himself to be his father's son, for, like Sir Austin's system, his chivalric notions stem from a fear of confronting man's potential for evil."[19] Rich-ard's knightly playacting, amusing and even at times attractive in the earlier part of the novel, takes on an increasingly foreboding aspect as he reaches manhood and must assume the responsibili-ties of husband and father.

Many readers have been disturbed, however, because Meredith

appears to provide Richard with a conversion from this theatrical behavior in the late "Nature Speaks" chapter, and then, in J. B. Priestly's phrase, "quite arbitrarily"[20] allows him to take up his heroics where he had left off as the novel moves to its tragic denouement. To view the failure of Richard's conversion as arbitrary, however, seems to me to involve a wish to impose a convention on the novel that is far more arbitrary than the form Meredith chose. The reconciliations and happy ending of romantic comedy, as is so evident in Shakespeare, are typically highly stylized, true to the comic mode that is by nature "arbitrary" in that it rules out treatment of the darker side of human experience and poses marriage as the ultimate resolution to problems of human interaction. If Meredith were to have brought his main characters together in reconciliation at the end of *Richard Feverel*, he would have in large part canceled the increasingly serious implications of the Systematic development of Richard's character and invalidated what David Foster has rightly called "the formative principle of the novel's structure"—its "shift from the comic mode to the tragic."[21] What I wish to argue here is that in the "Nature Speaks" chapter, Meredith is very much in an innovative mode as he proposes but veers away from a conventional romantic resolution, providing instead a recapitulation of the novel's central thematic opposition between nature and artifice, an opposition he effectively embodies in the style of the chapter itself.

Jacob Korg has observed that in *Richard Feverel* the "first function" of the narrative voice "is that of embodying the various states of mind represented in the novel in parodistic styles laced with irony,"[22] and while I think this is less consistently true than Korg suggests, it is precisely the technique at work at the beginning of "Nature Speaks." In an extravagant mock heroic style Richard is compared with Briareus of the hundred hands, "reddening angrily over the sea" (457), and Orestes, "the Furies howling in his ears" (458). It is a style that neatly sums up Richard's sentimental and rather excessively self-flattering view—"Had he not been nursed to believe he was born for great things?" (459)—a style that epitomizes the problem of monological artifice as departure from common sense:

> Far in the West fair Lucy beckons him to come. Ah, Heaven! if he might! How strong and fierce the temptation is! how subtle the sleepless desire! it drugs his reason, his honour. . . .

Ah, happy English home! sweet wife! what mad miserable Wisp of the Fancy led him away from you, high in his conceit? Poor wretch! that thought to be he of the hundred hands, and war against the absolute Gods." (457–58)

The ironic narrative tone is maintained for several pages as Richard is depicted with Lady Judith, speaking "of Italy in low voices," "adrift prone on floods of sentiment . . . , [h]imself on horseback over-riding wrecks of Empires!" or affecting a Carlylean melancholy as "[o]ften wretchedly he watches the young men of his own age trooping to their work. Not cloud-work theirs! Work solid, unambitious, fruitful!" (459). Once nature asserts herself in the Rhineland forest, however, Richard's titanic visions appear to vanish as the narrative makes its transition from a style that is, to borrow a phrase from the *Essay*, "overblown, affected, pretentious, bombastical . . . , pedantic, [and] fantastically delicate" (23:47) to one of direct simplicity: "the Spirit of Life illumined him. He felt in his heart the cry of his child, his darling's touch. With shut eyes he saw them both. They drew him from the depths; they led him a blind and tottering man. And as they led him he had a sense of purification so sweet he shuddered again and again" (465).

In this chapter, then, Meredith dramatizes, both stylistically and thematically, the opposition between the values fostered by Sir Austin and those represented in the novel by Lucy. What is often overlooked, however, is that there is no guarantee offered here that Richard's "conversion" from the style of the first part of the chapter to the simplicity and humbleness of the last part is in any way permanent. As Renate Muendel has observed, "we expect a happy end . . . because literary convention has taught us that moral conversions are total, permanent, and rewarded with domestic bliss."[23] But the picture of Richard as "a blind and tottering man" seems to prepare for something quite different. Besides specifically anticipating the last lines of the novel,[24] the image stresses Richard's passivity in the scene, suggesting that his "purification" is not self-achieved but comes from without. His return to familiar melodramatic form on receiving news of Mountfalcon's apparent indiscretions in the next chapter, then, seems consistent, not with the conventions of romantic comedy, but with the psychological portrait Meredith has provided of Richard's upbringing and character from the outset.

The final scene between Lucy and Richard produces the novel's most affecting contrast between naturalness and artifice, between her reasserted humane common sense and his sophistic notions of male honor as he prepares for his duel with Mountfalcon. Lucy's instincts are shown to be consistently sound: with Richard safely returned from the Rhineland, her entire purpose is to keep him with her and their child. When she says, "'Come: lie on my heart'" (488), her impulse is to follow nature, to heal the breach between herself and Richard through sexual union. Although he is strongly moved by Lucy's directness, Richard's response throughout the scene is characteristically centered in his ego as he turns away from dialogue: "He must stab her to the heart, shatter the image she held of him" (484). His effort to replace this "shattered image" with one even more exalted—that of avenging lover—completes his transition from the romantic and comic hero of the first part of the novel to the tragically misguided husband of the last part, hell-bent on pursuing his Systematized ideal of conduct at any cost: "It was over in an instant. She cried out his name, clinging to him wildly, and was adjured to be brave, for he would be dishonoured if he did not go. Then she was shaken off" (488).

6

The last words of *Richard Feverel* are given to Lady Blandish in a letter to Austin Wentworth. The linking of these two figures begins early in the novel when Lady Blandish takes Wentworth's side in opposition to Adrian Harley, whom Sir Austin prefers to Wentworth as Richard's tutor; by the novel's end, she and Wentworth have come to be Meredith's two chief touchstones of good judgment. Both are placed primarily in the role of nonparticipant commentator: Wentworth appears only briefly at the opening and close, and Lady Blandish is always in the shadow of Sir Austin. But as the novel progresses, their commentary—particularly that of Lady Blandish—becomes increasingly significant as an index of common sense and humane intuition against which to judge the sophistic arguments of Sir Austin, Richard, and Adrian. When Wentworth finally returns from South America and enters the action—to take Lucy to Raynham and seek out Richard in the Rhineland—he follows the judgment of Lady Blandish as well as his own. As is true throughout the novel, however, the wills of Sir Austin and then increasingly of Richard determine the final course of events: the conversion of good judgment into Wentworth's positive action at this late point cannot avert the tragic conclusion.

Lady Blandish is presented initially as an uncritical admirer of Sir Austin. Her name, straight out of Restoration and eighteenth-century comedy, bears the mark of her introduction among the crowd of caricatured feminists in the first chapter, but this is an association she is seen to outgrow rapidly. At first she regards Sir Austin as an intellectual knight (119), but the chivalric metaphor eventually comes to have the same ironic effect as when used to describe Richard: the distinction between knightly virtue and heroic posturing is one of Meredith's most persistent preoccupations in the novel. Lady Blandish's initial inability to perceive this distinction, Meredith implies, is due to her tendency to sentimentalize—to distort her clear-sighted intelligence with the romantic view she would prefer: "Lady Blandish had been sentimentalizing for ten years. She would have preferred to pursue the game" (226).

The first time her idealized view of Sir Austin is disturbed is on the occasion of Richard's illness after his attempted pursuit of Lucy, who has been sent away by Farmer Blaize. Lady Blandish, when she has seen Richard's serious condition, moves aside from Sir Austin and offers an independent judgment: " 'Mark!' said the Baronet to Lady Blandish, 'when he recovers, he will not care for her. . . .' 'Oh! what an iron man you can be,' she exclaimed, smothering her intuitions. She was for giving the boy his bauble; promising it him, at least, if he would only get well and be the bright flower of promise he once was." The narrator's rendering of Lady Blandish's thought here still suggests the strength of Sir Austin's influence: the cavalier use of "bauble" would be uncharacteristic later on. As for Sir Austin's response to the crisis, "his patient serenity was a wonder to all who knew him. Indeed to have doubted and faltered now was to have subverted the glorious fabric just on the verge of completion" (221). By the novel's end, Lady Blandish responds quite differently to the serene mask that is Sir Austin's means of maintaining the infallibility he claims for himself and his System: "I could hardly bear the sight of his composure. I shall hate the name of Science till the day I die" (489).

The conclusion to this first episode, however, is a satisfactory one for Sir Austin. As he has predicted, Richard seems to have forgotten Lucy altogether. Lady Blandish, still an "enslaved mind," accepts the defeat of her intuitions and the apparent victory of "Science" over romance:

She was rebuked for certain little rebellious fancies concerning him that had come across her enslaved mind from time to time. For was he not almost a prophet? It distressed the sentimental lady that a love like Richard's could pass off in mere smoke, and words such as she had heard him speak in Abbey-wood resolve to emptiness. Nay, it humiliated her personally, and the Baronet's shrewd prognostication humiliated her. For how should he know, and dare to say, that Love was a thing of the dust that could be trodden out under the heel of Science? But he had said so, and he had proved himself right. (223)

"Science," as the word is used here and elsewhere, and as I have already suggested, is for Meredith a convenient term to suggest Sir Austin's particular blend of patriarchal egotism and spiritual blindness combined with the naive presumptions of nineteenth-century scientific amateurism. What this "Science" means practically in Raynham Abbey is an absence of the dialogical values associated with Meredithian common sense and consequent enslavement, not only for Lady Blandish, but for the rest of Sir Austin's intimates as well. It is only later, after Richard's rebellion against these conditions has proven Sir Austin wrong, that Lady Blandish is provided the occasion to catalyze her "little rebellious fancies" into a true assertion of spiritual independence.

When news of Richard's wedding reaches the Abbey, "the author of the System was on trial under the eyes of the lady who loved him" (326). The "Nursing the Devil" chapter in which this trial occurs describes the turning point of Richard's as well as Lady Blandish's relation to Sir Austin. William Buckler has suggested in his essay on this chapter that at the beginning "the die is not yet cast—at the end of the chapter it is."[25] That is, if Sir Austin had decided to welcome Richard and Lucy back to Raynham, the story would end there with no tragedy. But everything we know about the Baronet would lead us to expect him to react precisely as he does, placing "Science" above the welfare of his son. In this sense, the die is cast much earlier. As is later to be the case with Richard, Sir Austin's greatest concern is with "honor" and the consistency of the image his lady holds of him:

[T]he poor gentleman tasked his soul and stretched his muscles to act up to her conception of him. He, a man of science in Life, who was bound to be surprised by nothing in Nature, it was not for him to do more than lift his eyebrows and draw in his lips at the news delivered by Ripton Thompson, that ill bird at Raynham.

All he said, after Ripton had handed the letters and carried his peni-
tential headache to bed, was: "You see, Emmeline, it is useless to base
any System on a human being." (327)

Lady Blandish's response throughout this chapter is to appeal to Sir
Austin's humanity—to the man behind the mask. Invoking an
image that reappears in various significant ways throughout the
later part of the text, she tells him, " 'Do not shut your heart!' He
assured her that he hoped not to do so, and the moment she was
gone he set about shutting it as tight as he could" (328).
The inhumanity of the Scientific Humanist is thus shown to become unavoidably evident to Lady Blandish. The only response to
her further pleas on Richard's behalf is patronizing sententious-
ness: " 'Consequences are the natural offspring of acts. My child,
you are talking sentiment, which is the distraction of our modern
age in everything—a phantasmal vapour distorting the image of the
life we live' " (334). Far from being a sentimentalist, however, Lady
Blandish by this point is actively exercising her intuition and common sense. Sir Austin, on the other hand, is shown "distorting the
image" repeatedly in his attempts to bring events and his system
into alignment. The immediate consequence is the dethroning of
the patriarch: "she was compelled to perceive that his heart was
at present hardly superior to the hearts of ordinary men, however
composed his face might be, and apparently serene his wisdom.
From that moment she grew critical of him, and began to study her
Idol—a process dangerous to Idols (335).
Toward the end of the novel Lady Blandish is joined with a formidable ally in the person of Mrs. Berry, whose clear-eyed view of affairs is not complicated by any romantic attachment to Sir Austin.
The narrator provides the essential information that her expulsion
from Raynham Abbey twenty years before was brought about when
she spied Sir Austin, without mask, shedding a tear over Richard's
cradle. In one moment Mrs. Berry has been brought to the same
point of understanding it has taken Lady Blandish years to attain.[26]
The result, in both cases, is considerable skepticism about Sir Austin's motives. Having given Mrs. Berry this background, Meredith
allows her to produce what amounts to a definitive analysis of Sir
Austin's character, along with a summary of the actions necessary
to set matters right:

"I'll say his 'art's as soft as a woman's, which I've cause for to know.
And that's it. That's where everybody's deceived by him, and I was. It's

because he keeps his face, and makes ye think you're dealin' with a man of iron, and all the while there's a woman underneath. . . .—he's like somethin' out o' nature. Then I say—hopin' be excused—what's to do is for to treat him *like* a woman, and not for to let him 'ave his own way—which he don't know himself, and is why nobody else do. Let that sweet young couple come together, and be wholesome in spite of him, I say; and then give him time to come round, just like a woman; and round he'll come, and give 'em his blessin', and we shall know we've made him comfortable. . . ."

Now Mrs. Berry only put Lady Blandish's thoughts in bad English. (396)

Both women by this point in the novel act as touchstones of natural sound sense in opposition to that which is "out o' nature"— epitomized in Sir Austin's failure to achieve self-integration of masculine "iron" and feminine "heart." His problem, then, is not that he is androgynous, but that he wants to deny his feminine side; rather than achieving a fully integrated male personality, he is "a man that's like a woman . . . , the puzzle of life!" When Mrs. Berry suggests treating him like a woman—not letting him have his way— she is cleverly proposing a solution that asserts feminine values under the guise of partriarchal authority in combination with a reversal of traditional gender roles. What Mrs. Berry has not been able to see sufficiently clearly, however, is how extensive the effects of Richard's unnatural education have been. "Wholesomeness" is a long way from Richard's own lack of self-integration, a lack reflected in the system of impossible heroic conduct he has concocted in rebellion against the original System.

By the time Bessie Berry's directives have been carried out by the intervention of Austin Wentworth, Richard has already initiated proceedings for his duel with Mountfalcon, which in turn puts his father in an extraordinarily awkward position: "Sir Austin detained him, expostulated, contradicted himself, confounded his principles, made nonsense of all his theories. He could not induce his son to waver in his resolve. Ultimately, their Good-night being interchanged, he understood that the happiness of Raynham depended on Lucy's mercy. He had no fears of her sweet heart, but it was a strange thing to have come to" (482). Forced finally to take the side of feminine "heart," the Baronet is right in his judgment of Lucy's capacity for mercy, but quite wrong in his assumption at this late hour that Lucy can alter the forces put to work long before in shaping the destiny of Raynham.

It is "heart" that Lady Blandish fastens on in her description of the final scene of the novel. Sir Austin, in spite of his newfound regard for Lucy, is seen finally by Lady Blandish to be without heart or understanding toward her. When Lucy is dangerously ill with brain fever, "he thought her to blame for not commanding herself for the sake of her maternal duties" (489). Worse, in Lady Blandish's view, he shows himself incapable of any tragic understanding when confronted by Lucy's impending death: "He could not even then see his error. . . . His mad self-deceit would not leave him" (490). Ripton Thompson, who has been held up by Sir Austin as an outstanding negative example of unsystematic education, nonetheless has shown himself to be more devoted to Lucy than either Feverel. On seeing him by the deathbed, Lady Blandish comments, "That poor young man has a true heart." As for the product of Systematic education, Sir Austin "has given the death-blow to his heart. Richard will never be what he promised" (492). The shutting of the father's heart has led, finally, to the death of the heart of the son.

7

A final illuminating case of corrupted patriarchal intelligence and heartlessness in the novel is that of Adrian Harley, a character whose sins of omission coincide with the more active intellectual blundering of Sir Austin and Richard to propel events from their comic beginnings to the novel's tragic denouement. Adrian's perverse male gaze is developed as the negative complement to his patron's "Science"; where Sir Austin is blind and acts decisively, Adrian sees relatively clearly and is content to look on in amusement. He is often used as a means to provide judgements of Richard and Sir Austin and, as Thomas Campbell has observed, Adrian's "analyses are invariably acute."[27] But these analyses are always made at a safe distance, in order not to threaten the security of his position. Adrian is both parasite and consummate hypocrite: the chief supporter of the System in public, he is its chief critic in private. For him, humanity is "a Supreme Ironic Procession, with Laughter of Gods in the background. Why not Laughter of Mortals also? Adrian had his laugh in his comfortable corner. He possessed peculiar attributes of a Heathen God. He was a disposer of men; he was polished, luxurious, and happy—at their cost" (34). The last phrase is important, for in it lies Adrian's condemnation. His view is that of Meredithian common sense gone bad, without the moral sense or humane optimism—without the heart—that assumes human beings capable of or worth redemption. "Adrian's laughter," as Mohammad Shaheen has put it, "is laughter of indifference."[28] The irresponsibility of his intellectual negativism, then, acts as a foil to the spirit of critical and emotional intelligence represented at significant moments by characters like Lady Blandish and Lucy, and embodied in the narrative voice of the novel, a voice that repeatedly alerts us to the dangers inherent in this perversion of common sense. Through his broad satiric treatment of the porcine "Wise Youth," the narrator illuminates Adrian's style of life for what it is—a constant violation of the "unwritten but perceptible laws binding [us] in consideration one to another" (23:47).[29]

The "unwritten but perceptible laws" referred to in the *Essay* are premised upon acknowledgment of the supreme importance of the powers of the intellect when tempered by knowledge of the heart and open to the polyphony of life. The persistent lack of "consideration" or compassion found in this novel's portraits of isolated patriarchal monologism—Adrian's comfortable cynicism, Sir Austin's demented theorizing, and Richard's self-indulgent heroic posturing—is a pattern of conduct that Meredith shows to be at once comic and potentially tragic; in this first novel social comedy, to use Scholes and Kellogg's terminology, is joined with a "tragic concern for the individual"[30] in a highly innovative manner that was to become distinctively Meredithian. Meredith works—and of course not always successfully—to evoke responses that dramatic tradition has schooled us to keep separate. Like Molière, he repeatedly dramatizes the tensions that develop in human relationships between common-sensical behavior—in the full sense of that term—and its opposites; unlike Molière, in *Richard Feverel* and a number of the novels that were to follow, Meredith pursues this subject to its full implications, a pursuit in which traditional boundaries between the worlds of comedy and tragedy simply become irrelevant.

3

The Adventures of Harry Richmond and the Disintegration of Identity

1

*T*HE ADVENTURES OF HARRY RICHMOND (1871) IS THE NEXT NOVEL IN the Meredith canon that I find to have substantial interest as experimental fiction. As in *Richard Feverel*, Meredith plays with an intermixing of genres, this time crossing picaresque romance and Bildungsroman with a comic plot centered on the royalist pretensions of one of his most outlandish and powerful creations—the picaro-extraordinaire, Richmond Roy. But perhaps the most intriguing element of innovation in *Harry Richmond* is Meredith's narrative experimentation, his use of a first-person unreliable narrator, Harry Richmond—the only such narrator in the canon—as the reflector of both Harry's and his father's picaresque careers. What is particularly striking is the way Meredith is repeatedly able to create an ironic tension between Harry's naive narrative observations and what the reader is able to infer from those observations. While one could argue that Meredith looked back to other recent contemporary first-person narrators—Thackeray's Barry Lyndon and Henry Esmond, Dickens's David Copperfield and Pip, Mrs. Gaskell's Mary Smith, the multiple narrators of Emily, Charlotte, and Anne Brontë are all obvious examples—there is an indeterminate play to Meredith's narrative irony that also anticipates early modernism. For example, the epistemological experimentation we find in the impressionist projects of Ford Madox Ford and Joseph Conrad almost two generations later show some striking similarities to the questioning of a definitive view of the world that we find in this novel. And as we shall see, in *Harry Richmond* the tendency to indeterminacy is also manifested in a resistance to traditional no-

63

tions of closure, fulfilled identity, and the monological voice of the autobiographer.

Before we look at *Harry Richmond*, however, a quick glance at Meredith's four intervening novels should be useful because in many respects they mark a retreat from our center of interest—the innovative impulse that makes *Richard Feverel* so remarkable. The story of the hostile reception of *Feverel*, including its being dropped by the all-important Mudie's lending library, is well known; Meredith's motivation for attempting less controversial and therefore more popular fictional forms seems quite understandable, especially because, like Hardy after him, he was attempting to underwrite his career as a poet with his fictional offerings.

Evan Harrington (1861), then, marks a departure from the experimental form of *Richard Feverel*. It is a novel at once less ambitious and more successful, in the sense of solving the artistic problems it poses, than its predecessor. In it Meredith set out in the traditional realm of domestic realism to write a comedy of manners in narrative and thus avoided the difficulties raised by the mixed genres of the previous novel. Because of its generic unity, *Evan Harrington* stands, along with *The Egoist*, as one of the two novels in the Meredith canon closest in spirit to the *Essay* and the comedies of Molière. The story plays on the time-honored themes of New Comedy: frustrated young love, blocking relatives, and the complications raised by class barriers. In fact, if it were not for Louisa, the sister of the titular hero, *Evan Harrington* might well be the most conventional and, in that sense, the most uncharacteristic of Meredith's novels. As it is, however, the Countess de Saldar de Sancorvo, as Louisa styles herself, is the true Molièrian figure of the comedy, an extraordinarily unconventional upholder of convention who provides the novel with its real distinction and center of interest. Thus, working within the safe confines of familiar comic structure, Meredith also produced one of his most original characterizations.

Evan Harrington is a new study in the egotistical perversion of critical intelligence, a study that is especially noteworthy because for the first time Meredith took as his major theme feminine egoism rather than masculine. The Countess de Saldar is a marvelous rendition of a Cinderella who has married nobility, albeit in the form of an impoverished and exiled count well beyond his prime, and then dedicated her life to covering the tracks leading back to her humble origin. Louisa is a consummate snob, worshipping the outward forms of aristocratic life to the exclusion of all else. She is also much more, however. As the heroine in the only novel of Meredith's early career that comes near to fulfilling the generic precepts he later set down in the *Essay*, Louisa presents a paradoxical blend of both the virtues and the vices sought out by the comic spirit. She possesses many of the intellectual capacities Meredith associated with the feminine figures he wished us to admire: like Noorna bin Noorka, Louisa is coolheaded, with an exceptional ability to maneuver men and women in accordance with her wishes. In moments of crisis, she is shown to have remarkable savoir faire, a trait that commanded Meredith's high approval; she is a superb tactician, "a born general" who achieves triumphs against impossible odds.

At the same time, Louisa's coolheadedness has little of the humane quality that Meredith characteristically associated with the term common sense—one reason why her intellect is clearly a perversion of Meredithian critical intelligence. In addition, the Countess entirely lacks the saving grace of intellectual laughter—the sine qua non of the comic spirit. Hardly the *raisonneuse* figure seen so often in Meredith's fiction, she is incapable of laughing at herself or viewing her own conduct with anything approaching detachment. The paradox she presents is that she is Meredith's only heroine who is both intelligent and ineducable. Despite her quick mind, at the end of the novel the Countess is shown to be as obtuse to the absurdity of her pretensions as she was at the beginning. She is one of Meredith's three most memorable comic creations, ranking in expansive ego with both Sir Willoughby Patterne and the outlandish Richmond Roy of *Harry Richmond*.

Meredith, then, showed himself to be an accomplished creator of comedy of manners in *Evan Harrington*, but this work did not bring him commercial success or launch him on a career as "comic novelist." All the fiction that followed during the next decade and a half moved away, in varying degrees, from the *Evan Harrington* model as Meredith continued to seek a means to a somewhat contradictory end: to achieve popularity and to express his decidedly unconventional vision. *Sandra Belloni*, which appeared in 1864 under the title *Emilia in England* and received its revised title as a reprint in 1886, is a study in depth of a central Victorian issue—the dangers of sentimental self-indulgence—but it is also an early explicit manifestation of Meredith's impulse to develop dialogic narration. There is a literal struggle between two narrators, the one, as

Allon White has observed, a conventional plot-oriented teller of tales, while the other is a "Philosopher," "a figure who tries to introduce a new level of analytical seriousness into the romantic drama."[1] In this novel it is as though Meredith plays at conceding to the demands of the wider audience he sought while he also provides a running critique of—and alternative to—such concessions to popular taste.[2] *Rhoda Fleming* (1865) is a less convoluted and self-defeating effort in the direction of a popular genre. As a "problem novel," it deals with an illicit love affair and a forced marriage, while *Vittoria* (1867), originally to have been entitled *Emilia in Italy*, is a historical romance about the further adventures of the heroine of *Sandra Belloni* in the Italian Risorgimento of 1848.

What all of the very different novels of this period have in common is their characteristic Meredithian preoccupation with the disastrous effects of deviations from a standard of enlightened common sense—seen most clearly in the self-preoccupied shortsightedness of the Pole family and the eventual suicide, Purcell Barret, in *Sandra Belloni*, the wrongheadedness of Rhoda Fleming, Mrs. Lovell, and others in *Rhoda Fleming* as they impose their conventional views on Rhoda's "fallen" sister, Dahlia, the dedicated but ill-conceived national passion of the Italian patriots in *Vittoria*, and, most memorable of all, in *Harry Richmond*, the demented machinations of Richmond Roy. As I have already suggested, however, it was not until this last work that Meredith made a positive advance over his first novel in terms of innovative technique. In *Harry Richmond* he was able, finally, to find a way to combine the imaginative power and shifting, sometimes contradictory narrative voices of *Richard Feverel* with the greater unity of tone found in *Evan Harrington*. He achieved this increase in unity by confining those conflicting voices to the utterance of a single, bemused first-person narrator who has to make his way through a paradoxical maze of indeterminate language and experience in an effort to discover who he is—and who he isn't.

2

Like *Shagpat*, *Feverel*, and, to a much lesser degree, *Evan Harrington*, *Harry Richmond* can be viewed as a novel of education, tracing the emotional and spiritual growth of a not particularly remarkable young man as he contends with the various tests that confront him. This novel is much more ambitious in range than *Evan Harrington*: Harry begins his history in the country-house world of comedy of manners, but then is almost immediately transported to "the brazen castle of romance" (9:14) as his adventures begin. Meredith had not forgotten the problems that arose from the ambitious scope of *Richard Feverel*, however. In spite of its wide range, there is very little of the shrillness and stylistic unevenness in *Harry Richmond* that characterize the shifts from comedy to romance or tragedy in the earlier novel—or in *Sandra Belloni*. A major reason for the consistency of tone, as I have just suggested, is the restraining effect imposed by the limitations of first-person narration, which begins in the second chapter. Also important to the novel's success was the way in which Meredith rediscovered the pattern he had used in *Shagpat* and *Feverel* and was to return to again and again in his later fiction—the basic opposition between the *raisonneuse* or, in this case, *raisonneuses*, and a figure (or figures) who is, in Molièrian terms, *déraisonnable*.

The introductory chapter of *Harry Richmond* presents the two worlds that are to vie for Harry's loyalty throughout the novel.[3] The first is that in which he has been brought up, the down-to-earth bourgeois world of his wealthy grandfather, Squire Beltham—the familiar territory of domestic realism. The second is an alternative world of romance, introduced in an astonishing manner by his flamboyant father, Richmond Roy. Both of these men are egoists who attempt to impose their visions of happiness on Harry, and it is only later that modified and common-sensical versions of the domestic world and the world of romance are discovered in the two principal heroines of the novel—Janet Ilchester and Princess Ottilia.

The two major male influences in Harry's life, then, act as exempla of world views perverted by egoism, while the two young women who figure predominantly in his history eventually provide more reliable guidelines that are to direct him toward rational conduct. But Harry is able to appreciate the views of Janet and Ottilia only after he has had his season of self-indulgence with Beltham and Roy as role models. What is new and significant here is that, through the first-person narrative, Meredith immerses us in Harry's self-indulgent and disoriented vision of things. Following Harry's inside view, the reader participates in his bewilderment as well as his intermittent advances in understanding; as a consequence, the problem of interpretation becomes a central issue—for the reader as well as for Harry. Even late in the narrative Harry is just beginning to get his epistemological bearings so he can address what L. T. Hergenhan has described as his "basic problem," "to free himself from his dependence on his family—here reduced to his father, and to some extent his grandfather—which has sapped his growth as an individual."[4]

The confrontation between Squire Beltham and Richmond Roy that begins the novel is narrated in the third person by the adult Harry, looking back on his experiences as a very young child. Meredith produces an effect here in some ways reminiscent of the one Dickens had created in the opening chapters of *David Copperfield* and *Great Expectations* a few years earlier—the effect of a child's perspective, looking up at an adult world, but at the same time rendering that world with the some of the coloring of adult judgment.[5] As the text progresses, however, and the first-person narration takes over, the point of view is restricted increasingly to Harry's perspective of the moment, with little interpolation of adult judgment. This technique produces a tension between the narrator's often disoriented attempts to understand his pilgrimage and the reader's own efforts at interpretation, an effect particularly important in the simultaneous rendering of Roy's mesmerizing power and manifest absurdity. By late in the novel, as I have suggested, the autobiographer has begun to gain a larger vision of things that more closely coincides with what the reader is able to see, but this is a vision that gains authenticity in part by its acknowledgment of how difficult it is to interpret the world—and especially Richmond Roy.

The reading experience here is in some ways similar to that of tracking John Dowell's story in *The Good Soldier*, where Ford is always emphasizing the problem of interpretation, both in relation to Edward Ashburnham, who exercises a power of fascination over Dowell not unlike that of Roy over Harry, and in relation to the meaning of human interactions in general. Paul Armstrong's comments on this aspect of modernist fiction has relevance to what I am saying about the narrative of *Harry Richmond*: "the function of narration in modern fiction is less to guarantee the authenticity of the tale than to make the reader reflect about meaning and interpretation through the challenges of the telling."[6] In this novel, the challenges posed by Harry's telling of his story direct us repeatedly to consider issues of meaning and interpretation—not with quite the same stress on indeterminacy that we find in the narratives of the Dowells and Marlows of impressionist fiction, but nevertheless in a way that points significantly in their direction.

The opening scene presents Roy in terms of an opposition that is to continue for the length of the novel. Young Harry, awakened in the middle of the night by a pounding on the hall-doors and talk of "audacious highwaymen" who are feared to be attacking Squire Beltham's Riversley Grange, is then told that a "gentleman wanted to see him: nothing more. Whether the gentleman was a good gentleman, and not a robber, he could not learn" (9:9). The intruder, as Harry soon discovers, is his dimly remembered father, come to claim him and thus not the audacious highwayman as feared. But the nagging question raised by Harry's later experiences is precisely whether or not Roy in fact may be a braggart confidence man and thief masquerading in the guise of "good gentleman." At this early point in the text, however, the question of Roy's identity is raised only to be deferred as Harry passes under his father's spell: "He found himself facing the man of the night. It appeared to him that the stranger was of enormous size, like the giants of fairy books: for as he stood a little out of the doorway there was a peep of night sky and trees behind him, and the trees looked very much smaller, and hardly any sky was to be seen except over his shoulders" (9:10).

The "man of the night" acts as a shape-changer out of fairy tale, a figure easily blending with a child's dreams. Harry is awestruck as Roy holds him in his arms and delivers a speech full of obscure but wonderful suggestions of the magnificent career that awaits the boy under his father's tutelage:

> "By heaven! his destiny is brilliant. He shall be hailed for what he is, the rightful claimant of a place among the proudest in the land; and mark me, Mr. Beltham, obstinate sensual old man that you are! I take the boy, and I consecrate my life to the duty of establishing him in his proper rank and station, and there, if you live and I live, you shall behold him and bow your grovelling pig's head to the earth, and bemoan the day, by heaven! when you—a common country squire, a man of no origin, a creature with whose blood we have mixed ours—and he is stone blind to the honour conferred on him—when you in your besotted stupidity threatened to disinherit Harry Richmond."
>
> The door slammed violently on such further speech as he had in him to utter. (9:13)

Richmond Roy outdoes even the Countess de Saldar in Meredith's gallery of snobs. Where Louisa Harrington's object was to move about on an equal footing "at a third-rate English mansion" (6:174), Roy's aim in life is nothing less than to gain recognition as a member of the royal family and thus his "Case" provides the basis for his regal manner and the flattering princely notions he pours into the ears of his son.[7] Observed progressively from the viewpoint of child and then adolescent, Roy powerfully exerts his spell, though Harry learns eventually to regard him with an increasingly critical eye. Point of view here is all-important: if Meredith had presented Roy by means of an Olympian and worldly-wise narrator like the one he later constructed for *The Egoist*, the extremes of his heroic posturing would have inevitably produced a study in comic caricature. But rendered through the sensibility of the growing boy, Roy is placed in a much more compelling perspective. He becomes a more disturbing, convincing, and potentially tragic figure than could be suggested by a reality-testing judgmental style that embodies Meredithian common sense. At the same time, our impression of Harry's developing consciousness is proportionately the richer for his fitfully changing impressions of his father. By novel's end, when the viewpoints of implied reader and narrator have moved more closely together, Meredith has provided us with a compelling sense of the tortured ambivalence Harry must necessarily feel towards Roy.

3

Harry's "adventures" are eventually to provide him with sufficient common sense to discern some of the insubstantiality of his father's—and his own—castles in the air, but the attainment of clearer vision is never an easy or definitive matter in this text. When, after a long separation, Harry is suddenly confronted by Roy in Germany, their extraordinary meeting provides a richly ironic moment in which the grandiose figure cast by Harry's imagination is first reinforced and then deconstructed before his eyes. It is also significant that this moment marks Harry's first meeting with Princess Ottilia.

The long journey towards this scene is rendered, appropriately, as a passage through literal darkness and obscurity, a pilgrimage that acts for Harry as a night journey of the soul. When he searches with his friend Temple for Roy in London, for example, Harry finds himself lost in the "subterranean atmosphere" of city fog. Their

destination is a meaningless abstraction—"the Bench"; all Harry
knows is that the Bench is part of the disorienting cityscape and in
some way associated with his father. As they keep up their spirits
with talk of the *Odyssey*, Harry flatters himself and Roy with comparisons to Telemachus and Ulysses. The dreamlike search goes on
through "a labyrinth of dark streets" (9:138) until the boys are finally confronted by the nightmarish spectacle of an enormous
house fire opposite "an immense high wall. . . . [with] a sombre
glow on it" (9:141). When this wall is identified by two passing girls
as the Bench—King's Bench Prison, one of London's three debtors'
prisons—the specter of the devouring fire is joined with the revelation that Roy's magnificence may not be all that it seems. Once
again, disorienting images are registered on Harry's consciousness,
but, as in a dream, he is much more observer than interpreter. Barbara Hardy has suggested that the critical insight that does allow
Harry to see his father more clearly comes only at the novel's end
with another conflagration—one that literally consumes Richmond
Roy himself.[8]

In the present scene, Harry's realization that his father has been
in debtors' prison is registered entirely by his visual impressions of
the glowing Bench, as it dawns on him that he may have been
robbed of his watch by the two girls:

The great wall of the Bench was awful in its reflection of the labouring
flames—it rose out of sight like the flame-tops till the columns of water
brought them down. I thought of my father and of my watch. The two
girls were not visible. "A glorious life a fireman's!" said Temple.

The firemen were on the roofs of the houses, handsome as Greek
heroes, and it really did look as if they were engaged in slaying an enormous dragon, that hissed and tongued at them, and writhed its tail,
paddling its broken big red wings in the pit of wreck and smoke, twisting
and darkening—something fine to conquer, I felt with Temple. (9:143)

The Homeric daydreams have thus been set aside for the more substantial heroism of the dragon-slaying fire fighters. In Squire Beltham's terms, the "real" has momentarily supplanted "artifice,"
but the significance of the images and thought patterns is, again,
left for the reader to discern. Harry continues on undaunted in his
dreamlike quest for his father, "not aware how frozen and befogged
my mind and senses had become until . . . the whole of our adventures . . . swam flashing before my eyes, and I cried out . . . , 'Well,
I'm awake now!' and slept straight off the next instant" (9:145).

When Harry's adventures lead him to Germany, he meets Clara Goodwin, a minor but nonetheless significant character who stands out clearly in Harry's hazy journey as a voice of common sense, one that tries to persuade him to give up his pursuit of his father. Her reason only becomes clear later: Roy has not only established himself on a false basis at the court of the Prince of Eppenselzen in Sarkeld, but he has also, to use Margaret Tarratt's term, become something very much like a court jester.[9] Harry responds to Clara's persuasive efforts with typical confusion: "Her voluble rattling succeeded in fencing off my questions before I could exactly shape them, as I staggered from blind to blind idea, now thinking of the sombre red Bench, and now of the German prince's Court" (9:170). True to form for a fledgling Meredithian hero, he turns his back on sound feminine intuition: "It was clear to me that she had joined the mysterious league against my father" (9:171).

The final stage of Harry's journey, in a coach packed with German travelers, reinforces the atmosphere of disorientation and nightmare that has preceded:

> The windows were closed, the tobacco-smoke thickened, the hides of animals wrapping our immense companions reeked; fire occasionally glowed in their pipe-bowls; they were silent, and gave out smoke and heat incessantly, like inanimate forces of nature. I had most fantastic ideas—that I had taken root and ripened, and must expect my head to drop off at any instant: that I was deep down, wedged in the solid mass of the earth. . . . The dim revival of light, when I had well-nigh ceased to hope for it, showed us all like malefactors imperfectly hanged, or drowned wretches in a cabin under water. (9:173–74)

The surrealistic quality of Harry's quest acts not only as an indication of the unacknowledged conflicts within his mind, but also as preparation for what is perhaps the most remarkable scene in all of Meredith. Rendered through the medium of young Harry's impressionistic consciousness and as the culmination of an increasingly mystifying night journey through half-comprehended images of smoke and fire, the scene of the son's confrontation with his father is orchestrated by Meredith to maximum effect.

Having arrived at Sarkeld, Harry and Temple find a crowd gathered to witness the unveiling of an equestrian statue of Prince Albrecht, the celebrated ancestor of the prince of Eppenwelzen. The boys catch a glimpse behind a protective cover of a splendid horse cast in bronze, but without rider. Intrigued, they join the crowd to watch:

> The cannon was fired and roared; the band struck up a pompous slow march: and the tent-veil broke apart and rolled off. It was like the dawn flying and sunrise mounting.
>
> I confess I forgot all thought of my father for awhile; the shouts of the people, the braying of the brass instruments, the ladies cheering sweetly, the gentlemen giving short, hearty expressions of applause, intoxicated me. And the statue was superb—horse and rider in new bronze polished by sunlight. . . .
>
> The horse gave us a gleam of his neck as he pawed a forefoot, just reined in. We knew him; he was a gallant horse; but it was the figure of the Prince Albrecht that was so fine. I had always laughed at sculptured figures on horseback. This one overawed me. The Marshal was acknowledging the salute of his army after a famous victory over the infidel Turks. He sat upright, almost imperceptibly but effectively bending his head in harmony with the curve of his horse's neck, and his baton swept the air low in proud submission to the honours cast on him by his acclaiming soldiery. (9:193–94)

In full sunlight, then, Meredith shows Harry confronted by an image that seems to fulfill all his romantic notions of the heroic. He is "overawed," just as he has been as a child in the presence of Roy, but here the majesty of the figure puts even Roy out of mind. When the statue is about to be re-veiled, Temple steps forward and calls out Harry's name:

> Little Temple crowed lustily.
> The head of the statue turned from Temple to me.
> I found the people falling back with amazed exclamations. I—so prepossessed was I—simply stared at the sudden-flashing white of the statue's eyes. The eyes, from being an instant ago dull carved balls, were animated. They were fixed on me. I was unable to give out a breath. Its chest heaved; both bronze hands struck against the bosom.
> "Richmond! my son! Richie! Harry Richmond! Richmond Roy!"
> That was what the statue gave forth. (9:197)

In an instant the image of extraordinary heroism is transformed into the public display of an imposter.[10] The confused obscurity of Harry's dreams is abruptly brought to a halt in the full light of day as all Roy's splendid romantic trappings turn out to be mere plaster and paint. The long-awaited reunion between father and son finally takes place: "We met at the ropes and embraced. All his figure was stiff, smooth, cold. My arms slid on him. Each time he spoke I thought it an unnatural thing" (9:197). Harry again proves capable of observing significant detail: "he was plastered and painted from head to foot. The fixture of his wig and hat, too, constrained his skin, so that his looks were no index of his feelings. I longed gloomily for the moment to come when he would present himself to me in his natural form. He was not sensible of the touch of my hand, nor I of his" (9:200). Roy's bizarre costume effectively sums up his compromised state: he is literally caught in the act of posturing as something he is not, which in turn is precisely what has prevented natural feelings between himself and his son. His pose as a bronze Prince Albrecht, while ostensibly part of a game to win the margravine's favor, also provides a most fitting symbol of his role at the court—and in life. Barbara Hardy has neatly recapitulated this effect: "the statue scene is the literal enactment of so much in Richmond Roy: mountebank, romantic, noble in appearance, unrealistic and false in aspiration. . . . The scene, like Roy's carefully manipulated rhetoric, marks the delicate poise which he maintains almost until the end, the poise between dignity and grotesque inflation."[11]

Harry, while not yet ready to recognize anything like the full significance of what has been so carefully and forcefully presented to the reader, has nevertheless begun to perceive with a new kind of vision. Even after his father has partially disencumbered himself, he finds that Roy is still not the man whom he has been seeking: "I had my father's living hand in mine to squeeze; feeling him scarcely yet the living man I had sought, and with no great warmth of feeling. . . . 'Richie, my little lad, my son Richmond! You found me out; you found me!' . . . I was now gifted with a tenfold power of observation, and let nothing escape me" (9:201). Harry *has* found Roy out and, by letting nothing escape him, begins the long and difficult process of adjusting his mind to the fact that beneath the facade of heroics and romance his father may cut a very diminished figure indeed. The great problem, as Meredith poses it, is that Harry is capable of responding with a "tenfold power of observation" only at extraordinary moments like this one. When the shock of recognition begins to wear off, he finds it all too easy to lose his grasp on his hard-won critical intelligence and to fall back into the old pattern of subservience to Roy's glittering personality.

4

Various elements established by this point in *Harry Richmond* are familiar ones in Meredith's early fiction. Richmond Roy, like Sir Austin Feverel and the Great Mel of *Evan Harrington*, is a larger-than-life study of patriarchal egoism. And, as in the preceding novels, the great task allotted to the son is that of developing a personal destiny independent of the father's overpowering influence. But what is especially interesting here, and suggests new aspects of the emerging modernist impulse in Meredith, is the way he returns relentlessly to a variety of "modern" problems—the difficulties of becoming oriented, of seeing clearly, of escaping ambivalence, of defining the characters of others, and of achieving something like self-identity. Harry Richmond's task is doubly difficult: he must try not only to understand his father's elusive character, which becomes increasingly a study in disintegrating subjectivity, but he must also exert some control over that character before he can effectively begin to determine his own. And the process of trying to view Roy dispassionately is further complicated by Harry's own romantic disposition. The power of the father over the son continues, in spite of the boy's glimpses behind the mask. It is for this reason that the two major female figures in the novel come to play such an important role in Harry's education. Ottilia and Janet, each in her own way, provide examples of youthful good sense and integrated subjectivity that eventually have a positive effect on Harry's vision and conduct, though they also serve, by the contrasts they provide, to highlight Harry's continuing disorientation.

Princess Ottilia, daughter of the Prince of Eppenwelzen, is first introduced just before the unveiling of the statue. Twelve or thirteen at this time—Harry is apparently a little older—she charms him at once with her self-possession and grace. And one of the vivid memories Harry later retains from the time of Roy's disastrous performance is his impression of the little princess, "eyeing us with an absorbed air quite unlike the manner of a child" (9:198). The look is characteristic. As Meredith begins to show at this early point, Ottilia combines romantic circumstances with a firmly grounded outlook—she is both a fairy princess and a young woman with "perspicacious clear eyes for the world" (*Essay*, 23:21). The one failure in her judgment, however, is a major one: she assumes Harry to be as independent-minded as she herself is.

When Harry and Ottilia meet again, they have reached young adulthood and Harry is on his grand tour, financed by Squire Beltham, while Richmond Roy, as domineering and magnetic as ever, has made an unauthorized reappearance. Roy manages to parry Harry's attempts to criticize him by veiled allusions to his "Case," and by the time they cross the Channel, the son's efforts to think independently are shown to have succumbed to his father and the charms of romance:

> Standing with my father on deck, and gazing on this fringe of the grand romantic Continent, I remembered our old travels, and felt myself bound to him indissolubly, ashamed of my recent critical probings of his character. My boy's love for him returned in full force. I was sufficiently cognizant of his history to know that he kept his head erect, lighted by the fire of his robust heart in the thick of overhanging natal clouds. . . . I chattered of anything but my feelings. (9:272)

But the imagery of fire and obscuring clouds, ostensibly emblems of heroism in Harry's mind, is also a reminder of the dominant metaphors of the novel that depict Roy's charlatanry and disgrace. Lingering in the background of Harry's admiration for his father remains the shadowy memory of the glowing Bench.

Ottilia, on the other hand, embodies a positive representation of romance in *Harry Richmond*. In contrast to Roy's self-deluded posturing, there is nothing bogus about her romantic enthusiasm—and she *is* an authentic princess. But, as Harry becomes increasingly involved with her, this is precisely the difficulty: "With what manner of face could I go before the prince or the margravine, and say, I am an English commoner, the son of a man of doubtful birth, and I claim the hand of the princess?" (9:322). In order to enter into his relationship with Ottilia with any degree of enthusiasm, Harry must try to put this question out of his mind, and he is able to do so only by fits and starts. Meredith, while presenting the princess and her world of romance in a highly attractive manner, is also at pains to show that this world is incompatible with the ordinary broad daylight of English bourgeois life to which Harry belongs and must return. The fairy tale marriages that end *Shagpat* and *Evan Harrington* are characteristic of Meredith's earlier, more permissive view of romance. By the time of *Harry Richmond*, an essential part of Meredith's moral vision, one that is clearly prefigured in *Richard Feverel*, was his insistence on what he saw as the necessary, unromantic realities. He continued to have a strongly romantic side to his imagination—a novel as late as *The Amazing Marriage* (1895) is full of exuberant romantic description—but the romance is always severely qualified by the constraints of quotidian circumstance. The escapist resolutions of *The Shaving of Shagpat* and *Evan Harrington* represented an extreme of artistic self-indulgence to which Meredith never permitted himself to return.

Harry Richmond's dim recognition that his romance with Ottilia flies in the face of a number of oppressive realities makes him an extraordinarily lethargic and passive lover. It seems to be either Ottilia or Richmond Roy who always takes the lead. In addition, Harry cannot seem to keep his two worlds of romance apart—the bogus world of Roy is constantly infringing on the world of romantic love. Meredith makes it clear, for example, that it is entirely through Roy's machinations that Harry has been able to become involved with Ottilia in the first place: "The margravine . . . sent me an imperious invitation from her villa, and for this fruit of my father's diplomacy I yielded up my daintier feelings, and my judgement into the bargain" (9:301). The affair, then, is doomed from the start: Harry cannot escape appearing an imposter himself while remaining in the German court as the father's ambiguous identity inevitably swallows up the identity of the son.

Ottilia, by contrast, is shown to have the high-spirited self-assurance and dedication of a Juliet. What seems remarkable is that she should be so seriously attracted to a young man who appears so much her inferior. The benefit of the relationship falls largely on Harry's side. Through his contact with Ottilia, he begins to gain some notion of what constitutes intellectual integrity and common sense. The "daintier feelings" and good judgment he yields up to Roy are precisely the attributes in which the princess excels, with the important exception, again, of her evaluation of Harry himself: "To her the escapades of foolish damsels were abominable. The laws of society as well as of her exalted station were in harmony with her intelligence. She thought them good, but obeyed them as a subject, not slavishly: she claimed the right to exercise her trained reason. . . . Nor would she have had cause to repent had I been the man she held me to be" (10:8).

Harry's contact with Ottilia and her Teufelsdröckhian tutor, Herr Professor von Karsteg, leads him to recognize that "I have not thought at all. I have been barely educated. I only know that I do desire with all my heart to know more, to be of some service" (9:316). His state of mind at Sarkeld fluctuates wildly between this kind of dedicated pronouncement, which is followed by a brief scholarly retirement to a nearby German university, and the complete abandonment of his slowly developing good sense to his father's lead: "My glorious future, he said, was to carry a princess to England and sit among the highest there, the husband of a lady peerless in beauty and in birth. . . . This led me to a luxurious sense of dependence on him, and I was willing to live on dreaming and amused, though all around me seemed phantoms" (9:336–37).

This dreamlike existence is a reversion back to the mood of Harry's search for his father, and is brought to an abrupt end when the worlds of Ottilia and Roy finally come into direct confrontation. Although Harry is vaguely aware that Roy intends somehow to witness the midnight scene in which he and Ottilia are to pledge their engagement, he nevertheless dreamily consents to go along with the performance. By this time Ottilia herself has become an increasingly indistinct figure to him. When, during their meeting in the palace library, she does give her word, Harry's sensations are described in an excess of romantic rhetoric worthy of Roy himself: "I looked: she swam in a mist. We had our full draught of the divine self-oblivion which floated those ghosts of the two immortal lovers through the bounds of their purgatorial circle, and for us to whom the minutes were ages, as for them to whom all time was unmarked, the power of supreme love swept out circumstance" (10:46).

As Meredith constructs the scene, the most immediate circumstance missed by Harry is the presence of unseen witnesses, including, as it turns out, the clownish Baroness Turckems, representing the prince's faction. Harry's ecstatic vision of himself and Ottilia as Paolo and Francesca is interrupted, appropriately, by real flames as the witnesses reveal themselves. Here Meredith utilizes a major shift in tone—the kind that at times marks uncertainty of execution in *Richard Feverel*—to the best advantage. What the autobiographer conceives of as sublime love-making is suddenly transformed into farce:

Baroness Turckems, desperately entangled by the sofa-covering, rushed into the ray of the lamps and laid her hand on the bell-rope. In a minute we had an alarm sounding, my father was among us, there was a mad play of chatter, and we stood in the strangest nightmare light that ever ended an interview of lovers. . . . The room was in flames, Baroness Turckems plucking at the bell-rope, my father looking big and brilliant. (10:48)

Roy, acting on impulse, has set the fire to account for the bell-ringing and thus foil the Baroness's attempt to betray the lovers. For Harry, who characteristically stands passively off to one side, the scene is another strategic moment of illumination, like his previous epiphanic encounters with the glowing Bench and the brazen statue. He feels "humiliated on Ottilia's behalf, and enraged on my own" (10:50), as well he might, for the "stupid burlesque majesty" of the father has now implicated the conduct of the son as well. Having supposed that he was meeting Ottilia on his own highly romantic terms, Harry now realizes to his dismay that he was in fact aping Richmond Roy. But this moment of identity confusion also suggests that Harry's regenerated capacity to see now includes a developing faculty of self-scrutiny, for Meredith the most essential aspect of the spirit of critical intelligence.

As the scene ends, Harry's thoughts are rapidly moving away from Sarkeld and the princess, back to England, Riversley, and the other major feminine player in the novel, his second cousin, Janet Ilchester. Thoughts of Janet suggest the antithesis of romance to Harry and, as Meredith is anxious to make clear, at this late stage of his adventures a good dose of the ordinary is precisely what he needs:

Thoughts of Janet . . . were singularly and refreshingly free from self-accusations. Some love for my home, similar to what one may have for Winter, came across me, and some appreciation of Janet as well, in whose society I was sure to be at least myself, a creature much reduced in altitude, but without the cramped sensations of a man on a monument. My hearty Janet! I thanked her then for seeing me of my natural height. (10:51–52)

As Jerome Buckley has said in commenting upon this passage, "Harry must be much less condescending than this, and his need for honest appraisal more acute, before he can claim Janet as his bride. But he does eventually learn by experience and example and is at last aware of the different person he has 'grown to be.' He comes then to cherish Janet's courage, realism, and unaffected grace as values far stronger than the illusions he once lived by."[12]

5

The recoil away from romance that occurs in *Harry Richmond* follows a characteristically Meredithian pattern. The world of romantic love is first rendered in a compelling and attractive manner and then shown to be an impossibility. Ferdinand and Miranda of *Richard Feverel* have their short respite of idyllic romance on Propero's Island while the reality of Raynham Abbey remains temporarily in the background; in the same way, shortly before the exposé in the palace library, Harry and Ottilia are shown isolated together in a scene of high romance. The scene begins when the lovers seek shelter from the rain during a summer storm. They pass an hour together in a natural setting that performs much the same symbolic function as does the island in *Richard Feverel*. Away from unnatural paternal influence, the heroes of both novels begin to respond to romantic love in a manner that is implied to be in harmony with nature. As Harry and Ottilia huddle together under an overturned boat watching the rain, the confrontation with wild nature acts almost as a religious purification, or "scourge," after the sham romance associated with Roy: "We had for prospect an ever-outbursting flame of foliage, and the hubbub of the hissing lake, crimson, purple, dusky grey, like the face of a passionate creature scourged. It was useless to speak. Her lips were shut, but I had the intent kindness of her eyes on me almost unceasingly. The good hour slipped away" (9:328).

This endorsement of romantic love—one of many instances of striking stylistic similarities between Meredith and D. H. Lawrence—is followed by an equally strong denial. The key to the failure of romance in both *Harry Richmond* and *Richard Feverel* is to be found in the state of mind of the hero when he permits himself to indulge in self-delusive visions that are essentially dishonest— that is, as Meredith might put it, when he drifts into disharmony with nature and betrays common sense. This is precisely the point in the "Prelude" to *The Egoist* when Meredith observes that the comic spirit "is not opposed to romance" per se: "You may love, and warmly love, so long as you are honest. Do not offend reason. A lover pretending too much by one foot's length of pretense, will have that foot caught in her trap" (13:4). Harry and Richard, as well as Sir Willoughby, err by a good deal more than a foot's length on the side of pretense. And when one considers the romantic relationships in the novels that follow *Harry Richmond*—Beauchamp and Renée de Croisnel, Sir Willoughby and Clara Middleton, Alvan and Clotilde in *The Tragic Comedians*, Percy Dacier and Diana Warwick in *Diana of the Crossways*—it is clear that dishonesty and pretense of one sort or another lie at the center of each of the relationships and thus eventually spell disaster to romantic love.

When one considers what amounts to an almost obsessive repetition of this theme, it is not irrelevant to recall Meredith's own unfortunate adventure in high romance. At the age of twenty-one, when he married Mary Peacock Nicolls, she was the most accomplished, magnetic woman he had ever met. Almost seven years his senior, she radiated wit and charm, and Meredith was apparently captivated at once. According to the tradition passed down by Nicolls's daughter, he made six offers of marriage before he was finally accepted.[13] That Meredith later took on a full share of responsibility for the marital disaster that followed seems clear from the way in which he handled figures in his own art like Sir Austin and Sir Willoughby, or the relationship of husband and wife in *Modern Love*. What also seems clear is how strongly Meredith must have later condemned himself for being a victim of romantic self-delusion.[14]

To return to the case of Harry Richmond, by the time he "secretly" meets Ottilia at midnight, sham romance and romantic love are so hopelessly mixed in his mind that real critical perception begins to seem an impossibility. The perception does come, finally, when the flames of the palace library illuminate the precise nature of his dishonesty. By assenting to Roy's theatrical plot, and then getting caught at it, Harry clearly demonstrates to himself that he is not the hero of romance Ottilia has been encouraged to take him for.

But what is of particular interest in Meredith's resolution of this situation is his use of the "unromantic" heroine—a figure to recur in *The Egoist* in the form of Laetitia Dale.[15] Janet Ilchester offers Harry a world untainted by Richmond Roy. Brought up at Riversley under Squire Beltham's supervision, she is at a pole in Harry's mind opposite to that occupied by his father—and Ottilia: Janet "did not raise a spark of poetical sentiment in my bosom" (10:53). And, as we have seen, the reason Harry thinks of Janet at Sarkeld when he feels the "cramped sensations of a man on a monument" is precisely because she views him without romantic exaggeration—"of my natural height." It is her model of intuition and common sense, finally, that he must follow in order to achieve independence from Richmond Roy.

Even by this late point in the text, Meredith is by no means finished with revealing just how deeply ingrained Harry's habits of self-delusion are, and in this respect he is much like Richard Feverel. He is shown drifting back into a half-hearted acceptance of his engagement to the princess as Squire Beltham, in true Squire Western form, gets scent of the arrangement and proceeds to do battle with what he correctly sees as the persisting influence of Richmond Roy:

> "Make a clean breast of it, Harry. You're not the son of Tom Fool the Bastard for nothing, I'll swear. All the same, you're Beltham; you're my grandson and heir, and I'll stand by you. Out with't! She's a princess, is she? . . ."
>
> "Do you find a princess objectionable, sir?"
>
> "Objectionable? She's a foreigner. I don't know her. I never saw her. Here's my Janet I've brought up for you, under my own eyes, out of the way of every damned soft-sawderer, safe and plump as a melon under glass, and you fight shy of her and go and engage yourself to a foreigner I don't know and never saw! By George, Harry, I'll call in a parson to settle you. . . . I'll couple you, by George, I will! 'fore either of you know whether you're on your legs or your backs." (10:66)

Beltham's strenuous efforts to foster his own brand of romance at Riversley are frustrated by Janet herself. Meredith carefully shows her refusal to be involved in any coercion of Harry as she renounces claim to him and enlists herself in the cause of the princess. By contrast, Harry repeatedly stands passively by as she performs a series of brilliant maneuvers aimed at what, on limited information, seems to her to be necessary for Harry's happiness. When a London newspaper arrives, linking the squire's name with Richmond Roy's and announcing that Roy "had joined the arms of England and a petty German principality stamped on his plate and furniture" (10:74), Janet saves the day: "The squire was waiting for her to hand the paper to him. . . . 'This paper,' she said, 'deserves to be burnt,' and she was allowed to burn it—money article, mining column as well—on the pretext of an infamous anti-Tory leader, of which she herself composed the first sentence to shock the squire completely" (10:73). Meredith's portrayal of Janet as the woman of common sense and action is further extended as she advises Harry to go at once to London to exert some control over Roy's extravagances. What she does not realize, of course, is what the reader has by now come to expect: when in Roy's presence, Harry's own judgment becomes paralyzed. When it is finally exerted, his control over his father and himself comes at a time when Janet stands directly beside him.

6

The final stage of the novel depicts the culmination of Roy's efforts to realize his visions of greatness—with Harry and Ottilia as his instruments. As so often happens in Meredith, comedy and romance begin to combine with tragedy when common sense has been thwarted too long. Meredith does not hesitate to cross generic lines in *Harry Richmond* any more than he did in *Richard Feverel*, but unlike *Feverel* the later novel maintains a unity of tone throughout due, as I have already suggested, to its narrative structure. Seen through the eyes of his bemused son, Roy is a figure large enough to combine the attractiveness of unlimited romantic aspiration, the comic absurdity of that aspiration in conflict with an increasingly tawdry reality, and, finally, the tragic dimensions of a man driven mad at the end by the failure of his overreaching imagination to transform the world to its desires. During this period, Harry strikes the keynote of our evolving view of his father: "Instead of a comic I found him a tragic spectacle; and his exuberant anticipations . . . were examples of downright unreason such as contemplation through the comic glass would have excused; the tragic could not. . . . I chafed at his unteachable spirit, surely one of the most tragical things in life; and the proof of my love for him was that I thought it so" (10:199).

As for Harry himself, it becomes increasingly clear that his affairs are eventually to be resolved in the usual New Comedy fashion, with his socially responsible marriage to Janet.[16] The mood in this last stage, however, is much like that in the last act of Shakespearean romance: the dominant tone is one of melancholic sobriety in contrast to the festive spirit of Shakespearean comedy—or of *Evan Harrington*.

Harry, on his return to London, seems almost to lose consciousness as he is again swept into his father's schemes; urban disorientation is once more the predominant note as his identity slides into a state of indeterminacy. The one image that does stand out clearly in his mind is that of Janet: "I remembered, when back in the London vortex, the curious soft beauty . . . and the brilliant direct beam of those thick-browed, firm, clear eyes, with her frown, and her set lips and brave figure" (10:137). When Meredith brings all the major actors of the novel together on the Isle of Wight for his *scène-à-faire*, Janet provides Harry with the council he needs to finally break the chains that link his fate—and his identity—with his father. Once again, it is the pattern set by Noorna bin Noorka and Shibli Bagarag. When Harry's mind flies off to the wild idea of a duel with his father, Janet brings him directly back "to the circumstances," adding, "But why should I speak to you as if you were undecided!" (10:238). What she really asks of him here is that he exert control over himself, that he declare independence from Roy and achieve the self-command of autonomous identity. Janet's final words, as Harry leaves to confront his father, are "come to us when you are at liberty" (10:239).

Harry does finally achieve liberty, although it takes considerably more than this single confrontation, which ends when Roy feigns sleep before his blustering, but finally active son. Roy's true defeat takes place in the climactic scene that acts as a complement to the opening of the novel as Squire Beltham confronts him with newly-discovered facts about himself and his "Case."[17] Roy, for the first time in the novel, is struck dumb, a "petrified large figure." Beltham, for his part, showers Roy with a string of epithets that sum up the role-playing that have characterized him from the very beginning—"stage lacquey," "low vulgar comedian," "keep your menagerie performances for your pantomime audiences" (10: 278; 279; 280). Employing the same metaphor that Meredith later used in describing Sir Willoughby, Beltham vows to Roy that he will "strip him stark" (10:282), and this is precisely what he does.[18]

Harry observes the scene with the same visual clarity that has accompanied the previous revelations of Roy, but it is an awareness that is now joined, finally, with something approaching mature judgment. In a few moments, Roy's masks have all fallen aside and Harry is able to see beyond Beltham's epithets to a pathetic old man whose fabricated personality is in the process of disintegration: "My father said: 'I am broken.' He put out a swimming hand that trembled when it rested, like that of an aged man grasping a staff. I feared for a moment he was acting, he spoke so like himself, miserable though he appeared: but it was his well-known native old style in a state of decrepitude" (10:286). In his transition from majesty to humbleness, there is something Lear-like in Roy—in imagination he has fallen as far. But, unlike Lear, as Harry has observed previously, Roy "clearly could not learn from misfortune" (10:199). A measure of tragic understanding comes, at last, not to the father but to the son.

The parting view of Harry, however, is no self-assured portrait of accomplished identity emerging from its *Lehrjahre*; rather than achieving self-realization, "this everlastingly recurring I of the autobiographer" continues to view himself as an identity in flux, resistant to the traditional summings-up of realistic fiction:

> The pleasant narrator in the first person is the happy bubbling fool, not the philosopher who has come to know himself and his relations toward the universe. The words of this last are one to twenty; his mind is bent upon the causes of events rather than their progress. As you see me on the page now, I stand somewhere between the two, approximating to the former, but with sufficient of the latter within me to tame the delightful expansiveness proper to that coming hour of marriage-bells and bridal-wreaths. (10:332)

Poised "somewhere between" "the happy bubbling fool," whose emphasis falls on plot and unreflective narration, and "the philosopher," whose interests are psychological and analytical, that is, focused on "meaning and interpretation,"[19] Harry's self-mocking valedictory nicely illuminates several aspects of Meredith's modernist impulse. This autobiographer undermines both the formal constraints of traditional closure and the confines of any definitive identity for himself as he acknowledges his indeterminate position. This is a good example of what Allon White has aptly described as a "warring doubleness" in early modernist literature—and in Meredith, James, and Conrad in particular. White finds this kind of uneasy attempted accommodation between "antagonistic voices"[20] laid out explicitly in the dual narratives of *Sandra Belloni* and *The Amazing Marriage* where, as we have seen, an analytically-inclined "philosopher" does battle with a second narrator bent on meeting the demands of conventional story telling. The conflicting voices we hear within Harry Richmond's narrative seem to me to be an interesting—and successfully articulated—variation of this same dialogic impulse, the impulse which, sometimes out of control, is so evident in the problematic narrative of *Richard Feverel*.

This account ends with its focus more on its most extraordinary player than on its autobiographer, as Meredith provides a final symbolic portrait of Richmond Roy in the novel's last pages. "The delightful expansiveness proper to that coming hour of marriage-bells and bridal-wreaths" is so "tamed" in this narrative that we come to know of Harry and Janet's marriage through a single reference to her as "my wife"—Harry never directly mentions the ceremony—as they return to Riversley Grange. The squire by this time having died, it is Roy, now a half-crazed old man, who is to greet them, but instead they are confronted by the sight of Riversley in flames. As Barbara Hardy has effectively demonstrated,[21] the scene acts as a culmination of the series of images associating Roy with the uncontrolled violence of fire. A showman to the very end, he has prepared an outlandish reception, replete with torches and fireworks, and it is these that have brought about the disaster: "The fire had broken out at dusk, from an explosion of fireworks. . . . The house must have been like a mine, what with powder, the torches, the devices in paper and muslin, and the extraordinary decorations fitted up to celebrate our return in harmony with my father's fancy" (10:342).

The novel comes abruptly to its close with the information, gathered from the servants, that "my father must have remained in the doomed old house to look to the safety of my aunt Dorothy. He was never seen again" (10:342). Dorothy, however, is miles from Riversley and thus, as Hardy has put it, "violence, grandiose futility, and heroics are all blended in this last scene."[22] Roy's identity, like Harry's, resists any simplistic summing up, but this last act is consistent with the rest of his career, which has been one confused course to theatrical self-destruction. Harry, marginalized as he is at the end, can be seen to have at last achieved something like independence, but he has had to witness the destruction of his father's overpowering personality in the process. The huge funeral pyre that confronts him at the end of the novel is a fitting symbol of what this independence has cost him. It is also a reminder that this is no conventional narrative; Harry doesn't bother to give us any suggestion of where his departure from romance into ordinary life is to take him and, as Conrad might put it, we have forgotten to ask.

4

The Egoist: The Female Hero
as Agent of Exposure

1

THE 1870S WERE YEARS OF MAJOR ACHIEVEMENT IN FICTION WRITING
for Meredith; the triad of novels produced in this period suggests
both the diversity and the continuity of his creative energies. A fictional autobiography as romantic antiromance, a novel of contemporary politics, and country-house comedy of manners—so *Harry
Richmond* (1871), *Beauchamp's Career* (1876), and *The Egoist*
(1879) could be described to stress their diversity, with attention to
the wide variance in type of hero, narrative technique, action, and
scene. But beneath the obvious dissimilarities of these three texts,
we also encounter major elements of continuity, one of the most
interesting of which is Meredith's increasing fascination with feminist issues. In *Beauchamp's Career* and especially *The Egoist*, the
strategic role of the female hero[1] in the conflict between Meredithian common sense and the full dimensions of sentimental male
egoism becomes even more pointed than in the previous fiction.
Beauchamp's Career is much more about Beauchamp's career with
women than his career with "the people" and the world of radical
politics, and *The Egoist* gains much of its grim comic poignancy
through Meredith's treatment of the interplay between Sir Willoughby Patterne's prodigious ego and the three women who are
candidates for the honor and trial of becoming Lady Patterne.

My intention in this chapter is to examine in this latter novel
how, midway in his career, as Meredith momentarily reined in his
impulse to challenge the traditional boundaries of genre with a
single-minded focus on comedy, he simultaneously pursued his interest in the role of women, in private relations and in society, with
a new sense of experimental possibilities. As this increase in em-

phasis occurs, we see Meredith turning away from his interest in the traditional youthful hero of the Joseph Andrews/Tom Jones variety—Shibli Bagarag, Richard Feverel, Evan Harrington, Harry Richmond, and Nevil Beauchamp can all be viewed as highly qualified nineteenth-century versions of the impulsive Fielding hero. Instead, we find most of the later novels concerned with the problem of the female hero's self-assertion in the modern world; however, the narrative focus in these texts is always divided, always directed in addition to a central blocking patriarchal figure who makes strong demands on our attention and, occasionally, on our sympathies.

Susan Morgan has pointed out that the later novels do not permit "heroic solutions for Britain" through the agency of the female hero any more than such a solution is achievable through a failed hero like Beauchamp. Rather, Morgan sees in the rest of the Meredith canon "some hope on the sidelines, in the only reform the story will define as progress, the growing mental freedom of women."[2] This Meredithian preoccupation with the story on the sidelines—the freeing of the feminine mind—will be my major concern in *The Egoist*. As a complement to this discussion, I shall also examine how Meredith's depiction of his egoist-patriarch's ill-fated desire to "control and direct" a stable definition of his own identity points in a modern—even postmodern—direction with the questions it raises about the provisionality of subjectivity. Such questions are, as we have already seen, important to the portraits of father and son in *Harry Richmond*; in *The Egoist*, these questions are even more central as Meredith focuses relentlessly on the process of exposure through which Willoughby Patterne's initially serene sense of self is destabilized. All the action leads to a remarkable final scene in which the protagonist is confronted by a determined Laetitia Dale bent on bringing transformation to Patterne Hall through a transformation in how Willougby himself is defined—a reconstitution of subjectivity that runs exactly counter to his increasingly frenetic efforts to maintain a stable Patterne before "the world."

Meredith's comic project in *The Egoist* is to show Sir Willoughby's egoism gradually stripped "stark naked," and all three women whom the egoist tries to entrap are shown to be agents of this process of exposure. In their relations with Willoughby, Constantia Durham, Laetitia Dale, and Clara Middleton undergo an intensive education in the intricacies of male egoism, an education that in

Clara's case also involves some significant depictions of female subjectivity in flux. The great difference between *The Egoist* and the
novels we have already examined lies in the new ways this familiar
pattern is executed—in particular, the ways in which Meredith increasingly directs us to identify with the plight of the female hero
and her development of "mental freedom" while we simultaneously maintain a comic distance between ourselves and the male
protagonist and his ego-driven machinations.

Judged on the basis of dramatic unity, the work in the Meredith
canon most like *The Egoist* in execution is the early *Evan Harrington* (1860). Both of these novels proceed by means of carefully restricted dramatic exposition: their characters move through a
series of comic confrontations, presented predominantly in dialogue, that eventually lead up to a *scène-à-faire*. In addition, there
is the same country-house setting that helps to confine the subject
of the two novels to "human nature in the drawing room."

But to mention *Evan Harrington* is also to highlight the striking
differences between it and *The Egoist*. Both novels are "comedies
in narrative" dealing in the exposure of self-defeating egoism, but
the handling of this theme in *Evan Harrington* clearly does not
raise the serious feminist issues that it does in *The Egoist*. The
Countess de Saldar is a deliciously comic figure, but her exertions
of egoism—her efforts to take Beckley Court by storm—are essentially benign: as presented, the moral significance of her scheme is
trivial. The moral significance of Sir Willoughby's egoism is by no
means trivial, and it is in this respect that the two novels part company thematically.

The rendering of the conflict between Willoughby's acquisitive
aggression and the awakening consciousness of the novel's female
heroes to their rights of spiritual equality is Meredith's most moving
and articulate treatment of one of the great themes of late Victorian
fiction. *The Egoist* is his contribution to the handful of novels written within this period—including *Middlemarch, Daniel Deronda,
The Portrait of a Lady,* and *The Wings of the Dove*—that present
this theme in definitive form.

At the same time, the mention of these novels also suggests how
Meredith's approach to the problems of the modern female hero in
The Egoist differs from that of George Eliot or Henry James. To put
the matter most simply and obviously, Meredith's experimentation
with strict comic limits in this novel places a constraint on his exe-

cution that is absent from the treatments we find in George Eliot and James. Meredith permits Clara Middleton to gain moral awareness without undergoing the horror that her marriage to Willoughby would surely have produced. George Eliot, on the other hand, does subject Dorothea Brooke and Gwendolyn Harleth to the horror of equally unsuitable marriages—marriages that make a mockery of their notions of freedom and epic achievement—yet she also allows them to escape the consequences of their choices through the device of "providential death."[3]

In *The Portrait of a Lady*, there is no such reprieve. As George Levine long ago pointed out, "Osmond does not die, and the only man through whom a genuinely rich life might have been made available to Isabel—Ralph Touchett—does."[4] In *The Wings of the Dove*, James's vision is even more somber. When Milly Theale "turn[s] her face to the wall,"[5] the act symbolizes not only spiritual death—the death of her ideal of freedom—but oncoming physical death as well. Her act of trusting herself to Merton Densher and her subsequent recognition of his betrayal are events as irrevocable as Isabel's marriage to Osmond: they occur when the time allotted Milly in which to fulfill her liberating visions has almost run out. Again, there is no possibility of a reprieve. But in the world of *The Egoist*, a mistake may be corrected, although the process of correction, as illustrated by the case of Clara Middleton, can be extremely difficult.

2

The precedent for a reprieve in relations with Sir Willoughby is set at the beginning of *The Egoist* in the example of Constantia Durham. Long after her brief appearance, Constantia's name recurs in the novel as an ironical reminder of Willoughby's sentimental ideal of stable identity and faithful womanhood as well as the potential reality of feminine inconstancy and revolt. Constantia is introduced in the first chapter after she has already become his "affianced," and at the moment she is beginning to regret it. This moment is marked by the arrival at the Hall of the sea-hero, Lieutenant Crossjay Patterne, of whom "young Sir Willoughby was fond of talking [as] his 'military namesake and distant cousin, Young Patterne—the Marine.'" When the aristocratic Patterne spies the Marine Patterne approaching, "decidedly *not* bearing the stamp of the

gentleman 'on his hat, his coat, his feet, or anything that was his,'"
the Marine is summarily dismissed with a curt "Not at home"
(13:8–9). This act of rudeness apparently marks the first time Constantia has perceived the Egoist as egoist and in itself, as Robert
Polhemus has suggested, it "defines the pattern of egoism."[6]

Meredith's handling of this incident at the end of Chapter 1 provides a convenient approach to the role of the female hero in this
novel, and also returns us to the question of Meredithian narrative
control explored in *Richard Feverel*. Constantia presents a portrait
in miniature of what is to be the dilemma and function of Clara
Middleton in relation to Sir Willoughby. At the same time, Meredith renders the incident in a style that demonstrates the modulations of the narrative voice in *The Egoist* when most effective—and
most problematic:

> He had been disappointed in the age, grossly deceived in the appearance of the man claiming to be his relative in this unseasonable fashion;
> and his acute instinct advised him swiftly of the absurdity of introducing to his friends a heavy unpresentable senior as the celebrated gallant
> Lieutenant of Marines, and the same as a member of his family! He had
> talked of the man too much, too enthusiastically, to be able to do so.
> . . . Considerateness dismisses him on the spot, without parley. It was
> performed by a gentleman supremely advanced at a very early age in
> the art of cutting.
> Young Sir Willoughby spoke a word of the rejected visitor to Miss
> Durham, in response to her startled look: "I shall drop him a cheque,"
> he said, for she seemed personally wounded, and had a face of crimson.
> The young lady did not reply.
> Dating from the humble departure of Lieutenant Crossjay Patterne
> up the limes-avenue under a gathering rain-cloud, the ring of imps in
> attendance on Sir Willoughby maintained their station with strict observation of his movements at all hours; and were comparisons in quest
> [sic], the sympathetic eagerness of the eyes of caged monkeys for the
> hand about to feed them, would supply one. They perceived in him a
> fresh development and very subtle manifestation of the very old thing
> from which he had sprung. (13:9–10)

The passage begins with the ironic refraction of Sir Willoughby's
interior monologue—a narrated monologue and psycho-narration,
to adapt Dorrit Cohn's description of Flaubert's technique in *L'Éducation sentimentale*, in which "the narrator will glide in and out of
[the protagonist's] mind at will, adopting his . . . inner language at

crucial moments, but always free to return to [the] objective narrative base. . . . Precisely because [narrated monologues] cast the language of a subjective mind into the grammar of objective narration, they amplify emotional notes, but also throw into ironic relief all false notes struck by a figural mind."[7] We are made privy here to Willoughby's thought processes, false notes and all, just as he might convey them to an intimate, up to the moment he registers but only begins to understand Constantia's response. As the narrative provides visual details—"startled look," "face of crimson"—we are made to realize, as Willoughby does not, that her eyes have been opened, that she is in the process of gaining the "perspicacious clear eyes" that mark the Meredithian female hero who becomes associated with the principle of common sense. This cinematic rendering of significant detail develops its irony with wonderful economy and precision in conjunction with revealing discourse: "her startled look" followed directly by " 'I shall drop him a cheque.' "

One may see a continuity here between Meredith's technique and similar essential tactics in, for example, James, Woolf, and Joyce, the narrated monologue acting, in Cohn's words, "as a kind of stylistic bridge that led from nineteenth- to twentieth-century fiction."[8] But it is equally important to note that this technique is to be found functioning in much the same way, not only in earlier nineteenth-century continental texts, as Cohn points out, but in many earlier English texts as well. A prime example is Jane Austen's use, in Wayne Booth's words, of "Emma's mind as a reflector of events—however beclouded her vision must be."[9] And this comment suggests still another strategic point—that the beclouding, whether in the mind of Emma Woodhouse (or Emma Bovary or Frédéric Moreau) or Willoughby Patterne, is rendered in such a way as to provide the reader with an understanding quite distinct from the protagonist's "false notes" of misjudgment and implied confusion.

In the passage under consideration, however, as the narrator goes on in the final paragraph to veer away from direct presentation of Willoughby's colossal arrogance and Constantia's awakening sensibilities, something goes wrong. The problem is not that Meredith is shifting from drama to summary; like Austen, he is fully capable of effective "panoramic" as well as "scenic" narration. Rather, the problem is a stylistic one, as the brisk and devastating comic narrative gives way to a self-conscious cleverness epitomized by the leering "imps." It is precisely this kind of striving for clever effect that has disturbed readers of *The Egoist* since the novel first appeared. Even William Ernest Henley, one of the growing circle of intellectuals in the late '70s who were becoming "true-blue Meredith persons,"[10] leavened his enthusiastic praise of *The Egoist* at the time of its publication by mentioning its "freakishness" and suggesting that "its peculiarities of form are such as must stand inevitably in the way of its success."[11] A major source of this "freakishness," I would argue, is to be found in Meredith's unwillingness to observe consistently in *The Egoist* a central distinction he makes between comedy and satire in the *Essay*.

In Chapter 2 of *The Egoist*, Meredith defines his imps as the "pets of the Comic Spirit" (13:10)—that is, the agents of comedy. At the same time, however, the imps, "squatting . . . on their haunches" (13:6), are also clearly the crude agents of satire; their function, as in the passage quoted from Chapter 1, is to cast ridicule on Sir Willoughby's antics—"falling foul of the ridiculous person with a satiric rod" (*Essay*, 23:41). But the *Essay* unequivocally states that the comic "is not to be confounded" with satiric ridicule (*Essay*, 23:42). My point here is that when Meredith *chooses* to write within the generic limits of the *Essay*, conflicts between theory and practice may then produce genuine difficulties. Typically, when the narrator treats a character—particularly Willoughby—with open scorn, the style becomes supercilious, coy, and artificial. This is one of those cases, then, where Meredith's experiments with a self-reflexive style may be damaging rather than liberating or evidence of his having "gone ahead by at least fifty years."[12] The effect is not so much to create the appropriate distance and steadiness of vision he associates with comedy as to annoy us with his strenuous effort to turn Willoughby into a ridiculous object: "If you detect the ridicule, and your kindliness is chilled by it, you are slipping into the grasp of Satire" (*Essay*, 23:41).

Wayne Booth observed in *The Rhetoric of Fiction* that "how we feel about generalizing commentary will depend . . . basically on the author's skill in suiting its quality to the quality of the dramatic portions."[13] The narrator's impish sarcasm on the theme that Willoughby is descended from an ape, and is acting like one,[14] is not only unsuited to the dramatic portions—it is gratuitous. The moral and psychological situation has already been rendered with simple effectiveness by such lines as "I shall drop him a cheque" and "the young lady did not reply." As is the case here, however, effective narrative balance and stylistic control are particularly evident in this text when Meredith is intent on dramatizing the assertive roles played by the novel's female heroes. It is to this area of substantial achievement in *The Egoist* that much of the subsequent discussion will be devoted.

3

Of the three women in *The Egoist* who undergo the ordeal of receiving Sir Willoughby Patterne's amorous attentions, Clara Middleton is clearly the central figure and I will examine her role presently. But Laetitia Dale also plays an intriguing and strategic part that deserves full attention. When her role has been examined by critics, the treatment has tended either to be perfunctory or to go to one of two extremes: laments over the tragedy of her fate or strictures against Meredith's handling of her unconvincing behavior.[15] I would argue that, viewed within the historical constraints of the novel's Victorian setting, there is nothing tragic or even pathetic about Laetitia's marriage to Willoughby and, further, that her conduct throughout *The Egoist* is not only plausible but consistent with George Meredith's development of both her character and the overall form of the novel. Most importantly, Meredith develops Laetitia's character in such a way as to make her, by novel's end, the primary character to speak for the critical intelligence that is the essence of the comic spirit.[16]

From the beginning of *The Egoist* Laetitia Dale provides a counterpoint of constancy to Willoughby in contrast to the independent attitudes developed by Clara and Constantia. What is particularly interesting about Laetitia is that her constancy does not in any sense preclude criticism of her hero, whereas both of the other women appear to have become involved with Willoughby in a wholly uncritical manner. Meredith makes a point of stressing this distinction early: "Clara Middleton did not study and know him like Laetitia Dale" (13:41). The fact that Laetitia's eyes are at least partly open from the beginning of the novel allows her to act for the comic spirit as a relatively sympathetic critic of the lord of Patterne Hall. Her point of view is a primary means by which Meredith manages to keep our critical responses to Willoughby under control, and it helps to explain how it is that such a man, as Lionel Stevenson has put it, "eventually emerges as a truly pathetic figure."[17]

Laetitia's awareness also helps, I think, to explain a point that has baffled many readers—why it is that Meredith condemns her to marry Willoughby after his egoism has been stripped bare at the novel's end. As Willoughby himself says to Laetitia at that time, "you are the woman of all the world who knows me" (14:323); the irony is that her essential knowledge is of the precariousness of Willoughby's public persona—the instability of the self definition he is so anxious to maintain. Yet if there is to be any hope left for him at the end, it resides in this very sense of precariousness, that is, in his potential openness to a changing view of what it means to be lord of Patterne Hall.

As for Laetitia, her decision finally to marry Willoughby is based on a number of factors, all related to her increasingly clear appraisal of his character—and her own situation. First, one gets the strong impression by the end of the novel that she regards her relations to Willoughby as a challenge—granted an enormous one—to her considerable powers of common sense and clear-sightedness. A second and related point is that Laetitia, unlike Constantia and Clara, does not see Willoughby's faults as "monstrous" but rather as the unfortunate result of his being "nurtured in idolatry." Third, and equally important, is the fact that Laetitia, at the age of thirty, has a great deal to gain by an alliance with Willoughby: his money will provide her with new freedom—"the wings to fly abroad over lands which had begun to seem fabulous in her starved imagination" (14:320). And, lest one should disparage such a materialistic basis for conduct, this very Jamesian phrase helps to recall that it is precisely money that permits James's Isabel and Milly the opportunity to exercise their imaginations. The great difference between Laetitia and James's protagonists—and Clara and Constantia as well—is that Laetitia is devoid of illusions by the time she consents to marry Willoughby and thus acquire her "wings": she recognizes exactly what she is in for. One has the strong sense that she can handle being Lady Patterne in a way that the other two leading women of *The Egoist* could not.

Willoughby's affluence is also important to Laetitia because her position in life, unlike that of Constantia or Clara, is precarious: " 'I am glad of a fireside, and not sure of always having one. . . . My father has very little money. We subsist on what private income he has, and his pension: he was an army doctor. I may by-and-by have to live in a town for pupils. I could be grateful to any one who would save me from that' " (13:187–88).[18] Hers is the position of Charlotte Lucas, Elizabeth Bennet's friend in *Pride and Prejudice* who is (relatively) poor, unmarried, and twenty-seven years old. What Jane Austen's narrator says about the social realities of Charlotte's Regency world applies just as much to the rural Victorian world of Laetitia Dale: marriage "was the only honourable provision for well-educated young women of small fortune, and however uncertain of giving happiness, must be their pleasantest preservative from want."[19]

Finally, there is something refreshing, after all the suffocating false sentiment that surrounds Willoughby, in Laetitia's extraordinarily unromantic view of things: "I crave for money. I should marry to be rich. I should not worship you. I should be a burden" (14:323). It would seem by the novel's end that such a burden is precisely what Willoughby most deserves—and needs.

4

Laetitia does not arrive at this realistic appraisal of matters all at once, however. Early in the novel she is described by Meredith as perceiving Willoughby at moments with great clarity, yet she is still subject to her childhood adulation of him. An amusing early episode, occurring just after Willoughby—and no one else—has learned of Constantia's elopement with Harry Oxford, illustrates Laetitia's ambivalence as well as Willoughby's dedication to preserving the illusion of his imperturbability:

> Sir Willoughby met [Laetitia] on a Sunday morning, as she crossed his park solitarily to church. They were within ten days of the appointed ceremony. He should have been away at Miss Durham's end of the county. He had, Laetitia knew, ridden over to her the day before; but here he was; and very unwontedly, quite surprisingly, he presented his arm to conduct Laetitia to the church-door, and talked and laughed in a way that reminded her of a hunting gentleman she had seen once rising to his feet, staggering from an ugly fall across hedge and fence into one of the lanes of her short winter walks: "All's well, all sound, never better, only a scratch!" the gentleman had said, as he reeled and pressed a bleeding head. Sir Willoughby . . . went on talking in the church porch, and murmuring softly some steps up the aisle, passing the pews of Mrs. Mountstuart Jenkinson and Lady Busshe. Of course he was entertaining, but what a strangeness it was to Laetitia! (13:23)

This episode sums up Willoughby and Laetitia's relation to him as neatly as anything in *The Egoist*, and also provides another good example of Meredithian narrated monologue/psycho-narration. Willoughby, staggering from Constantia's jilt, has one thought in mind: above all, keep up appearances—don't let the Mrs. Mountstuart Jenkinsons and Lady Busshes of the world[20] have the satisfaction knowledge of his predicament would surely give them. Laetitia, and Laetitia only, has been the true object of his affections. Willoughby sneers at the world, but as the narrator notes later, he is at the same time terrified "lest he should be the victim of a sneer of the world he contemned" (13:54). Laetitia, while still savoring the "enchanting romance" of the past, is shown to see at once the intrinsic absurdity of Willoughby's conduct. But, as the comparison with the reeling and bleeding huntsman suggests, she also recognizes that Willoughby is in some way hurt. Her natural reaction in both cases is to question the "strangeness" of covering up one's true feelings with a theatrical display. Willoughby's instinct (like Sir Austin Feverel's) is at all costs to escape shame[21] and preserve his mask; Laetitia's instinct is to reach out to the man behind the mask, but it is not until the end of the novel that he permits her to begin to do so.

Although her perception is sharp in this scene, Laetitia does not act here as an agent for the comic spirit. Without the supernatural powers of a Noorna bin Noorka, she responds to what is Willoughby's most chilling—and characteristic—remark about the Durham affair by assuming that he is not responsible for it: "One question she asked: 'Miss Durham is well, I trust?' And he answered: 'Durham?' and said: 'There is no Miss Durham to my knowledge.' The impression he left with her was, that he might yesterday during his ride have had an accident and fallen on his head" (13:24). And the point, of course, is that the "accident" has damaged Willoughby's ego rather than his head, and that his response to this damage is a mental trick that amounts to a kind of spiritual murder—"there is no Miss Durham." Constantia is guilty of the same sin as is Lieutenant Crossjay Patterne—both have threatened Willoughby's appearance before "the world." If they don't continue to serve the predictable function of helping to maintain a coherent Patterne, they are simply obliterated from existence, as far as Willoughby is concerned. It is no coincidence that Constantia's action was initially instigated by her observation of Willoughby's unsettling habit of consigning dissidents to oblivion. Indeed, at one time or another in *The Egoist*, all the major figures are threatened with "extinction" by Willoughby's dedication to preserving appearances and the status quo. And, as I have already suggested, this threat includes Willoughby himself, since as the novel progresses his attempts to remain a fixed identity propel him towards spiritual self-destruction: "Through very love of self himself he slew" (13:6).

Still another revelation of this aspect of his personality occurs when he responds to Clara Middleton's suggestion that Vernon Whitford might desire to leave Patterne Hall in order to begin his career as a writer in London:

> "Supposing he goes, he offends me; he loses a friend; and it will not be the first time that a friend has tried me too far; but, if he offends me, he is extinct."
> "Is what?" cried Clara, with a look of fright.
> "He becomes to me at once as if he had never been. He is extinct."
> "In spite of your affection?"
> "On account of it, I might say. Our nature is mysterious, and mine as much so as any. Whatever my regrets, he goes out." (13:105–6)

Clara's "look of fright" here is a direct reminder of Constantia's earlier "startled look" under very similar circumstances. As is suggested by Willoughby's obscurantism—"Our nature is mysterious"—the true despot stands revealed.

Laetitia herself is not in the least immune to this kind of treatment, in spite of her apparent constancy and its usefulness to Willoughby's notions of a stable identity. This becomes clear when Clara makes "her first direct leap for liberty" (13:150). Her tactic is to suggest discreetly that Laetitia might make a more suitable wife for Willoughby than she herself could ever be. Clara's efforts to free herself and allow him to save face at the same time—a tact not exercised by Constantia Durham—are treated by Willoughby as a simple case of feminine jealousy. His response is first to declare, in words that he must later eat, his absolute dedication to the project of marrying none other than Clara—"'I repeat. *I could not marry Laetitia Dale'*"—and second, to make Laetitia's expendability entirely clear: "'There are times when, I confess, I require a Laetitia Dale to bring me out, give and take. I am indebted to her . . . , but if she is displeasing in the sight of my bride by . . . by the breadth of an eyelash, then . . .' Sir Willoughby's arm waved Miss Dale off away into outer darkness in the wilderness. Clara shut her eyes and rolled her eyeballs in a frenzy of unuttered revolt" (13:151).

Not unlike Browning's Duke of Ferrara, Willoughby regards an attractive woman as an objet d'art whose sole function is to "bring out" the possessor. And, if the object ceases to perform its proper function, he, like the duke, can give "commands." However—and it is in this respect that Meredith maintains his comic note—the "outer darkness" would be banishment from the Patterne estate rather than the implied fate of the duke's last duchess. And, as long as Laetitia does not "displease" and performs the rites Willoughby "requires," she is preserved even from the fate of banishment. Laetitia's important and primary role in life to Willoughby's eyes is that of providing him with illumination, which in a different sense is also the role assigned her by the comic spirit: "The presence of Miss Dale illuminated him as the burning taper lights up consecrated plate. Deeply respecting her for her constancy, esteeming her for a model of taste, he was never in her society without that happy consciousness of shining which calls forth the treasures of the man" (13:94). Laetitia's illumination, at once flattering Willoughby's egoism and revealing it for what it is, is yet another example of how Meredith's delicate irony functions through a narrative style that simultaneously provides access to Willoughby's self-congratulatory view and a devastatingly more critical comic perspective.

Willoughby stands displayed in the above passage as a type of male egoism that recurs often in later Victorian fiction—Edward Casaubon, Henleigh Grandcourt, and Gilbert Osmond come to mind at once. Osmond's egoism in particular is rendered by James in terms strikingly similar to those used by Meredith:

> What could be a happier gift in a companion than a quick, fanciful mind which saved one repetitions and reflected one's thought on a polished, elegant surface? Osmond hated to see his thought reproduced literally—that made it look stale and stupid. . . . His egotism had never taken the crude form of desiring a dull wife; this lady's intelligence was to be a silver plate, not an earthen one. . . . He found the silver quality in this perfection in Isabel; he could tap her imagination with his knuckle and make it ring.[22]

But, again, the comparison also recalls an important distinction: Meredith's tone, in the above passage as well as in the rest of *The*

Egoist, is essentially comic. The style encourages us to smile inwardly at Willoughby, even when he is most inhumane, because we are made to anticipate that the women he tyrannizes will eventually take the upper hand—with a vengeance. There are no such comic expectations encouraged by James's style. The "ring" that Osmond imagines producing by tapping Isabel's imagination suggests an outcome altogether different from the one Meredith prepares for from the beginning of *The Egoist*.

5

When Meredith introduces Clara Middleton, he stresses her inexperience and youth—she is eighteen, while Willoughby is thirty-two. She is everything he is not: she embodies youthful high spirits and views life as an adventure of growth and discovery. Willoughby by contrast is prematurely aged: for him life is a fixed system in which every move is calculated for effect. Trapped within solipsism and monologue—"I never quarrel. It is a characteristic of mine," he later tells Clara (13:177)—social forms exist for him as the means to self-aggrandizement and the exercise of his will. For Clara, social forms are simply the means to interacting with the world she finds all before her—the world in which she seeks a life worthy of her considerable imagination. She is poised for a relation with society based on what she calls "real talk" (13:86), communication that, as Randall Craig has argued, is the dialogical opposite to Willoughby's monologism: "it is creative, not merely reflective, and interactive, not simply active."[23]

Initially, Meredith makes it clear that the great problem for Clara is that in her inexperience she fails to recognize the distinction between Willoughby's views on communication, the self, and society and her own. It is a distinction, however, that the reader is made to see from the moment she is introduced:

> [Willoughby] looked on her, expecting her to look at him. But as soon as he looked he found that he must be in motion to win a look in return. He was one of a pack; many were ahead of him, the whole of them were eager. He had to debate within himself how best to communicate to her that he was Willoughby Patterne, before her gloves were too much soiled to flatter his niceness, for here and there, all around, she was

yielding her hand to partners—obscurant males whose touch leaves a stain. Far too generally gracious was Her Starriness to please him.

Perceived as fulfilling Willoughby's financial, Darwinian, and aesthetic criteria—"she had money and health and beauty, the triune of perfect starriness" (3:42)—Clara and her innocent enjoyment of her first appearance in society here are neatly played off against the psycho-narration of his reluctant participation in a degrading and indecorously promiscuous display of primitive sexual selection. Again, particularly in the last line, one is reminded of the view of decorum dramatized by Browning's Duke of Ferrara. By the time Willoughby remarks late in the novel, "I will not consent to a violation of decorum" (14:168), it has become quite clear to Clara that his views of decorous behavior are a matter of the strictest religious orthodoxy—and that he is his own self-appointed high priest. The education she undergoes at his temple, then, is a process of learning precisely what "he was Willoughby Patterne" means.

Clara's education in Willoughbyhood proceeds by stages. After it has been demonstrated to her over a month's time that Willoughby "had a leg," that is, "a style, a tone, an artist tailor, an authority of manner" (13:43), she is "implored to enter the state of captivity by the pronunciation of vows—a private but binding ceremonial" (13:44). In other words, Willoughby is no longer interested in loose verbal understandings of the Constantia Durham variety. Confirmed in his monologism and, as Randall Craig has put it, "fully believing in the power of language to convey and to fix meaning, he takes espousal to be tantamount to marriage and impervious to time and change."[24] From the very beginning, the keynote of his relation to Clara is one of coercion toward such a "binding"—a wonderfully multivalent term—but a coercion always exerted through the proper, "ceremonial" forms. When Clara pleads a "desire to see a little of the world before she plighted herself," Willoughby is ready with a rebuttal of the highest propriety—filial duty: "Willingly would he obey her behests, resignedly languish, were it not for his mother's desire to see the future lady of Patterne established there before she died. . . . The plea of urgency was reasonable" (13:44).

Later, once Clara has "submitted"—not chosen—"to stand engaged," Willoughby returns to the theme of his mother's failing health and from there, with a very definite proprietary goal in mind, moves to the subject of "his own death to come, carelessly, with a

philosophical air" (13:56). The highly comic interchange that en-
sues provides us with another one of those electric moments in *The
Egoist* when a female hero has her first full look at Willoughby's
ego in all its extraordinary acquisitive splendor as he moves "from
elaborate disguise to self-revelation":[25]

> "All of us must go! our time is short."
> "Very," she assented.
> It sounded like want of feeling.
> "If you lose me, Clara!"
> "But you are strong, Willoughby."
> "I may be cut off to-morrow."
> "Do not talk in such a manner."
> "It is as well that it should be faced."
> "I cannot see what purpose it serves."
> "Should you lose me, my love!"
> "Willoughby!"
> "Oh, the bitter pang of leaving you!"
> "Dear Willoughby, you are distressed; your mother may recover; let
> us hope she will; I will help to nurse her; I have offered, you know; I
> am ready, most anxious. I believe I am a good nurse."
> "It is this belief—that one does not die with death!"
> "That is our comfort."
> "When we love?"
> "Does it not promise that we meet again?"
> "To walk the world and see you perhaps . . . with
> another!"
> "See me?—Where? Here?"
> "Wedded . . . to another. You! my bride; whom I call mine; and you
> are! You would be still—in that horror! But all things are possible;
> women are women; they swim in infidelity, from wave to wave! I know
> them."
> "Willoughby, do not torment yourself and me, I beg you."
> He meditated profoundly, and asked her: "Could you be such a saint
> among women? . . . Be mine beyond death?"
> "Married is married, I think."
> "Clara! to dedicate your life to our love! Never one touch! not one
> whisper! not a thought, not a dream! Could you?—it agonizes me to
> imagine . . . be inviolate? mine above?—mine before all men, though I
> am gone:—true to my dust? Tell me. Give that assurance. True to my
> name!" (13:56–57)

This brilliantly comic dialogue, playing as it does on Willoughby's
voracious desire for a kind of psychological suttee[26] on Clara's part,

tells almost as much about her as it does about him. Her responses to his rhapsody of self-love are consistently common-sensical, and as she dodges around his increasingly direct appeals for her "oath" to future self-immolation, Clara demonstrates the emerging independent will and self-reliance that are to be tested to the upmost later on.

One of Meredith's most effective touches in this scene as well as in others is to show the content of Clara's statements apparently escaping Willoughby who, always desiring to be the monologist,[27] listens only to the sound of his own voice: "It has haunted me ever since we joined hands. To have you—to lose you!" "Is it not possible that I may be the first to die?" said Miss Middleton. "And lose you, with the thought that you, lovely as you are, and the dogs of the world barking round you, might . . . Is it any wonder that I have my feeling for the world?" (13:58). Clara, with her critical faculties awakening, is shown by contrast to be increasingly alert to all that Willoughby says. By the time this scene is almost over, she has reached a very significant conclusion: "Our views of the world are opposed, Willoughby" (13:59). This recognition is a strategic step for her on the road to understanding him and, just as importantly, herself.[28] Meredith drives his feminist point home repeatedly in just this way, with closed masculine monologue played off against a feminine "view of the world" defined by openness and the possibility of change. This latter view is taken to its extreme at the novel's end when Laetitia Dale launches a concerted effort to break through Willoughby's monologue and initiate real change in him—a project of truly heroic proportions.

Meredith created in Willoughby an epitome of aristocratic English egoism, a Barbarian of perhaps greater completeness and perfection than Matthew Arnold ever imagined, or one could ever hope to meet. But if more archetypical than typical, Willoughby, like Don Quixote, nonetheless lives as a complex psychological being in his fictional world. And much of the comic fascination exerted by *The Egoist* is derived from our knowledge, as the novel progresses, that he is moving steadily toward a confrontation with the inadequacy of his view of the universe. What gives this aspect of the comedy particular psychological interest is that by midway Willoughby himself is shown to recognize such a confrontation as inevitable. As Neil Roberts has suggested, "Willoughby's utterances . . . are, in fact, tense with involuntary dialogic relations."[29] The grotesque contortions he undergoes to preserve his "look of indignant contentment" (13:64) are as much efforts at self-deception as efforts to deceive the world: "He desired to be deceived . . . , [and] above all desired that no one should know of his being deceived" (14:49).

6

Once Clara Middleton has begun to see Willoughby's view of the world for what it is, she does not immediately turn revolutionary as Constantia Durham has done before her. In fact, Clara's efforts for release remain within the bounds of social propriety until it becomes clear—after his midnight proposal to Laetitia—that Willoughby himself has acted dishonorably, in breach of his own ostensible rules of conduct. Before this occurs, however, Clara's first response to her newly acquired knowledge of Willoughby's character is a vague "wish to run to Switzerland or Tyrol and see the Alps" since "very few weeks were left to her" before the date set for her marriage (13:62). The urge for open spaces and mountain air is countered by the imagery characteristically associated with Willoughby: "To be fixed at the mouth of a mine, and to have to descend it daily, and not to discover great opulence below; on the contrary, to be chilled in subterranean sunlessness, without any substantial quality that she could grasp, only the mystery of inefficient tallow-light in those caverns of the complacent talking man" (13:65).

Meredith's rendering of the confinement and "sunlessness" Clara encounters in her relation to Willoughby and his endless monologue is, again, strikingly similar to moods evoked by George Eliot and Henry James in their treatment of the threat of a proprietary male ego to an expansive feminine imagination. Edward Casaubon in particular shares Willoughby's dreary subterranean quality—a quality that in *Middlemarch* and *The Egoist* leads increasingly to a sense of claustrophobia:

> Dorothea had not distinctly observed but felt with a stifling depression that the large vistas and wide fresh air which she had dreamed of finding in her husband's mind were replaced by anterooms and winding passages which seemed to lead nowhither. . . . Poor Mr. Casaubon himself was lost among small closets and winding stairs. . . . With his taper stuck before him he forgot the absence of windows, and in bitter manu-

script remarks on other men's notions about solar deities, he had become indifferent to the sunlight.[30]

In the chapter entitled "The Betrothed," Meredith delicately suggests Clara's similarly developing but "not distinctly observed" consciousness of her position: "She knew of nothing but her mind at work, objecting to this and that, desiring changes. She did not dream of being on the giddy ridge of the passive or negative sentiment of love, where one step to the wrong side precipitates us into the state of repulsion" (13:66). Meredith characteristically draws the reader in at the end of the passage through use of the first-person plural, conveying instinctive sexual antagonism with remarkable force. But what is most interesting as the chapter proceeds is how, through narrative tactics that anticipate the dramatization of consciousness in modernist writers, Meredith provides direct access to Clara's troubled and extremely conflicted state of mind as he depicts what is presumably her first experience of physical intimacy. Willoughby, in order to be alone with her, "dispatches" young Crossjay to order tea:

> Clara saw herself without a shield. . . .
> "My dearest Clara! My bride!" said he. . . .
> Why would he not wait to deserve her!—no, not deserve—to reconcile her with her real position; not reconcile, but to repair the image of him in her mind, before he claimed his apparent right!
> He did not wait. He pressed her to his bosom.
> "You are mine, my Clara—utterly mine; every thought, every feeling. We are one. . . . I have been longing for you, looking forward. . . . My dearest!"
> She came out of it with the sensations of the frightened child that has had its dip in sea-water, sharpened to think that after all it was not so severe a trial. Such was her idea; and she said to herself immediately: What am I that I should complain? . . . She did not blame him; she fell in her own esteem; less because she was the betrothed Clara Middleton, which was now palpable as a shot in the breast of a bird, than that she was a captured woman, of whom it is absolutely expected that she must submit, and when she would rather be gazing at flowers. (13:67–68)

Through modulations between various forms of narrated and quoted interior monologue (especially suggestive of such tactics to come later in Virginia Woolf) Clara emerges here as a portrait of self-contradictory subjectivity, an important motif we shall return to later. As she experiences outrage at Willoughby's sexual aggressiveness she also tries in her mind's eye to protect him from the implications of his actions by blaming herself for her own failed attempts to accommodate to societal expectations of the "captured woman"—and all the while she "would rather be gazing at flowers." Further, as Susan Payne has pointed out in her useful discussion of this chapter, "the comic twist is given by the narrator's allowing access to the thoughts of both the characters concerned, but giving pre-eminence to the female viewpoint." Willoughby, Payne goes on, entirely misreads Clara's silence and blush of shame—"a misreading caused by the strength of both social and literary convention":[31] "Sir Willoughby was enraptured with her. Even so purely, coldly, statue-like, would he have prescribed his bride's reception of his caress. The suffusion of crimson coming over her subsequently, showing her divinely feminine in reflective bashfulness, agreed with his highest definitions of female character" (13:68–69).

As Clara begins to piece together the fragments of Willoughby's character appearing beneath the "highly civilized" exterior, the process is of course greatly accelerated by Willoughby himself. Repeatedly Meredith's prime method of providing comic revelations about his hero is the dramatic process of Willoughby's unwitting self-exposure. When Willoughby, angered at losing the lead in conversation at table, turns to Clara and tells an anecdote about a selfish husband, his object is to recapture her entire attention and dazzle her "little brain." In a famous passage, Willoughby sums up his story by saying, " 'Now, there, Clara, there you have the Egoist. . . . The man was utterly unconscious of giving vent to the grossest selfishness.' 'An Egoist!' said Clara. 'Beware of marrying an Egoist, my dear!' He bowed gallantly; and so blindly fatuous did he appear to her, that she could hardly believe him guilty of uttering the words she had heard from him" (13:115).

It is also evident, however, that Willoughby as Egoist[32] is not simply a supremely fatuous man; he is in addition an extremely dangerous one. Meredith never lets us forget that Willoughby operates from a position of real power, and that, with the exception of Constantia Durham, he has been extraordinarily successful at treating people as objects all his life. As the narrative traces Clara's thoughts following the above passage, we become increasingly aware of her deepening sense of isolation: "She looked at Vernon, she looked at her father, and at the ladies Eleanor and Isabel. None of them saw the man in the word, none noticed the word" (13:115). Janet Horo-witz Murray has remarked that "Meredith walks a thin line in keep-ing us amused with Willoughby, and yet letting us see Clara's increasing desperation."[33] Much of the poignancy of her position is derived from her being surrounded by people who are willing to ac-cept Willoughby at face value, and who would regard her thoughts of release, as Dr. Middleton puts it much later, as a "flagrant breach of duty and decorum" (14:203). Even when Vernon Whit-ford finally comes rather lamely to her aid, it is still she who must fight the major battle with Willoughby's ego.

In this earlier scene, the thought of what lies ahead produces in Clara's mind a terrifying image of the crude violence inherent in Willoughby's sense of "duty and decorum": " 'Beware of marrying an Egoist.' Would he help her to escape? The idea of the scene en-suing upon her petition for release, and the being dragged round the walls of his egoism and having her head knocked against the corners, alarmed her with sensations of sickness" (13:115–16). Charles J. Hill, in noting the recurrence of such imagery of vio-lence, points out Meredith's indebtedness to Darwin and Mill and proposes that "the informing idea in Meredith's novel [is] the con-ception of egoism as a survival of primitive brutishness."[34] Jona-than Smith has extended this way of reading *The Egoist* by suggesting that "Meredith's target is the view of the sexes endorsed or enabled by Darwin's culturally powerful voice." Willoughby, as an "amateur scientist obsessed with finding a mate whose health will insure the continuation of the Patterne line and whose beauty will provide proof of his own superiority,"

> tells Laetitia that "Science . . . deals with facts, and having mastered them, it masters men," but his actions show that what science really masters is women. It does so "not with a stupid, loud-mouthed arro-gance" (14:83) but in a civilized manner, slowly and subtly; yet Wil-loughby is not above claiming that what the intractable Clara needs is "a whipping to bring her to the understanding of the principle called mastery, which is in man." (13:268)[35]

Similar images of violence abound in *The Egoist*, acting not only as a leitmotif for Willoughby's wish to be the "fittest" patriarch/sci-entist but also for his growing desire to smother Clara's rebellious imagination and offer up the remains to his injured pride:

> [H]e had an infinite thirst for her misery, that he might ease his heart of its charitable love. . . . An illness, fever, fire, runaway horses, personal

disfigurement, a laming, were sufficient. And then a formal and noble offer on his part to keep to the engagement with the unhappy wreck: yes, and to lead the limping thing to the altar, if she insisted. His imagination conceived it, and the world's applause besides. (14:61–62)[36]

Desire to do her intolerable hurt became an ecstasy in his veins, and produced another stretching fit, that terminated in a violent shake of the body and limbs; during which he was a spectacle for Mrs. Mountstuart at one of the windows. (14:164)

He slew imagination. There is no direr disaster in love than the death of imagination. He dragged her through the labyrinths of his penetralia, in his hungry coveting to be loved more and still more, more still, until imagination gave up the ghost, and he talked to her plain hearing like a monster. (14:183)

These gothic passages[37] graphically suggest the tragic implications of Meredith's subject; at the same time, by context and the wonderful ironic excessiveness of the imagery, the treatment also remains brilliantly comic and helps prepare for Clara's escape at the novel's end.

Willoughby's crucial error in his relations with Clara is to assume that she is incapable of opposing him; this, in turn, is based on the assumption, as Meredith puts it in the *Essay*, that she is "the pretty idiot, the passive beauty, the adorable bundle of caprices, very feminine, very sympathetic, of romantic and sentimental fiction" (23:14). Just how incorrect this assumption is becomes increasingly clear: "Was it possible he did not possess her utterly? He frowned up. Clara saw the lift of his brows, and thought: 'My mind is my own, married or not.' It was the point in dispute" (13:88). As she recognizes the nature of Willoughby's assault on her mind, Clara joins rank with the women praised in the *Essay* who "use their wits, and are not wandering vessels crying for a captain or a pilot. Comedy is an exhibition of their battle with men, and that of men with them" (23:14–15).

One could say that Willoughby the sentimentalist is a would-be pilot crying out for a wandering vessel. Perhaps the most striking quality of his extraordinary "arts of self-defense" (13:233) is the manner in which he perpetuates his sentimental image of Clara in spite of the increasing evidence to the contrary:

"Whenever the little brain is in doubt, perplexed, undecided which course to adopt, she will come to me, will she not? I shall always listen," he resumed soothingly. "My own! . . ."

"Willoughby . . .—will you listen? I am so commonplace that I shall not be understood by you unless you take my words for the very meaning of the words. I am unworthy. I am volatile. I love my liberty. I want to be free . . ."

"Flitch!" he called.

It sounded necromantic.

"Pardon me, my love," he said. "The man you see yonder violates my express injunction that he is not to come on my grounds, and here I find him on the borders of my garden!"

Sir Willoughby waved his hand to the abject figure of a man standing to intercept him.

"Volatile, unworthy, liberty—my dearest!" he bent to her when the man had appeased him by departing, "you are at liberty within the law, like all good women; I shall control and direct your volatility; and your sense of worthiness must be re-established when we are more intimate; it is timidity. The sense of unworthiness is a guarantee of worthiness ensuing. I believe I am in the vein of a sermon!" (13:126–27)

Flitch, the Patterne coachman previously consigned to oblivion for voicing absurd notions of independence, is indeed a necromantic invocation on Willoughby's part. He manages to threaten Clara with this example of abject disobedience at the same time he tries to dismiss her plea for liberty by deconstructing "the very meaning" of her words to indeterminacy as he sermonizes on his own determinate text of "worthiness," patriarchal "law," and "good women." But Willoughby's words are also a prime example of what Gary Handwerk has called the "linguistic self-deception"[38] of the characters in this novel; in the words of Alanna Kathleen Brown, "he uses language to shield himself from his own self-knowledge."[39]

As for Clara, the term "volatile" and the shifting of identity it implies in the above passage returns us to an interesting dynamic of Meredith's experimental impulse. We can see him here challenging certain realist conventions of characterization even as he is also exerting an increase in conventional control over his narrative materials in other respects—in his adherence to the limits of comedy, for example. Hillis Miller has explored Meredith's experiments in characterization somewhat later in the text by closely examining Chapter 21, "Clara's Meditations," in which Clara is shown coming to the inevitable conclusion that "the structure of assumptions presupposed in [her] promise to marry was false. Basic to this structure was the presupposition that she had a solid character on the basis of which promises could be made and kept."[40] Miller argues that

Clara's volatility, her "multitude of flitting wishes" as she realizes she must break her promise, creates an instability that deconstructs traditional notions of "fixed character" and shows "the procedures of realism dismantl[ing] themselves." Clara's "nature," then, is displayed as "an anonymous and shapeless energy which cannot be outlined. It must be compared, incoherently, to fire, to liquid, to the formless wind, to a featureless desert, or to unshaped stone. It changes from moment to moment."[41]

Gary Handwerk has a similar point in mind when he takes Clara Middleton as a model of Lacanian "liquidation of the traditional subject."[42] Handwerk suggests that Meredith's ironic treatment of Clara's relations with the other characters in the novel—and with Willoughby as "egoist" in particular—displays the intersubjective dynamics that for Lacan mark the vanishing of "the old stable ego of character."[43] As I have begun to suggest earlier in this chapter, Willoughby's repeated attempts to maintain *his* volatile persona as "fixed character" provide an even more central model of instability of subject. As in the scene I have just discussed, beneath his coercive tactics he is shown to be in a state of nervous dependency on others for reassurance that his rigid definitions of relationship are still in place. And of course what in fact Meredith brilliantly dramatizes for us are the ways in which those relationships are more and more in ironic flux, both in spite of and because of Willoughby's ingenious—and frantic—efforts to "control and direct" them. Thus it is that he feels "an appalling fear on behalf of his naked eidolon, the tender infant Self swaddled in his name before the world." His "dread of stripping in a wintry atmosphere" (14:50) is precisely a dread that his name will no longer signify the static ideal he assumes as his birthright in the enclosed world of Patterne Hall. In Lacanian terms, Willoughby is increasingly forced into confrontation with the radical provisionality of his own subject and its dependency "for its status at any point in time . . . [on] the sum of its interrupted encounters with all its significant others."[44] The only hope we are given for Willoughby at the novel's end (and it is a very modest and provisional hope) is premised on the possibilities of positive change to be generated by such encounters—in particular, his encounters with Laetitia Dale.

7

When Clara Middleton voices the "commonplace" words, "I want to be free," she makes her difficult but determined resolve to define herself anew in relation to Willoughby. At the same time, she is taking the steps that identify her as a distinctly modern female hero. But I also want to argue that Laetitia Dale, in her own manner, begins to display a "modern" sensibility as she confronts and eventually starts to exercise some control over the world of male coercion embodied in Willoughby. Laetitia's innate intelligence—as "illumination" of Willoughby's ego—comes progressively more into play as the novel proceeds. Once she has heard Clara's expression of distaste and cry for liberty in Chapter 16, Laetitia begins to see the incongruity between her adolescent idealization of Willoughby and the realistic glimpses of him provided her all along by her critical faculties. Chapters 31 and 32, narrated from Laetitia's point of view, give a running account of this process: as Willoughby pontificates in his accustomed style during their first midnight interview, "he seemed to her to justify Clara's feelings and her conduct: and her own reawakened sensations of injury came to the surface a moment to look at him, affirming that they pardoned him, and pitied, but hardly wondered" (14:83); "It saddened her that she knew so much" (14:88); "she was thinking that . . . his manner of talking to women went to excess in the artificial tongue—the tutored tongue of sentimental deference of the towering male: he fluted exceedingly" (14:89). And later, "she was endowed to feel that she had power to influence him, because now . . . she felt some emancipation from the spell of his physical mastery. He did not appear to her as a different man, but she had grown sensible of being a stronger woman" (14:99).

The process being described in these two chapters is of central importance to *The Egoist*—the shift in the woman's role from one of uncritical admiration to one that approaches a position of spiritual equality. As I have suggested in Chapter 1, this is a direction that, for the comic spirit, is the sine qua non of true comedy—and true civilization.[45] Laetitia, then, is undergoing the transformation already seen in Constantia and Clara, but with an essential difference: she retains her delicate sense of "pardon" and "pity" for Willoughby throughout his ordeal—a delicacy that, as I have already mentioned, has an important effect in controlling the reader's responses. In addition, Meredith analyzes the evolution of Laetitia's relationship to Willoughby just as thoroughly as he does that of Clara. This analysis centers on the tension that develops between her old and new attitudes: "Laetitia's habit of wholly subservient sweetness, which was her ideal of the feminine, [was] not yet conciliated with her acuter character" (14:96). Laetitia's long-standing "ideal of the feminine" is directly linked with Willoughby's assumption of the "sentimental deference of the towering male," and it is her "acuter character," finally, which throws down a challenge to the sentimental arrogance that Meredith saw as endemic in the Victorian male ego.[46]

The conflict between these two points of view is summarized with neat irony close to the end of the first midnight interview when Laetitia tells Willoughby that she is straining to pardon his conduct—an implicitly critical statement that the reader will relate to her newfound "acuteness." Willoughby, responding in his usual monological manner to words he does not wish to hear, simply fails—or chooses to fail—to grasp her meaning: "He had heard something; he had not caught the words, but they were manifestly favorable; her sign of emotion assured him of it and of the success he had sought. . . . He had inspired one woman with the mysterious man-desired passion of self-abandonment, self-immolation! The evidence was before him. At any instant he could . . . command her enthusiasm" (14:91). Here, as with Sir Austin Feverel, Willoughby's deficiency in Meredithian critical intelligence is fully displayed: his lack of emotional intelligence[47] is highlighted (again) in a parody of empathetic response—"her sign of emotion assured him"—while we are also reminded of his posturing as disinterested amateur scientist—"the evidence was before him"—along with his lust for the "good woman" who is ready to perform the rite of suttee before his "mysterious" ego.

In the famous second midnight interview (Chapter 40) Willoughby attempts to take complete command of Laetitia's enthusiasm and learns, to his horror, how fully her "wholly subservient sweetness" has given way to an "acuter character." Throughout this scene the ironic repetition of the word "constancy" acts to recapitulate Willoughby's sentimental ideal of womanhood:

> "You were and are my image of constancy!"
> "It is an error, Sir Willoughby; I am far from being the same." (14:190)
> "You carry in your bosom the magnet of constancy, and I, in spite of apparent deviations, declare to you that I have never ceased to be sensible of the attraction. . . . You teach me the difference of an alliance with a lady of intellect. . . . I have, as it were, gone the tour, to come home to you—at last?—and live our manly life of comparative equals." (14:191)
> "I was prouder of your constancy than of anything else that I had on

earth. It was a part of the order of the universe to me. A doubt of it
would have disturbed my creed. Why, good heaven! where are we? Is
nothing solid on earth? You loved me! . . . You loved me passionately!
. . . You cannot blot out the past: it is written, it is recorded."
(14:193–94)

The point is summed up concisely when Willoughby tells Laetitia
"that it is on your head if my ideal of women is wrecked" (14:196).
The wrecking of his ideal—his Willoughby-centric and, one might
add, logocentric view of the universe—is, of course, what *The Egoist* is all about. Laetitia's refusal of Willoughby's proposal is based
in large part on her clear knowledge that he makes his offer on exactly the same sentimental terms that were the basis of his previous
relationships with Constantia, Clara—and Laetitia herself. He can
be accepted only if he shows a willingness to change—that is, a willingness to adapt to a past, present, and future whose "written" and
"recorded" meanings may be deconstructed to yield, not simply his
own expedient interpretation, but a range of possible viewpoints in
a universe whose order is dynamic rather than static. Laetitia's
constancy after this second interview, then, is dedicated, not to the
Willoughby of the present but to the better man Willoughby might
become.[48]

8

One of Meredith's cleverest strokes in *The Egoist* is to embody
Willoughby's desired view of the world—the static world for which
he performs his rituals of propriety—in the person of Mrs. Mountstuart Jenkinson. One of this woman's functions in relation to Willoughby is summed up in her wish, for her own amusement, "to
keep him in love with himself" (14:331). But through a wonderful
irony it is precisely Willoughby's fear of committing a breach in the
decorum of self-love before Mrs. Mountstuart and her "world" that
finally permits Laetitia to begin to initiate change in him. By the
end of *The Egoist*, Willoughby's responses to Mrs. Mountstuart's
"incantation-summons" have become a frenetic caricature of his
accustomed sallies of wit. A single word—"Twice"—representing
an uncharitable count of jilts received is enough to reduce him to
"the affectation of a staring stupidity" (14:116). And much of the
dramatic intensity of the novel's *scène-à-faire* is derived from Wil-

loughby's terror lest Mrs. Mountstuart should be able to raise her count to "Thrice."

Having failed in all his attempts to gain Laetitia's consent to marry him and faced with Clara's desertion to Vernon Whitford, Willoughby has the added discomfort of knowing that Mrs. Mountstuart is to arrive at Patterne Hall at noon to greet Laetitia as his new fiancée. It is under this pressure that he begins, finally, to lower his mask before her: "In a fit of supplication, upon a cry of 'Laetitia!' twice repeated, he whimpered" (14:319). And Laetitia, as she scrutinizes Willoughby in this last scene, now takes center stage as Meredith's primary agent for the spirit of critical intelligence: "If her sentiment for this gentleman was gone, it was only a delusion gone; accurate sight and knowledge of him would not make a woman the less helpful mate. That was the mate he required: and he could be led. A sentimental attachment would have been serviceless to him. Not so the woman allied by a purely rational bond: and he wanted guiding" (14:320).

As he brings this novel to its close, Meredith's antisentimental stance is essential to his overall design and helps to explain why he goes as far as he does in denying the conventional romantic expectations of his audience. When Laetitia says, "I have lost faith in romance" (14:323), she sums up the essential change that is to provide a basis of very modest hope for both her and Willoughby. She then goes on to describe herself as prospective bride in the most unsentimental terms possible: "the skeleton is present with me all over life. . . . I should be a burden, barely a living one, irresponsive and cold. . . . I was once a foolish romantic girl; now I am a sickly woman, all illusions vanished" (14:323–24).[49]

Before she will submit to engage herself to Willoughby, Laetitia takes the very important step of insisting that he too begin to acknowledge his illusions and thereby recognize his faults for what they are—publicly. The precedent for the possibility of Patterne-changing in their married life is set as the mood becomes increasingly that of the last act of a comedy by Congreve or Molière:

"I believe I do not know myself. Anything you will, only give me your hand; give it; trust to me; you shall direct me. If I have faults, help me to obliterate them."

"Will you not expect me to regard them as the virtues of meaner men?"

"You will be my wife?"

Laetitia broke from him, crying: "Your wife, your critic! Oh! I cannot think it possible. Send for the ladies. Let them hear me."

"They are at hand," said Willoughby, opening the door. (14:323–24)

With his aunts in attendance, and with Mrs. Mountstuart's arrival drawing closer every minute, Willoughby is shown to listen to Laetitia, as one may imagine, more intently than he has ever listened to anyone:

"I can endeavor to respect him, I cannot venerate."

"Dear child!" the ladies gently remonstrated.

Willoughby motioned to them. . . .

"I have a hard detective eye. I see many faults."

"Have we not all of us faults, dear child?"

"Not such as he has; though the excuses of a gentleman nurtured in idolatry may be pleaded. But he should know that they are seen, and seen by her he asks to be his wife, that no misunderstanding may exist, and while it is yet time he may consult his feelings. He worships himself."

"Willoughby?"

"He is vindictive."

"Our Willoughby?"

"That is not your opinion, ladies. It is firmly mine. Time has taught it me. So, if you and I are at such variance, how can we live together? It is an impossibility."

They looked at Willoughby. He nodded imperiously. (14:324–25)

Thus Laetitia makes it clear that she intends her becoming the new Lady Patterne to mean the beginning of a different way of life at Patterne Hall.[50] Her exposure of Willoughby goes on, as do his imperious nods to his aunts—demands for unquestioning agreement, even when it is to his own faults. Willoughby is still Willoughby; at the same time, as I have suggested, his trial by the comic spirit through the agency of Laetitia also offers some mild hope for his gradual compliance to "the unwritten but perceptible laws binding [us] in consideration one to another (*Essay*, 23:47). As Mrs. Mountstuart's carriage rolls up to Patterne Hall, Willoughby steps forward with Laetitia as his promised bride, "making her hand his own, and warming to his possession as he performed the act."[51] The acquisitiveness of the Egoist remains, but as the narrator laconically notes, once again including the reader in his generalization, "he was to learn the nature of that possession in the woman who is our wife" (14:327).

The marriage of Laetitia Dale and Willoughby Patterne, then, seems an appropriate if somewhat painful culmination to *The Egoist*; it also provides important insight into Meredith's basic attitudes. Laetitia, like so many other Meredithian female heroes, has the gifts of honesty and good sense, which are the traits most highly prized in the novels. And Willoughby, like so many other Meredithian heroes, is an extraordinary combination of dishonesty and bad sense, which are the traits most sought out by the spirit of critical intelligence for exposure and correction. By bringing together these two in marriage at the end of his comic masterpiece, Meredith reaches a conclusion about the human condition that is relentlessly anti-sentimental and, at the same time, guardedly—very guardedly—optimistic.

5

One of Our Conquerors: The Anatomy
of a Marriage

Meredith's preoccupation with feminist concerns in *THE Egoist* can be seen as a leitmotif that continues to the very end of his career. He experiments, in the five novels that follow in the eighties and nineties, with situations and characters that pose increasingly provocative questions about Victorian gender relations in the private sphere, but a private sphere always threatened with exposure in the public world. While *The Egoist* (1879) and *The Tragic Comedians* (1880) deal with complications of courtship, the last four novels are directly concerned with what Meredith calls, in a 1902 letter, "the present rough Marriage system."[1] More specifically, it is the "possessive marriage," to use Barbara Hardy's term,[2] that Meredith anatomizes in these novels. The pattern is repeated in various forms but remains essentially the same: a male figure whose powers of self-examination are stunted—in typical Meredithian monological fashion—and who is (or is to be) socially and economically prominent, marries (or cohabits with, in Victor Radnor's case) a young woman who then grows beyond him in her powers of viewing the world, her marriage, and herself. Augustus Warwick's arrogant attempts to limit Diana's freedom and identity in *Diana of the Crossways*[3] (1885) are echoed in much greater detail in the relations between Victor and Nataly in *One of Our Conquerors* (1891), Lord Ormont and his Aminta in the novel of that name (1894), and Lord Fleetwood and Carinthia in *The Amazing Marriage* (1895). The tensions and contrasts between characters who are closed and those who are open to change and growth in marriage are at the psychological center of each of these novels.

One of Our Conquerors is the only one of the last four novels to provide a strong emphasis on the male perspective in its study of the psychology of a troubled marriage. At once Meredith's most difficult and, in a number of respects, his richest novel, it extends the boundaries of many of the areas of experimentation we have been examining. Issues of genre, narrative technique, particularly as evocation of psychological state, and a variety of linked feminist concerns, including a devastating critique of Victorian upper-middle-class domesticity and the construction of the role of wife,[4] are all approached by Meredith in significantly new ways as he anatomizes a marriage that is also, literally speaking, not a marriage.[5]

This novel, like *Richard Feverel* over thirty years before, begins on a burlesque note and then proceeds relentlessly to show that what strikes us as funny or grotesque may eventually be seen as part of a larger pattern giving intimations of tragedy. Victor Radnor's pratfall on the opening page allows Meredith to take that classic joke-accident—one that somehow always manages to evoke the combined responses of laughter and concern—and develop it as a brilliant metaphor for Victor's career.[6] This is a career in the overlapping territories of marriage, business, society, and politics, one whose blind optimism in no way prepares for even the possibility of a fall.

Victor, the conqueror of the novel's ironic title, combines the familiar vices of the Meredithian sentimental egoist with the virtue of genuine concern for the well-being and happiness of those around him: "the aim of his life was at the giving and taking of simple enjoyment" (17:51). This combination of traits, in fact, provides Meredith with the essential paradox of Victor's character and the key to his eventual and, as we begin to realize, inevitable collapse. Considerably more than any of Meredith's previous male protagonists, Victor has a talent for friendship, generosity, and love; consciously he is continually preoccupied with schemes for pleasing Nataly and enhancing his relationship with her, their daughter Nesta, and his friends. Yet his schemes are also clearly shown to be those of the self-aggrandizing egoist, a perspective that Victor's sentimentalism effectively blocks him from perceiving. In this novel, however, an almost complete lack of disinterested sanity does not produce an insensible monster, as in the case of Willoughby Patterne; rather, Meredith presents us with a fallible, even likeable, human being whose headlong course to destruction, under the guise of worldly success, can be understood with remarkable fullness by the novel's end.

Although initially confusing, even irritating, the first chapter of *One of Our Conquerors* provides a richly ironic exposition for all that is to follow. Here Meredith is clearly continuing and advancing his experiments with narrative voice, creating effects that in some ways anticipate the equally difficult opening Henry James was to develop a decade later to convey—also in medias res—the convoluted state of mind of Lambert Strether in *The Ambassadors*. Once we get our bearings and recognize that the narration of Victor's actions and thoughts are rendered through the voice of an amused but not unsympathetic observer and, briefly, the view of the crowd as rendered ironically by this observer, confusion gives way to illumination. As we move in and out of Victor's mental stream during and after his slip on a discarded peel while he is walking on London Bridge, we are given a detailed sense of how he confronts his world:

> He was unhurt, quite sound, merely astonished, he remarked, in reply to the inquiries of the first kind helper at his elbow; and it appeared an acceptable statement of his condition. He laughed, shook his coat-tails, smoothed the back of his head rather thoughtfully, thankfully received his runaway hat, nodded bright beams to right and left, and making light of the muddy stigmas imprinted by the pavement, he scattered another shower of his nods and smiles around, to signify, that as his good friends would wish, he thoroughly felt his legs and could walk unaided. And he was in the act of doing it, questioning his familiar behind the waistcoat amazedly, to tell him how such a misadventure could have occurred to him of all men, when a glance below his chin discomposed his outward face. "Oh, confound the fellow!" he said, with simple frankness, and was humorously ruffled, having seen absurd blots of smutty knuckles distributed over the maiden waistcoat. (17:1–2)

The elevated style attempts to deny the commonplace and embarrassing nature of the event at the same time that it mocks such an attempt. As Donald Stone has pointed out, "the mock epic tone [of the opening] perfectly suits the self-styled conqueror who is supremely vulnerable"; Victor is a man who will be seen to practice, as Stone puts it, the "rhetoric of evasion," one who cannot "recognize his human frailty and hence [cannot] conquer himself."[7] Victor's shower of "bright beams . . . , nods and smiles around" to "his good friends" asserts that he is as he has imagined himself before, impervious, superior, and surrounded by uncritical admirers; at the same time, the throbbing head, blotted waistcoat, and irreverent comments of "the fellow" in the crowd with "smutty knuckles" all combine to challenge Victor's "maiden" assumption of invulnerability. We may see the beginnings, then, of a significant linkage between Willoughby Patterne and Victor—as another Meredithian study in the precariousness of subjectivity.

2

What we have in *One of Our Conquerors* is a portrait of the egoist in middle age, but a portrait presented through a narrative style that creates a relationship between reader and protagonist strikingly different from what we find in *The Egoist*. While we are made very conscious by the comic tone at the opening of the earlier novel that we are encouraged to maintain our critical distance in relation to Willoughby, from the outset of *One of Our Conquerors* our relation to Victor Radnor is both critical *and* intimate. Meredith's style repeatedly accomplishes a major rhetorical effect: we are made to participate in Victor's self-deceptive habits of mind while we are permitted to see them, with increasing clarity, for what they are. Although we also see this process at work from time to time in Meredith's presentation of Willoughby, the narrative structure of *The Egoist*—in particular its firm direction of our sympathies away from the hero and toward his female antagonists—keeps him, finally, at a distance and definitively comic. The narrative of *One of Our Conquerors*, on the other hand, immerses us consistently and closely in the protagonist's view and thus helps to evoke our concern for him as an isolated individual. If the reader gains some sense of tragic dimension to Victor's career, however, this is a dimension he himself is shown to be incapable of grasping—to the novel's bitter end.

In the opening scene on London Bridge, what is shown to be especially disruptive to Victor's equanimity is the marvelously appropriate parting shot of the helpful "fellow"—"'And none of your dam punctilio'":

> He abominated the thought of an altercation with a member of the mob; he found that enormous beast comprehensible only when it applauded him; and besides he wished it warmly well; all that was good for it; plentiful dinners, country excursions, stout menagerie bars, music, a dance, and to bed . . . : and in endeavouring to get at the grounds of his dissension with that dirty-fisted fellow, the recollection of the word *punctilio* shot a throb of pain to the spot where his mishap had rendered him susceptible. Headache threatened—and to him of all men! But was there ever such a word for drumming on a cranium? (17:3)

Again and again the throbbing of Victor's "punctilio bump" (17:43) acts as a reminder of this disconcerting incident, reviving in him an insistent but undefined and mystifying sense of disquietude, while the reader's understanding of the event—and of Meredith's portrait of this paradoxical blend of liberal impulse and conservative instinct—is progressively enhanced at each reference.

The immediate meaning of punctilio here is something like gentlemanly arrogance, presumption, and posturing. The speaker in the crowd is shown to see through Victor's "condescending grins" at once to "the total deficiency of gratitude in this kind of gentleman's look and pocket" (17:2). But the more literal sense of the word also comes into play with ironical force—punctilio as conduct in precise accordance with convention. The central problem of Victor's life is that, in spite of his appeals to "Nature's laws" (17:13) against the forces of convention that condemn the "one error of his youth" (17:12), he is, as Donald Stone has pointed out, in other respects *entirely* conventional.[8] Thus he wants to live and flourish punctiliously, strictly by the protocol of success as defined by the moneyed classes. At the same time, however, he is living in the aftermath of his youthful impetuosity—the fact that he has in one major respect defied "punctilio" for twenty years by being married to one woman while living with another and having a child by her. Like the "mob" on the bridge, society for Victor is only comprehensible when it applauds him.[9] And despite his warm good wishes and determined efforts to irritate no one, he has managed to affront society repeatedly by ignoring the irreconcilability of his family arrangements with his grandiose social and, more recently, political aspirations. Just as his efforts to be punctilious with the "mob" fail, so his attempts at once to accommodate the demands of society and to maintain certain aspects of his private life as a separate sphere are shown inevitably to be subject to failure. And, as is made progressively clearer, the primary cause of this failure is Victor's absolute lack of the self-assessing vision Meredith equates with common sense.

Through the length of the novel Victor is unable "to read the riddle of the application of [punctilio] to himself" (17:4), though he is haunted by the glimmering of an "Idea" that, he thinks, will explain all when he grasps it completely. When he makes "a short run or attempt at running after the idea," however, it ends with a "pain to his head near the spot where the haunting word punctilio caught at any excuse for clamouring" (17:9–10). Meredith here has set the pattern for the entire text. As we slowly learn, Victor's "volatile idea" (17:11) involves a deeply repressed intuition that he must repudiate the worldly visions of success associated with his punctiliousness in order to achieve the "morality, humanity, fraternity—nature's rights" (17:9)—that would win some freedom and peace of mind for himself and his family. Fabian Gudas has effectively summed up this idea, which we perceive only piecemeal as we read the novel:

> It prescribes self-conquest over the animal; an end to philandering; a contempt for luxury, wealth, and position. It fixes new responsibilities on the rich: "We the wealthy will not exist to pamper flesh, but we live for the promotion of brotherhood" (17:485). Finally, it envisions a "society based on the logical concrete of humane considerateness" (17:444) and condemns the manipulation of people for selfish ends or even for the purposes of some Utilitarian ethic.[10]

The ironies associated with this idea are multiple. The notion of brotherhood and "humane considerateness" is introduced on the first page, not by Victor but by the workingman who comes to his aid. And it is this spirit of cooperation, as Gillian Beer has suggested, that is driven away at once by Victor's response—the "class tension epitomized in the word 'punctilio.'"[11] Further, part of the reason Victor has trouble in grasping "his" idea is that in the concrete it strikes him as too commonplace, too much "like a paragraph in a newspaper, upon which a Leading Article sits" (17:493) instead of the "great thing done to the flash of brilliant results" (17:494) that his ego demands. But, as the narrator suggests in a pompous phrase that nicely evokes Victor's proprietary and regal tone as well as the paradox of his situation, "We cannot relinquish an idea that was ours" (17:10).

Like Oedipus, Victor is shown in quest of a truth whose revelation would involve a repudiation of what he thinks he is. Unlike Oedipus, however, once the revelation comes, Victor is unable to find coherence or wisdom; Meredith insists that this modern hero, with all his limitations, is to find only madness and death. The true pathos of Victor's history, then, resides in the fact that he never clearly grasps his idea or its direct relevance to the quality of his own life. He is so caught up in his schemes of happiness that he fails to comprehend the significance of the unhappiness of those with whom he is most intimately connected.

3

In Chapter 2, Victor, "still but little more than midway across London Bridge (17:10), daydreams about Nataly and Nesta as the providers of domestic retreat, evoking what Elizabeth Langland has described as "the mystique of the happy, harmonious Victorian home as a refuge from the competitive sphere."[12] Ironically, this domestic scene also provides a refuge from the idea Victor simultaneously pursues and flees. In this section Meredith sums up with devastating clarity just how deeply seated are Victor's quintessentially Victorian notions of the robust male and the ministering protected/protective female in her private sphere:

> After his ineffectual catching at the volatile idea, Mr. Radnor found repose in thoughts of his daughter and her dear mother. They had begged him to put on an overcoat this day of bitter wind, or a silken kerchief for the throat. . . . Mechanically now, while doting in fancy over the couple beseeching him, he loosened the button across his defaced waistcoat, exposed a large measure of chest to flaws of a wind barbed on Norwegian peaks by the brewers of cough and catarrh—horrid women of the whistling clouts, in the pay of our doctors. He braved them; he starved the profession. He was that man in fifty thousand who despises hostile elements and goes unpunished, calmly erect among a sneezing and tumbled host, as a lighthouse overhead of breezy fleets. . . .
>
> Naturally he was among the happiest of human creatures; he willed it so, with consent of circumstances; a boisterous consent, as when votes are reckoned for a favourite candidate. (17:11–12)

Meredith provides us here with an informative portrait of the assumed invulnerability of the conquering Victorian male. Exulting is his sense of power like a small boy facing the rains without his boots, Victor presumes that the sheer force of his will is the route to happiness: "Mr. Radnor could rationally say that he was made for happiness; he flew to it, he breathed, dispensed it" (17:13).

This bravado and its complement—the pattern of difficulty avoided by the reassurance of retreat to the private sphere—are essential characteristics of the way Victor's mind works and they immediately reappear in a new and revealing variation. The simile of the "favourite candidate" is linked with Victor's thoughts of his actual ambition to stand for Parliament and the "small band of black dissentients" (17:12) who will try to block his candidacy with an uncharitable view of his personal life. But then Victor's narrated monologue moves impulsively past such a "temporary disturbance, ending in [the vision of] a merry duet with his daughter Nesta Victoria: a glorious trio when her mother Natalia, sweet lily that she was, shook the rainwater from her cup and followed the good example to shine in the sun. He had a secret for them" (17:13–14). The greatest irony in this self-assured pattern of habitual escape is, of course, that it is no escape at all: Victor's most serious problems, just intimated by the suggestion of Nataly's continuing sadness in the metaphor of the rain-filled lily, are at home, where the imagined polyphony of "a glorious trio" is still one more way in which he effectively conceals from himself the true nature of his unvarying monologue of self-worship. And at the center of this monologue is his "secret"—not his irregular union with Nataly, but the enormous country mansion he has had built as a surprise and styled "Lakelands"—a secret that acts as Meredith's most telling symbol of Victor's self-defeating attempts to fortify himself and his family against the threat of an unhappiness that lies, inevitably, within.

It has been Lakelands, it turns out, that was on Victor's mind on London Bridge in a pre-lapsarian vision of self-aggrandizing magnificence: "Just before the fall, the whole drama of the unfolding of that secret was brilliant to his eyes as a scene on a stage" (17:14). What we have here is a vision of success much like that so aptly described by Walter Houghton as the Victorian "bourgeois dream":

> The ambitious merchant or manufacturer . . . , even as he threw himself ardently into his work, longed for a life of ease. Not of mere ease— luxurious ease. At the heart of the bourgeois dream was the ideal of gracious living, symbolized by the country house. The middle-class businessman longed to escape from drudgery in hideous surroundings into a world of beauty and leisure, a life of dignity and peace, from which sordid anxieties were shut out.[13]

The shutting out of sordid anxieties is in particular what Victor aspires to. He describes Lakelands to his friend Simeon Fenellan— metaphorically, one assumes—as "a castle with a drawbridge: no exchanging of visits, as we did at Craye Farm and at Creckholt; we are there for country air; we don't court neighbours at all—perhaps the elect; it will depend on Nataly's wishes. . . . You see, that was my intention—to be independent of neighbouring society" (17:23). The pattern in the past, at Craye Farm and Creckholt, has been one of hesitant attachment and then abrupt departure, once the "neighbouring society" has caught wind of the special nature of the Radnor ménage. The pattern being set for the future is one full of ominous contradiction, not the least of which is Victor's cavalier reference to "Nataly's wishes." When she is introduced with Nesta in Chapter 6 in conversation about the new house, Nataly's true wishes are indicated in her very first words—"Not a cottage?" The "secluded modest cottage" (17:49) she pines for is her own imagined remedy for the precariousness of their position, but it is a remedy that, given Victor's rage of "ascension from heights to heights" (17:51), is a clear impossibility. Nataly indulges here in what had become an urban Victorian cliché, one that Victor himself, in his own very different way, invokes in his vision of Lakelands as place of rural retirement: "I get back to primal innocence in the country" (17:24). Both Victor and Nataly, then, entertain notions of Wordsworthian retreat in response to the extraordinarily difficult position in which their fall from innocence has placed them in modern society. The radically different ways in which they envision this retreat, however, begin to suggest the agonizing case of mutual incompatibility Meredith gradually reveals in this relationship as the novel progresses.

4

Just as the opening chapters show Meredith developing extended narrative techniques that provide intimate revelation of Victor's self-deceiving thought processes, so Chapter 6 acts to evoke the characteristic pattern of Nataly's mind in ways that are strikingly innovative. As her attempts to cope with the implications of Victor's latest scheme for happiness are developed, the narrative depicts her tortured ambivalence in a style that at times brilliantly prefigures the delicate accretion of psychological detail, phrase upon phrase, one finds in modernist writers such as James, Lawrence, Joyce, and especially Virginia Woolf. While Nataly muses on *her* secret—the "false position" she occupies—her narrated monologue and psycho-narration is in counterpoint to Victor's voice ringing through the house as he, mindful of the impending triumph of his own secret of Lakelands, intones Donizetti's "*Il segreto per essere felice*":[14]

> She heard his voice on a carol. Men do not feel this doubtful position as women must. They have not the same to endure; the world gives them land to tread, where women are on breaking seas. . . .
> He sang: he never acknowledged a trouble, he dispersed it; and in

her present wrestle with the scheme of a large country estate involving new intimacies, anxieties, the courtship of rival magnates, followed by the wretched old cloud, and the imposition upon them to bear it in silence though they knew they could plead a case, at least before charitable and discerning creatures or before heaven, the despondent lady could have asked whether he was perfectly sane.

Who half so brilliantly!—Depreciation of him, fetched up at a stroke the glittering armies of her enthusiasm.—He had proved it; he proved it daily in conflicts and in victories that dwarfed emotional troubles like hers: yet they were something to bear, hard to bear, at times unbearable.

But those were times of weakness. Let anything be doubted rather than the good guidance of the man who was her breath of life! Whither he led, let her go, not only submissively, exultingly. (17:50–51)

Much as in his first novel, Meredith develops here the theme of a woman of superior intuition trapped into compliance with the overbearing dictates of a man whose inflexible devotion to his own heroic image will eventually destroy her—and him. For Nataly "credulity—the continued trust in the man—is the alternative of despair" (17:56), while Lucy Feverel has to "shut out Wisdom: accept total blindness, and be led by [Richard]."[15] The mode of presentation, however, is altogether different. While we rarely get very close to Lucy, and she remains something of a generalized Miranda and Juliet, Nataly is portrayed in a fashion that is highly individuating. As we have just seen, her thoughts tend to operate in a painful tension between recognition of the essential reality of her situation and attempts at denial. Meredith dramatizes Nataly's profound ambivalence in several episodes of self-contradictory behavior, thought, and speech, such as this one, a technique we have already seen him utilizing to evoke Clara Middleton's awakening consciousness and one that Virginia Woolf was later to use repeatedly from early in her career—for example, in the abrupt changes in attitude she conveys in characters like Katharine Hilbery, Ralph Denham, and William Rodney in *Night and Day*.

Unlike Victor's mind, which is shown to be "rosily oratorical" (17:5), evasive, and prosaic, Nataly's mental stream is characteristically rendered in poetic form—often in metaphors and similes that graphically suggest her sense of beauty and exaltation along with the perception of peril in her life with Victor. "Women are on breaking seas" is a characteristic figuration of Nataly's position—of her entire unstable sense of identity, really; she, like Victor, is another Meredithian study of a disintegrating subject, but with the significant difference that she is shown to be nervously aware of the threat of imminent breakdown while Victor is always caught off guard by any disruption of his plans—as with his slip on the novel's opening page.

Nataly's surrender to Victor and the twenty years of stress that follow are like "the detachment of a flower on the river's bank by swell of flood: she had no longer root of her own; away she sailed, through beautiful scenery, with occasionally a crashing fall, a turmoil, emergence from a vortex, and once more the sunny whirling surface. Strange to think, she had not since then power to grasp in her abstract mind a notion of steadfastness without or within" (17:51). The metaphoric content of her mental stream, often evoked in narrated monologue and psycho-narration, repeatedly suggests this same lack of autonomy, as she is swept along by forces beyond her control. She sees herself driven "on the breakers" by her love for Victor; "the philtre was in her veins, whatever the directions of the rational mind. Exulting or regretting, she had to do it, as one in the car with a racing charioteer. Or up beside a more than Titanically audacious balloonist" (17:51). As for the balloonist-charioteer "bent on his goal," when Victor encounters Nataly in Chapter 6 and attempts to dismiss the most sensitive of topics—her fears over the possible disruption of the Lakelands scheme by Mrs. Burman—we are told that his words "received strong colouring from midday's Old Veuve in his blood." Nataly's Isolde, then, encounters more Bacchus than Tristan in her Victor, but nonetheless "his voice and words had a swing of conviction: they imparted vinousness to a heart athirst" and she is once again "captivated by his rare theatrical air of confidence. . . . When the sensations are spirited up to drown the mind, we become drift-matter of tides" (17:55).

Meredith makes it clear that Victor's confidence about their situation is based on his own wishes rather than any concern for mundane facts, and thus his resistance to providing Nataly with specifics about Mrs. Burman. Chapter 6 ends with a final image of water—this time as literal tears in Nataly's eyes—and an ironic narrative shift from her melancholic poetry to Victor's self-assured prose, a shift that neatly sums up his psychological state by displaying the ways in which he manages at once to misunderstand, sentimentalize, and dismiss Nataly when she shows herself as an individual whose mind and heart run counter to his:

He loved the eyes, disliked the water in them. With an impatient, "There, there!" and a smart affectionate look, he retired, thinking in our old satirical vein of the hopeless endeavor to satisfy a woman's mind without the intrusion of hard material statements, facts. . . . It would almost appear that man is exclusively imaginative and poetical; and that his mate, the fair, the graceful, the bewitching, with the sweetest and purest of natures, cannot help being something of a groveller.
Nataly had likewise her thoughts. (17:57)

5

Once having firmly established the nature of Victor and Nataly's troubled relationship, Meredith moves to a major dramatization of his primary concerns by depicting the Radnors and their set in a four-chapter sequence at Lakelands. Chapter 9, "An Inspection of Lakelands," opens this sequence in a marvelously pompous style that evokes Victor's well-intentioned pride in his mammoth creation, rather in the manner of a high-toned real estate broker who has been reading Ruskin:

One may not have an intention to flourish, and may be pardoned for a semblance of it, in exclaiming, somewhat royally, as creator and owner of the place: "There you see Lakelands."
The conveyances from the railway station drew up on a rise of road fronting an undulation, where our modern English architect's fantasia in crimson brick swept from central gables to flying wings, over pents, crooks, curves, peaks, cowled porches, balconies, recesses, projections, away to a red village of stables and dependent cottages; harmonious in irregularity; and coloured homely with the greensward about it, the pines beside it, the clouds above it. Not many palaces would be reckoned as larger. (17:81)

Reactions to this Victorian Blenheim on its 370 acre plot vary, though Victor, "like a swimmer in the morning sea amid the exclamations encircling him," is prepared only to acknowledge awe-struck wonder. We also see Nataly, surrounded by friends, having to stage-manage her enthusiasm: "She sent the expected nods to Victor's carriage" (17:82). Meredith again uses a contrapuntal technique in this chapter for psychological revelation. Nataly's appearance—"She summoned her smile"; "her face had the air of a smiling general satisfaction" (17:89; 93)—is countered by glimpses of the confused feelings of anger at Victor that she cannot quite acknowledge: "She would have given the whole prospect for the covering solitariness of her chamber. A multitude of clashing sensations, and a throat-thickening hateful to her, compelled her to summon . . . a groundless anger, directed against none, against nothing, perfectly crazy, but her only resource for keeping down the great wave surgent at her eyes" (17:82).

Linked with Nataly's anger is her instinctive sense of connection with her close family friend, Colney Durance. The first instant she views Lakelands, "her next look was at Colney Durance" (17:82). In Colney she knows she will find a ready, understanding response to her pain, and in this sense he acts as a touchstone of clear vision in the novel. But as Judith Wilt has shown, Colney's role in *One of Our Conquerors* is highly problematic, primarily because his attitude is that of the satirist who operates epigrammatically from a distance. Colney "has tried in his satiric withdrawal to contribute clarity and sanity to Victor's self-image and has only helped drive him deeper into madness."[16] The same may be said of his relation to Nataly. As Wilt points out, Colney serves the very dangerous function of allowing both Victor and Nataly to hear the uncomfortable truth and at the same time to set it aside as the exaggerated satire of a bachelor-theorist: "A thirst she had to hear the truth loud-tongued from him, together with a feeling that he was excessive and satiric, not to be read by the letter of his words. . . . But in very truth she was a woman who loved to hear the truth; she was formed to love the truth her position reduced her to violate" (17:117). This paradox sums up Nataly's untenable position: she is drawn toward Colney for his understanding but she feels at the same time she must reject that understanding due to its barbed criticism of Victor. And because of her difficult social position, Nataly regards the world as the "circumambient enemy"; even Colney, among "the dearest of her friends, belonged to that hostile world. Only Victor, no other, stood with her against the world. Her child, yes; the love of her child she had; but the child's destiny was an alien phantom" (17:116). With a sense of claustrophobia, then, Meredith allows us to see how completely Nataly is trapped since she does not have the will or the strength to stand alone.

All this lies behind the outwardly comic action at Lakelands as Victor leads his guests on their "admiratory stroll . . . , perpetually at the gape in laudation" (17:91). Colney, whom the "sight of Lakelands had gripped . . . with the fell satiric itch" (17:84), is driven "half way to frenzy behind his placable demeanour" (17:86) as he must discharge his spleen in random shots rather than in direct attack upon his host. What Colney is shown to see with absolute clarity is the repetitive and self-destructive character of Victor's grandiose "plan." For Victor, Lakelands is to be the means, not only to political and social triumph but also to his daughter's legitimization—all occurrences that are premised on the assumption of imminent death for Mrs. Burman. But as Colney says when Nataly asks him directly about the health of Victor's wife, " 'You catch at delusions, to excuse the steps you consent to take. Or you want me to wear the blinkers, the better to hoodwink your own eyes. You see it as well as I:—If you enter that house, you have to go through the same as at Creckholt' " (17:116).

The imagery associated with clarifying vision here is, once again, symptomatic of Meredith's emphasis on the primary role of critical intelligence in the responsible life. As I have been arguing, from *Shagpat* forward, the importance of common sense—the effort to view the world without blinkers—is at the center of all the novels. The particularly dark and modern quality of *One of Our Conquerors* comes from the fact that seeing more clearly in the world of the Radnors usually does *not* solve problems or lead to purposeful action. As Meredith has constructed this novel, Victor's obtuse, optimistic nature, which refuses to take any view divergent from his own seriously, imbues his career with its quality of tragic inevitability. Nataly's options, given her allegiance to Victor, are so severely limited that even when she does "see it as well as" Colney she is typically described in the metaphorical terms I have already discussed—as entrapped by forces over which she has no control.

There is, however, one important avenue of action Meredith does allow Nataly and that concerns Nesta's on-again, off-again fiancé, Dudley Sowerby. Victor has chosen to dazzle this stiff young aristocrat with Lakelands so that he may then, of his own free self-seeking will, give Nesta the benefit of his unchallengeable (though ominous-sounding) name. After Nataly's talk with Colney and her acceptance of an unblinkered appraisal of her relation to Dudley, she is faced with a question, as stated in her narrated monologue in Chapter 11, at once difficult and disarmingly simple: "How was the young man to be warned?" (17:121). This question is shown to haunt her over an extended period, as it is played off against Victor's monomaniacal preoccupation with Lakelands, which "had him fast, and this young Dudley was the kernel of Lakelands"

(17:211). It is much later in the novel, after Victor has once again sidestepped her efforts to prompt him to enlighten Dudley about Nesta's illegitimacy, that Nataly is finally moved to act in a decisive manner in a scene that provides her finest moment, one that also underscores Meredith's feminist critique of her disadvantaged position in the convoluted politics of late Victorian gender relations.

6

Chapter 25, "Nataly in Action," dramatizes more pointedly than anything that precedes it the impossible position Nataly is placed in by Victor's passion to be one of our conquerors.[17] We see her in a state of crisis, almost succumbing to the hostile forces that surround her, followed by a moment when, like a gallery of Meredithian female heroes before her, she is able to break out of her self-imposed passivity—if only for the moment.

Meredith's preparation for this scene is interesting: Nataly is described entertaining guests, her "own people," in the assumed sanctuary of her London home, but among the guests is a yet unknown threat bearing the appropriately Dickensian name of Mrs. Blathenoy, a woman who holds two important pieces of information. First, we have been told earlier (17:285) that she knows the Radnors' secret but has been enjoined by her politic husband to keep silent. Second, she knows of the death of Dartrey Fenellan's wife. Captain Fenellan, brother of Victor's close friend Simeon, is the vigorous man of advanced views and occasionally priggish nature one finds represented in almost all of Meredith's novels. Like Austin Wentworth, Vernon Whitford, Tom Redworth, Matey Weyburn, and Gower Woodseer, he acts the role of *raisonneur*, the foil of rational enlightenment who illuminates the irrational minds of Meredith's central male figures. Nataly has vaguely daydreamed about Dartrey as the ideal mate for her daughter, who admires him, but his unhappy marriage (disastrous marriages are epidemic in this novel) has prevented Nataly from anything but dreaming. Victor has been told about Mrs. Fenellan's death by Simeon months before (17:34), but he has not chosen to tell Nataly, who remains in ignorance.

It is within this carefully developed context that Meredith shows Nataly having to endure the shock of receiving this important information from none other than Mrs. Blathenoy in a scene that, among other things, nicely illustrates Meredith's capacity to intertwine narration, psycho-narration, narrated monologue, and stichomythic dialogue:

> Nataly's own people were about her and she felt at home.
> Mrs. Blathenoy pushed a small thorn into it, by speaking of Captain Fenellan, and aside, as if sharing him with her. Nataly heard that Dartrey had been the guest of these Blathenoys. Even Dartrey was but a man!
> Rather lower under her voice, the vain little creature asked: "You knew her?"
> "Her?"
> The cool counter-interrogation was disregarded. "So sad! . . . Poor woman!"
> "Who?"
> "His wife."
> "Wife!"
> "They *were* married?" [Italics added]
> Nataly could have cried: Snake! Her play at brevity had certainly been foiled. She nodded gravely. . . . Victor must have known it.
> Her duties of hostess were conducted with the official smile. (17:302–03)

The revelation of Dartrey's freedom and Victor's manipulative silence—Nesta's engagement with Dudley has just been confirmed—alters Nataly's relations with all those closest to her; like Julien Sorel, in a radically different context, "toutes ses idées changèrent."[18] The force of the revelation, combined with the humiliation of having to suffer Mrs. Blathenoy's patronizing chatter, is shown to almost kill Nataly. The heart disease hinted at earlier now becomes explicit: "her heart set to a rapid beating, a fainter, a chill at the core. She snatched for breath. . . . Then came sighs. The sad old servant in her bosom was resuming his labours. But she had been near it—very near it? A gush of pity for Victor, overwhelmed her hardness of mind" (17:303). It is in this condition— even in extremis Nataly's feelings toward Victor are marked by profound ambivalence—that she resolves to enlighten Dudley as soon as she is physically able.

In this anatomy of a troubled Victorian marriage, Meredith reaches a decisive—almost archetypal—point of feminine awakening in later nineteenth-century fiction. Like Dorothea Brooke on her honeymoon in Rome, or Isabel Archer sitting up all night before the fire in Chapter 42 of *The Portrait of a Lady*, Nataly is portrayed here trying to come to terms with a major shift in her perception of her husband and her world. As she oscillates between "pity" and "hardness of mind," she considers the step she is about to take, a step ironically associated in her mind with her last free move twenty years before, "less independently then than now; unregretted, if fatal. . . . She had lived with him and suffered intensely" (17:305–6).

In Nataly's narrated monologue, Meredith plays on the ways in which her increasingly critical view of Victor mingles with an increasingly clear and damning view of her own role—"an abasement beneath his leadership, a blind subserviency and surrender of her faculties to his greater powers, such as no soul of a breathing body should yield to man. . . . She had seen into him. The reproach on her was that she, in her worship, had been slave, not helper."[19] As Nataly recalls that "her intellect had sometimes protested" and then she had been "moved . . . to swamp it" (17:306), the imagery of a sweeping torrent is reinvoked: she "swam whirling with a pang of revolt . . . , swept onward; and she was arrested now by an accident, like a waif of the river-floods by the dip of a branch" (17:307). This difficult "accidental" opportunity is the one prepared for almost two hundred pages earlier at the end of the Lakelands sequence when Victor is compared with "a torrent of persuasion," while Nataly resembles "a log of the torrent. It is borne along; it dreams of a distant corner of the way for a determined stand; it consents to its whirling in anticipation of an undated hour when it will no longer be neutral" (17:122–23).

But an essential problem facing Nataly in her break from neutrality is similar to that which encumbers a long line of awakening female protagonists in the novel tradition—scant knowledge of the world. Dorothea Brooke, to take one familiar example from two decades earlier, has been "fed on meagre Protestant histories and on art chiefly of the hand-screen sort,"[20] while, to take another, Isabel Archer has spent her time reading miscellaneous volumes with attractive frontispieces in the "office" of her grandmother's house in Albany. In many respects different from Nataly in their youthful vigor, both of these female heroes are also like her in that they are poignantly mis- and uninformed. The disasters they all must endure are in large part brought about by the linking of their large imaginations with inadequate experience and information, and en-

lightenment, when it does come, is not necessarily a source of em-
powerment.

The poverty of women's education, one of Meredith's obsessions,
is attacked in *One of Our Conquerors* by Colney Durance, but Nataly, in her neutrality, "had not agreed with him." Again, it is his
satirical style that has allowed her to gloss over the significance of
his words: "He presented stinging sentences, which irritated more
than they enlightened." But it is these same sentences Nataly re-
members as she steels herself to act independently: "Now it
seemed to her that the model women of men make pleasant slaves,
not true mates: they lack the worldly training to know themselves
or take a grasp of circumstances" (17:307). Nataly, after twenty
years of subservience to Victor, is ready for revolt, but as Meredith's
imagery and context suggest, the real possibilities for meaningful
change in her life are both meager and dangerous. It is in her
daughter Nesta, to whom I shall turn shortly, that Meredith portrays some substantive hope for future change.

Nataly's confrontation with Dudley Sowerby occurs in a terse interchange at the end of Chapter 25, an interchange that, like the
one between Nataly and Mrs. Blathenoy, again displays Meredith's
capacity to produce charged meaning within apparently trivial dialogue, a tactic Henry James and Virginia Woolf were also to develop
with extraordinary proficiency. Dudley, whose only distinctive
characteristics are his overly methodical flute playing and his anticipation of an earldom, embodies the conventional world Victor aspires to and fears; it is before this world that Nataly now compels
herself to be exposed. As is true throughout this novel, the most
commonplace usages of surname and terms of family relationship
are a source of embarrassment and an invitation to petty deception,
and it is on this level that Nataly now refuses to deceive any further:

> "Your husband is quite well?" [Dudley] said, in affection for the
> name of husband.
> "Mr. Radnor is well; I have to speak to you. . . . Mr. Sowerby, you
> have done my daughter the honour to ask her hand in marriage. . . .
> You have not known of any circumstances that might cause hesitation
> in asking?"
> "Miss Radnor?"
> "My daughter:—you have to think of your family."
> "Indeed, Mrs. Radnor, I was coming to London tomorrow, with the
> consent of my family."

"You address me as Mrs. Radnor. I have not the legal right to the name."

"Not legal!" said he, with a catch at the word.

He spun round in her sight, though his demeanour was manfully rigid.

"Have I understood, madam . . . ?"

"You would not request me to repeat it." (17:311–12)

Dudley's comic astonishment and "face of wet chalk" counter Nataly's pain in this scene: "A surge of impossible questions rolled to his mouth and rolled back. . . . He mounted horse, raised hat, paced on, and again bowing, to one of the wayside trees, cantered" (17:313). As for Nataly, Colney Durance observes at the end of Chapter 27 "that Victor was killing her." Finally, in an ironical narrative summing up, we are told that "after her interview with Dudley, there had been a swoon at home; and her maid, sworn to secrecy, willingly spared a tender-hearted husband—so good a master" (17:329).

7

In the last third of *One of Our Conquerors,* Nataly tends to recede into the background as Nesta[21] comes forward to take a central role. When we do see Nataly, the aftermath of her efforts at self-assertion seem to be practically more than she can bear; one result is that she adopts a much more conservative position in relation to Nesta and becomes obsessed with her daughter's vulnerability. In this mood Nataly becomes another Meredithian study in self-contradiction as she shifts to favor Dudley over Dartrey because marriage to the former would not expose Nesta to public scrutiny in the way marriage to the outspoken and occasionally radical Dartrey would. This is simply one manifestation of the sad state Nataly is shown to come to as the novel moves to its conclusion; having exposed herself, she wishes above all to protect her daughter from anything like similar humiliation, even though it means promoting a marriage she doesn't believe in.

In Meredith's portrait of Nesta, however, we have a young woman of a markedly different nature. Nesta's character moves in the direction set by earlier independent-minded feminine characters in Meredith like Noorna bin Noorka, the Princess Ottilia, and

Diana Warwick, and takes it further; more than any previous Meredith woman, Nesta embodies the free spirit and vigorous temperament that one associates with the emerging "New Woman" of the eighties and nineties, a temperament one encounters again in Meredith's last two female protagonists, Aminta Farrell and Carinthia Kirby. Victor is shown to be uneasily aware of this quality when he asks himself, "what if his Fredi turned out one of the modern young women, who have drunk of ideas? He caught himself speculating on that, as on a danger" (17:204). Much later, Victor has gone some way toward accommodating himself to his daughter's clearheaded unconventionality when he tells an exasperated Dudley Sowerby that "she belongs to her time. I don't mind owning to you, she has given me a lead" (17:471). It is to Victor's credit toward the end of the novel that he does take his lead from Nesta on several important issues, including his disentanglement from the seductive Lady Grace Halley. But Meredith characteristically is not interested in providing anything like easy answers to the difficult issues he has raised here: Victor's acquiescence to Nesta's independent critical judgment comes too late and in too incomplete a form to alter his race to self-destruction.

At the novel's opening, we find that Nesta has been kept in complete ignorance of the irregularity of her parents' union; "her quick wits" (17:73), however, perceive the many incongruities and problems, and attempt to provide explanations and solutions. Practically the first thought we hear expressed by her takes form in one of the novel's central metaphors as she speaks of the Radnors' need to "strike roots"; Victor, full of his Lakelands plans and self-deluded as always about this central source of his family's unhappiness, responds, "Fixed this time; nothing shall tear us up" (17:48). When it comes to the visit to Lakelands itself, we are told that Victor "was blind to [Colney's and Simeon Fenellan's] reading of absurdities which caused Fredi's eyes to stream [in laughter]. . . . Young Sowerby appeared forgiving enough—he was a perfect gentleman: but Fredi's appalling sense of fun must try him hard" (17:92–93).

Earlier it is precisely this "appalling sense of fun" and the critical intelligence that informs it that allows Nesta to see through this "perfect gentleman." When Dudley is first introduced to the Radnors, Victor, quick to scent the possibility of an aristocratic alliance, reproaches Nesta for ignoring the young man. She, though not interested in him in the slightest, nevertheless proves that she has observed him with penetration by reproducing a "copy of the sugared acid of Mr. Dudley Sowerby's closed mouth: a sort of sneer in meekness, as of humility under legitimate compulsion . . . : the wonderful mimicry was a flash thrown out by a born mistress of the art, and her mother was constrained to laugh, and so was her father; but he willfully denied the likeness" (17:74). What Nesta's mimicry says, of course, is that the humorless Dudley is entirely inappropriate for her. In spite of their laughter, Victor and later Nataly both deny the truth that Nesta, "with perspicacious clear eyes for the world" (*Essay* 23:42), grasps at once. In this late novel, openness to life's polyphony and the healing powers of the comic spirit are reserved for the younger generation. Meredith seems to be saying that given the extreme self-deception of a Victor, or the poignantly entrapped position of a Nataly, even the energies of a comic intelligence like Nesta's can do little to avert a tragic outcome for those who cannot share her liberating vision. This is nowhere better summed up than when Victor, intent on gaining Nesta's approval of Dudley, confuses her blush of embarrassment for her father's schemes with an affirmative response. Victor, Willoughby-like, "was naturally as deceived as he wished to be" (17:290).

Linked with her problems involving Dudley Sowerby is Nesta's friendship at Brighton with Judith Marsett, a character who looms larger than one might wish in the last third of the novel. As the mistress of a philandering army captain, Mrs. Marsett occupies the painful position of the "fallen woman"—painful in another sense to the reader leery of Victorian clichés. Meredith's treatment of Mrs. Marsett—in contrast to his extraordinary treatment of Nataly— never quite breaks free of its hackneyed antecedents; her character, nonetheless, does provide a strategic device for illuminating the major figures in the novel, Nesta in particular. With her instinctive warmth and egalitarian spirit, she befriends Mrs. Marsett as a lonely woman in need of human contact. When Nesta learns more, her loyalty and friendship become all the firmer while Judith plays her part as a kind of cramming tutor in the realities from which Nesta has been shielded. Victor, we have been told earlier, viewed such shielding as necessary—"repression and mystery he considered wholesome for girls" (17:148)—but Nesta has managed to avoid going "through the various Nursery exercises in dissimulation; she had no appearance of praying forgiveness of men for the original sin of being woman" (17:145–46). Victor, on the other hand, is shown to be a thorough sentimentalist on this count, an admirer of "the shining simplicity of our dear young English girls!" (17:148).

Much later, Nesta seems to speak to Victor's attitude specifically as she talks with Judith and expresses her impatience with such passive "simplicity": " 'There cannot be any goodness unless it is a practiced goodness. Otherwise it is nothing more than paint on canvas. You speak to me of my innocence. What is it worth, if it is only a picture and does no work to help to rescue?' " (17:341). Warming to this topic in Judith's presence, and referring to her feminist friend, Louise de Seilles, Nesta then articulates the position toward which she herself is moving: " 'She will never marry until she meets a man who has the respect for women, for all women. We both think we cannot separate ourselves from our sisters. . . . She wants women to have professions. . . . Things are improving for them, but we groan at the slowness of it' " (17:341–42). Meredith here anticipates other outspoken heroines of the nineties, like Gissing's Rhoda Nunn and Mary Barfoot or Hardy's Sue Bridehead, but significantly he also manages to give us a young woman of advanced ideas who is psychologically whole and who does not feel the need to convert her views into an all-consuming profession.

Nesta's developing credo of self-denial, absolute honesty, unconcern for established shibboleths, and active caring for others is, as Victor dimly recognizes (17:479–80), quite in tune with his suppressed "Idea." But it is her translation of such principles into action, of course, that fills Nesta's parents with awe and trepidation. Victor tells Dartrey, " 'I positively doubt whether any of us could stop her, if she had set herself to do a thing she thought right' " (17:467). Nataly, alluding to Nesta's assimilation of forbidden knowledge from "the dreadful woman," Mrs. Marsett, says simply, " 'She frightens me' " (17:446). And a little later, Victor, viewing the estrangement between Nataly and Nesta over Mrs. Marsett with alarm, and increasingly but still ineptly concerned for Nataly's health, speaks more truth than he can recognize: " 'The best cure for mama would be a look into Fredi's eyes!' he said, embracing his girl, quite believing in her, just a little afraid of her" (17:448).

An honest look into Nesta's eyes—or even better, with Nesta's eyes—would reveal to Nataly that her daughter's partisanship for Mrs. Marsett is premised upon an instinctive response that excludes consideration of ready-made patriarchal social definitions.

And it is precisely such definitions, embodied in the looks of the Mrs. Blathenoys and Dudley Sowerbys, that increasingly obsesses Nataly as the Radnor "secret" becomes public property at the novel's end. Nesta's clear-eyed love for her mother—the same kind of direct, unbiased response found in her relationship with Judith Marsett—could be an avenue of escape for Nataly from her obsessions; instead, Meredith shows her locking her door to her daughter in anger, feeling that Nesta's unconventional friendship is going to produce the chorus of judgment summed up in Nataly's "cry of despair: 'The mother!—the daughter!'" (17:447). Because of her inability to escape such banal social judgments—that is, because of her inability to see herself independently as Nesta sees her—Nataly is shown in the novel's last chapters moving increasingly into painful isolation: "Her one great affliction, the scourging affliction of her utter loneliness;—an outcast from her family; daily, and she knew not how, more shut away from the man she loved; now shut away from her girl;—seemed under the hand of the angel of God. The abandonment of her by friends, was merely the light to show it" (17:449).

The torture of such a sense of abandonment as Meredith presents it is strikingly similar in some ways to that which Tolstoy depicts for his Anna Karenina; in fact, Tolstoy's comments to his wife about Anna's suffering, made when he was finishing the novel, shed light on the situation Meredith, who felt great admiration for Tolstoy, is evoking here:

> There exists a whole world of woman's work, fashions, ideas, by which women live. All that must be very cheerful, and I understood that women could love this and occupy themselves with it. . . . Anna is deprived of all these joys of occupying herself with the woman's side of life, because she is alone. All women have turned away from her, and she has nobody to talk to about all that which composes the everyday, purely feminine occupations.[22]

8

We also find Judith Marsett acting as a touchstone in Nesta's relations with Dudley Sowerby. As *One of Our Conquerors* progresses, Dudley becomes increasingly the novel's centerpiece portrait of unreflective Victorian patriarchal attitudes. And yet, from his view-point, he is shown to have huge obstacles to overcome in his dealings with the Radnors, whom he comes to regard as "a set of Bohemians" (17:472). Even before the complications introduced by Mrs. Marsett, Dudley has to endure "enormous internal conflict . . . [before] he had mastered [the] distaste" brought on by news of his fiancée's illegitimacy. Assistance in his appreciation of Nesta, we are assured, is provided by a reminder of Victor's millions—"money is the imperious requirement of superior station" (17:397). Dudley's impression of Nesta as they are reunited pro-vides a typical instance of the narrator's comic assumption of his point of view: "Her features, her present aristocratic deficiency of colour, greatly pleased him; her character would submit to mould-ing. Of all young ladies in the world, she should be the one to shrink from a mental independence and hold to the guidance of the man ennobling her. Did she?" (17:398). Here Dudley's narrated mono-logue shows he at least has the perception to dread "some intrepid force" behind Nesta's calm demeanor, and he is shown at this point to have enough sense to keep his thoughts for the most part to him-self—his conversation with Nesta is full of wonderfully pregnant ellipses.

Once he catches wind of her friendship with Mrs. Marsett, how-ever, we see Dudley displaying his colors more clearly in a flutter of tortured ambivalence and righteous indignation: "An alliance with her was impossible. So said disgust. Anger came like a stronger beast . . . , growing so excessive as to require tempering with drops of compassion; which prepared the way for a formal act of cold for-giveness . . . ; and [he] did it on a grand scale, and dissolved his heart in the grandeur, and enslaved himself again (17:415). His sentimental reverie, glorying in magnanimous self-sacrifice, sounds much like Willoughby Patterne's rhapsody of self-love as he envisions himself united to a vindictively disfigured Clara, leading "the limping thing to the altar, if she insisted" (*Egoist*, 14:62). But Willoughby, true to form, manages to maintain a facade of decorum with Laetitia and Clara, even when most ignominiously beaten; Dudley, on the other hand, gives up decorum altogether when he sees that Nesta is in no way influenced by his conventional views.

The *scène-à-faire* between the two occurs in Chapter 39—"In the Shadow of Mrs. Marsett"—where Dudley and Nesta are made to illuminate one another with dramatic fullness:

"Are you—I beg to ask—are you still:—I can hardly think it—
Nesta!—I surely have a claim to advise:—it cannot be with your mother's consent:—in communication, in correspondence with . . . ?" [sic]

Again she bowed her head, saying: "It is true."

"With that person? . . . I beg to know whether this correspondence
is to continue?" said Dudley.

"All my life, if I do not feel dishonoured by it."

"You are. . . . And you do not agree with me?"

"I do not."

"Do you pretend to be as able to judge as I?"

"In this instance, better."

"Then I retire. I cannot retain my place here. You may depend upon
it, the world is not wrong when it forbids young ladies to have cogni-
zance of women leading disorderly lives."

"Only the women, Mr. Sowerby?"

"Men, too, of course."

"You do not exclude the men from Society."

"Oh! one reads that kind of argument in books."

"Oh! the worthy books, then. I would read them, if I could find
them."

"They are banned by self-respecting readers."

"It grieves me to think differently." (17:475–76)

There is something here of the spirit of Elizabeth Bennet's confrontation with Lady Catherine De Bourgh towards the end of *Pride
and Prejudice*[23]—the same opposition between entrenched aristocratic presumption and the free play of youthful intelligence and
self-possession. What Nesta forces Dudley to do, of course—just as
Elizabeth forces Lady Catherine—is to be explicit about assumptions that won't bear explicitness. Two value systems are in direct
conflict: one system, to use Northrop Frye's terms for defining traditional comedy, embodies the values of "a society controlled by
habit, ritual bondage, arbitrary law and the older characters"—both
Dudley and Lady Catherine in their rigidity are "older" in this
sense; the other value system is that of a "society controlled by
youth and pragmatic freedom,"[24] the new society centered in
Nesta, Dartrey, and the other "free" characters in *One of Our Conquerors*—Louise de Seilles, Simeon Fenellan, and, to some degree,
Colney Durance. The "new society" counterparts in *Pride and
Prejudice* are those who inhabit Pemberley at the novel's end:
Darcy, Elizabeth, and Darcy's sister Georgiana, along with those
most welcome there—Elizabeth's sister Jane, Bingley, and Mr. and

Mrs. Gardiner, the major figures from the older generation who embody the virtues of the new. In both Austen's and Meredith's novels, the older society, controlled by habits and attitudes toward tradition that are precisely a kind of monological "ritual bondage" and "arbitrary law," gives way to a new social group that presumably, in its pragmatism, would be open to "arguments in books" and would continue to be capable of growth and change.

Pride and Prejudice ends with its focus firmly upon the new society at Pemberley where Elizabeth's "lively, sportive manner"[25] reigns. Rosings and Longbourn have moved to the periphery, although, in the spirit of comic reconciliation, Lady Catherine and Mrs. Bennet are permitted to visit—and leave. The ending of *One of Our Conquerors* is much more problematic. If our focus were entirely on Dartrey and Nesta—"often in the rebel ranks; . . . dissatisfied with matters as they are; . . . restless for action, angry with a country denying it" (17:461),[26] we would have an exemplary case of Frye's vision of comedy as the assertion of a new order premised upon pragmatic freedom and escape from ritual bondage. But our real concern at the end is much more for those characters trapped between the new and the old, and this, in part, is what strikes the characteristically modernist note of this text. Victor and Nataly, like Arnold's alpine climber, discover themselves "wandering between two worlds," and both succumb. They are shown, twenty years before, to have made an effort at breaking from the old world of arbitrary law, but they fail because they do not have the breadth of vision and self-command—values enshrouded in Victor's lost "Idea"—that we find in Nesta and Dartrey. Meredith highlights the irony of Victor's confused combination of rebellion and utter conventionality as he becomes progressively more tragic in stature in the novel's concluding section.

Close to the time of her death, Nataly's narrated mental stream reverts again to the novel's central metaphor when she observes that Nesta "had inherited from her father something of the cataract's force which won its way by catching or by mastering, uprooting, ruining!" (17:470). She is half right. Nesta has the force of her father but, as the primary and most dynamic figure in the novel associated with the values of Meredithian critical intelligence, her control and direction of the cataract's force are repeatedly seen as creative and humane. It is Victor who, without Nesta's sane judgment, uproots and ruins. In an early revealing use of water imagery, Colney refers to Victor's lack of clear vision and direction as "his

insane itch to be the bobbing cork on the wave of the minute"
(17:237).[27] This is precisely the point Victor uneasily registers late
in *One of Our Conquerors* when he makes the effort to view himself
as Nesta does—her "perception of the point where submission to
the moods of his nature had weakened his character. . . . An effort
to imagine a reproof, showed him her spirit through her eyes: in
her deeds too: she had already done work on the road. . . . Victor
could no longer so naturally name her Fredi" (17:481–82).

Again, in spite of his usual lack of self-discernment, Victor cannot be classed simply as a fixed "older character." As here, Meredith allows us to see him in several ways advancing under Nesta's
tutelage. Not only does he allow her to deflect him from his liaison
with Lady Grace Halley (who, as the sponsor of Dudley Sowerby, is
firmly in the camp of the "fixed" characters), but he also takes a
commendable role in the rehabilitation of Mrs. Marsett. Just after
his interview with Captain Marsett, during which he extracts the
man's not unwilling promise to marry her, Victor tells Dartrey, "I
come round to some of your ideas on these matters. It's this girl of
mine, this wee bit of girl in her little nightshirt with the frill, aston-
ishes me most:—'thinking of the tops of the mountains at night!'
She has positively done the whole of this work—main part. I smiled
when I left the house, to have to own our little Fredi starting us all
on the road" (17:466). But as Victor's habit of viewing Nesta as a
child rather than an adult suggests, his start "on the road" of dialogical reform is still marked by profound ambivalence. And, as one
would by this time predict, he does not "come round" enough to
significantly alter his relation to the two women with whom he has
longest been in conflict—Nataly and his Nemesis, Mrs. Burman
Radnor.

9

Victor and Nataly's visit to Mrs. Burman close to the end of *One
of Our Conquerors* provides our only direct view of the figure whose
presence haunts the entire novel. Indirect glimpses come at various times earlier through the reports of Victor's friends and
through Victor's and Nataly's obsessive thoughts of her. Victor operates under the pretense of a sentimental concern for Mrs. Burman's welfare—"her health is awful: yes, yes; poor woman! we feel
for her" (17:55)—while at the same time he is in a frenzy of antici-

pation over predictions of her imminent death and the end, as he sees it, of his problems. Nataly's relation to Mrs. Burman is more subtle and self-conscious than Victor's but, due to the pressures involved, amounts in the end to the same thing: "Part of her prayer was on behalf of Mrs. Burman, for life to be extended to her, if the poor lady clung to life—if it was really humane to wish it for her: and heaven would know: heaven had mercy on the afflicted. Nataly heard the snuffle of hypocrisy in her prayer. She had to cease to pray" (17:81).

It is precisely the hypocrisy of her prominent social position and of her relation to Mrs. Burman that causes Nataly so much pain; ironically, the solution to this problem offered by both women is the same—that Nataly and Victor should, as Mrs. Burman puts it, "live in obscurity." When Victor reports this suggestion, relayed to him by Mrs. Burman's factotum, he does not even hear Nataly's response—"May we not think that she may be right?"—as he storms on about the "'outrageous tyranny of a decrepit woman naming herself wife'" (17:263). Obscurity, for Victor, is shown to be literally a fate worse than death.

The portrait of Mrs. Burman Meredith provides through indirection is rather different from the vindictive and obtuse harpy of Victor's imagination. Not only is she literally quite correct in naming herself his wife, she has also apparently adapted to the situation to the extent that it is only the couple's "living in *flagrant* sin" (my italics) that brings on her intrusions into their life through the dispatching of emissaries and pronouncements. Victor's mania for being in the limelight exposes Mrs. Burman's impossible social position just as cruelly as it does Nataly's. Both women have in common, then, the suffering brought on by Victor's insensitivity. In addition, Nataly is able to see beyond Victor's mental caricature of the woman to Mrs. Burman herself. She tells Dartrey at one point that Victor's wife "'does not, I am now convinced, mean persecution. She was never a mean-minded woman. Oh! I could wish she were'" (17:361).

But what gives us our most distinct glimpse of Mrs. Burman before the late scene comes relatively early in the novel from Simeon Fenellan:

"Three or four days of the week the lady . . . drives to her chemist's, and there she sits in the shop; round the corner, as you enter; and sees all Charing in the shop looking-glass at the back; herself a stranger spectacle, poor lady . . . , with her fashionable no-bonnet . . . and a huge square green shade over her forehead. Sits hours long, and cocks her ears at orders of applicants for drugs across the counter, and sometimes catches wind of a prescription and consults her chemist, and thinks she'll try it herself. It's a basket of medicine bottles driven to Regent's Park pretty well every day." (17:130–31)

The picture of the old woman "under the beetling shade" (17:134), grasping at pharmaceutical straws and viewing the world at second hand like some antiquated Lady of Shallot, provides a bizarre image that neatly embodies Victor's confused sense of Mrs. Burman—at once pathetic, grotesque, and menacing. As he passes the chemist's, he is horrified that "the woman might be inside there now! She might have seen his figure in the shop-mirror!" (17:134). Victor's terror at the "henbane visage" (17:136) is terror at the unexplored and suppressed realities and responsibilities of the past—"those days of the monstrous alliance" (17:137). His characteristic mental response is, again Willoughby-like, simply to try to think away "the woman" along with the house in Regent's Park: "having shaken-off that house, he had pushed it back into mists, obliterated it. The woman certainly had a power. He shot away to the power he knew of in himself; his capacity for winning . . . warm supporters" (17:135), and so on. But, like Victor's punctilio bump, the thought of Mrs. Burman cannot be obliterated and at the same time a direct confrontation, until the end, is always evaded. As Donald Swanson has aptly noted, "Victor has a genius for the undefined . . . , much to his cost, since the suppression is not, and, Meredith dramatically suggests, cannot be total: that which is not made conscious haunts Victor on a level where it gains a great, almost supernatural, power."[28]

This is one important reason why, at the novel's end when Victor receives a summons to appear at Regent's Park, the scene is so charged with emotion. After twenty-one years of evasion, he finally and inevitably must confront his past and its implications—a "powerful formless vapour rolling from a source that was nothing other than yonder weak lonely woman" (17:136). Like the sentimentalists of Sir Austin Feverel's aphorism, Victor has sought " 'to enjoy Reality without incurring the Immense Debtorship for a thing done,' "[29] and as with Sir Austin himself, to whom the maxim applies as exactly as it does to Victor, the result that finally must be endured is infinitely worse than an earlier honest "payment of debts" (17:136).

On his way with Nataly to Mrs. Burman's, Victor tries to trivialize what lies ahead—they are going to "express penitence and what not, and hear words of pardon" (17:485). In the remarkable scene that follows, much of it rendered as Victor's narrated monologue and psycho-narration, Meredith maintains our sense of Victor's trivializing consciousness while we also see him, for the first time, completely at a loss:

> They were in the drawing-room. It was furnished as in the old time, gold and white, looking new; all the same as of old, save for a division of silken hangings; and these were pale blue: the colour preferred by Victor for a bedroom. He glanced at the ceiling, to bathe in a blank space out of memory. Here she lived, here she slept, behind the hangings. . . .
> Mrs. Burman was present; seated. People may die seated. . . . No voice came. They were unsure of being seen by the floating grey of eyes patient to gaze from their vast distance. Big drops fell from Nataly's. Victor heard the French time-piece on the mantel-shelf, where a familiar gilt Cupid swung for the seconds: his own purchase. The time of day on the clock was wrong; the Cupid swung. . . . He forgot his estimate of the minutes, he formed a prayer, he refused to hear the Cupid swinging, he droned a sound of sentences to deaden his ears. Ideas of eternity rolled in semblance of enormous clouds. Death was a black bird among them. The piano rang to Nataly's young voice and his. The gold and white of the chairs welcomed a youth suddenly enrolled among the wealthy by an enamoured old lady on his arm. Cupid tick-ticked.—Poor soul! poor woman! . . . Plunging through a wave of the scent of Maréchale, that was a tremendous memory to haul him backward and forward, he beheld his prayer dancing across the furniture; a diminutive thin black figure, elvish, irreverent, appallingly unlike his proper emotion; and he brought his hands just to touch, and got to the edge of his chair, with split knees. At once the figure vanished. By merely looking at Nataly, he passed into her prayer. A look at Mrs. Burman made it personal, his own. He heard the cluck of a horrible sob coming from him. (17:486–89)

In this moment of psychological time, an "intermingling past, present, and imagined future"[30]—"Death was a black bird among them"—merge in Victor's mind in a montage effect that is strikingly "modernist," suggestive especially of associative styles to be developed by Woolf, Richardson, Joyce, and Proust. This is a particularly richly allusive moment for Victor, when he might come to some recognition of the significance of his actions, both toward

Mrs. Burman and toward Nataly. Surrounded by emblems of the past that he has so carefully suppressed for half a lifetime, he has his chance to see himself more clearly and to make a gesture of expiation. But self recognition is not what Meredith has schooled us to expect of Victor. Now, just as in the earlier scene when he stretches his mind to consider Mrs. Burman's pathetic figure in the chemist's shop, he "made no advance. He stopped in a fever of sensibility" (17:136). The "cluck of a horrible sob" is the closest we come to acknowledgment on his part of responsibility or penitence.

When the black bird of death calls not only Mrs. Burman but Nataly as well, Victor's moral confusion—his lack of the self-assessing powers of Meredithian common sense—leaves him altogether defenseless. He succumbs for a short time to literal madness, obsessed with thoughts of his half-formed "Idea," punctilio, and marriage—the very same confused associations we find in his mind when the novel begins. Meredith makes it clear that Victor is no nearer understanding now than he was then. In spite of his enormous energy and spirit of good will, then, this "abstract Optimist" goes to his death with his life still essentially unexamined. While tragic understanding is denied to the father, however, this is not the case with the daughter. As becomes characteristic in the late works, we are directed at the very end to look to the novel's central young woman to gain a sense of possibility and progress. Nesta Victoria, with "her gathered knowledge of things and her ruthless penetrativeness" (17:513), promises to lead a creative life in which the errors of father and mother cannot be repeated. But, as Susan Morgan has suggested, Nesta's marriage to Dartrey Fenellan and the marriages that close the other late works have the effect of "tidy, cheerful endings" appended to "chaotic and despairing novels."[31] Our sense of progress as we close *One of Our Conquerors* is a muted and marginal one at best.

6

Lord Ormont and His Aminta: Escape from Patriarchy and the Problem of Narrative Dissonance

1

W<small>HAT ESPECIALLY INTERESTS ME ABOUT</small> *LORD ORMONT AND HIS AMINTA* (1894) is the way in which it displays impulses in Meredith—now in his mid-sixties—that are at once characteristically avant garde *and* regressive. By the novel's second half, its female hero, Aminta Farrell, has embraced progressive ideas about gender relations, education, and the class system that go well beyond those held by any of her Meredithian predecessors. As we move into the nineties, we see Meredith feeling increasingly able to depict the full-scale revolt of a woman who discovers her life to be a denial of subjectivity and self-respect. In addition, he continues to experiment with technique in interesting and compelling ways, extending the narrative tactics he had developed in *One of Our Conquerors* to convey complicated—especially contradictory and transitional—states of mind in his characters. But we may also see him at times, especially late in the text, presenting us with a different kind of contradictoriness—a curious and disquieting narrative dissonance that produces the regressive side of the novel. This dissonance occurs at those moments when the narrative voice seems to slide into the very patriarchal/sentimental attitudes it is so critical of elsewhere. At points like these it is hard to argue with E. M. Forster's devastating remark about Meredith's "heavy attacks on sentimentality"— that one "is apt to suspect anyone carrying a blunderbuss of being a sentimentalist himself."[1] But more on this problem later in the chapter.

Lord Ormont has been given minimal attention by critics, especially in the last quarter century or so.[2] And as I've just indicated,

148

there are some good reasons for this neglect. The novel does bear evidence of waning imaginative powers and there is at times a tendency to oversimplify, but to do as one modern critic has done, to dismiss *Lord Ormont* (along with *The Amazing Marriage*) as "literary abominations,"[3] is to miss much of real value and interest—as I hope to show. Coming from the complexities and richness of *One of Our Conquerors*, one may at times find the narrative style of *Lord Ormont* flat in its relative straightforwardness, but one may also experience some elation at the clarity of this novel's shallows after contending with the depths of its predecessor—a novel that Gillian Beer has aptly termed "a strange, compelling, hideously difficult experiment."[4]

In *Lord Ormont*, Meredith examines the role of a woman who develops the vision and courage to break away entirely from a demeaning marriage by establishing herself in a relationship that is premised on a renewed sense of self-worth. It is not going too far, I think, to suggest that Meredith had brooded close to four decades over Mary Meredith's abortive attempt in precisely this direction before he was able to translate it into fictional terms of success and fulfillment. Earlier figures—the wife in "Modern Love," Lady Feverel, Clara Middleton, and Diana Warwick—all suggest partial portrayals of Mary's break for freedom. Meredith's sympathetic treatment of Aminta's awakening and escape, then, marks another significant point in his personal and artistic development; it also suggests, as I have already implied, that in the changing climate of the nineties he was able to feel confident that he had an audience capable of responding to the subject of adultery without the hysteria that greeted *Richard Feverel* thirty-five years earlier.

By opening *Lord Ormont* with the school days of Aminta Farrell and Matey Weyburn, Meredith is able to establish a set of schoolboy attitudes—misogyny, military hero-worship, stress on athletic prowess, disdain for marriage and non-military careers, etc.—that he then ironically plays against through the rest of the novel. The development of Matey and Aminta involves their growing beyond the limitations of these views; their childhood hero, Major General Lord Ormont, on the other hand, tends to remain static for most of the novel, entangled in unexamined adolescent values rather similar to those of the schoolboys, though he is more than forty years their senior. Like Achilles, however—with whom he is several times compared—Ormont at the last is shown to grow beyond his narrowness and egotistical petulance to generosity and forgiveness, but, again like Achilles, not before his actions have resulted in the loss of the person who has come to mean the most to him.

We first hear of Ormont as a larger-than-life figure, the "pattern of a warrior" (18:8) for Matey, head boy at Mr. Cuper's school. Aminta, at the neighboring Miss Vincent's school, also has a mind "bent on [Ormont's] heroical deeds" (18:7), and this shared adulation is shown to kindle the already strong attraction between the two. However, mixed with the schoolboy talk of Ormont's cavalry exploits, his caring for his men and his "Christian" treatment of his horses, are references to his notorious duelling, linked with his callous mistreatment of women, all of which the adolescent Matey is eager to endorse: "somehow, the sacrifice of an enormous number of women to Lord Ormont's glory seemed natural. . . . It brightens his flame, and it is agreeable to them. That is how they come to distinction; they have no other chance; they are only women; they are mad to be singed, and they rush pell-mell, all for the honour of the candle" (18:11–12).

As we learn more of Ormont, we increasingly see beyond this hero worship to the man who "had a funny pride, like a boy at a game" (18:29). Ormont is displayed in a fit of pique against his country: having led a victorious cavalry charge in India, contrary to the orders of the provincial commissioner, he has been the recipient of an official reprimand and negative criticism in the press and elsewhere. Ormont's response is, Achilles-like, to withdraw from society, but not before he has fired off an angry letter to an offending journal. The narrative summary of the letter's effect sums up Ormont's mind with precision:

> The printing of it was an act of editorial ruthlessness. The noble soldier had no mould in his intellectual or educational foundry for the casting of sentences; and the editor's leading type to the letter, without further notice of the writer—who was given a prominent place or scaffolding for the execution of himself publicly, if it pleased him to do that thing— tickled the critical mind. Lord Ormont wrote intemperately.
>
> His Titanic hurling of blocks against critics did no harm to an enemy skilled in the use of trimmer weapons, notably the fine one of letting big missiles rebound. (18:23)

The rest of Ormont's history is a working-out of the rebounding consequences of his intemperate behavior—behavior that does indeed tickle the critical mind.

What follows involves an increasing testing—and then the eventual overturn—of Matey's and Aminta's childhood adulation. Years later, when Aminta becomes Ormont's wife while in Spain, he does not publicly acknowledge her as such on his return home because to do so, in his view, would be to pander to popular opinion. What Ormont fails to recognize until too late (in a characteristic act of Meredithian masculine insensibility) is the suffering this supposed act of vengeance against the British public imposes on Aminta. We are permitted to see this suffering with increasing clarity through the eyes of Matey; he is introduced into the household as Ormont's secretary by Lady Charlotte Eglett, Ormont's fiercely loyal sister, who hopes, by means of Matey's clearheaded editorial talents, to tame Ormont's memoirs and, presumably, to block any further acts of epistolary self-immolation.

In Chapter 9, "A Flash of the Bruised Warrior," Weyburn's boyhood enthusiasm for Ormont reasserts itself for a time as they work together over a period of days drawing up an elaborate plan for the defense of London. Once he has completed the plan, however, Ormont methodically places it on the fire. The long passage that follows this act combines narrative analysis with a suggestive evocation of Weyburn's mental stream as he tries to understand Ormont's self-indulgent destructivity along with his—and Weyburn's own—relation with Aminta, whom Matey has not consciously recognized from their schooldays. In Weyburn's mind these issues are all dimly related; as he gropes for the connection, he daydreams, envisioning himself and an unnamed woman—transparently Aminta—twirling in a dance as a "counter demonstration" to the madness of Ormont's inability to forgive his country's censure. As we've seen him do in *One of Our Conquerors*, Meredith evokes several levels of consciousness here with techniques we usually associate with modernist narrative, "more inchoate than rational verbalization—those levels on the margins of attention,"[5] but nonetheless essential and illuminating to the attentive reader:

> Praise the dance of a woman and the man together high over a curmudgeonly humping solitariness, that won't forgive an injury, nurses rancour, smacks itself in the face, because it can't—to use the old schoolboy words—take a licking!
> These were the huddled, drunken sensations and thoughts entertained by Weyburn, without his reflecting on the detachment from his

old hero, of which they were the sign. . . . The person criticized was manifest. Who was the woman he twirled with? . . . She murmured, or seemed to murmur—for there was no sound—a complaint of Lord Ormont . . . , [who] had no understanding of how to treat a woman, or belief in her having equal life with him on earth. . . . [H]er life was wasting.

Was not she a priceless manuscript cast to the flames? Her lord. . . . took her for his own, and he would not call her his own. . . . Could anything account for the behaviour of so manly and noble a gentleman?—Rhetoric made the attempt, and Weyburn gave up the windy business.

Discovering that his fair partner of the wasting life was—he struggled to quench the revelation—Aminta, he stopped the dance. (18:118–20)

Matey's youthful approval of women as moths to be singed by Ormant's flame becomes windy rhetoric—the "unwonted argumentative energy" of Mr. Cuper's boys—to his newly critical mind, while Aminta, and the manuscript with which she is compared, become emblems of the pernicious effects of Ormontian caprice. Directly linked with this revelation is the amusing play between Weyburn's subconscious and conscious mind, between his natural sexual attraction to Aminta and his circumspect address, when he encounters her, to "Lady Ormont": the vision of himself and the "unfeatured, undistinguished" woman who "twirled on his arm, uninvited; accepted, as in the course of nature; hugged . . . , and going now at desperation's pace" (18:119) is posed against the self-righteous dismissal of the daydream ("he stopped the dance") when Aminta's role is consciously acknowledged.

This sequence, with its inside view of Weyburn's ambivalence, prepares for the novel's main action, but the narrator's insistence that at this point Matey still remains quite limited in his understanding of Ormont is also significant:

> a little patient unemotional watchfulness might have intimated to him something besides the simple source of the old hero's complex chapter of conduct. As it was, Weyburn . . . moralized and disapproved; telling himself, truly enough, that so it would not have been with him; instead of sounding at my lord's character . . . , who compressed, almost repressed, the roar of Achilles, though his military bright name was to him his Briseis. (18:120)

Weyburn, then, even though his newfound awareness is leading him to sympathetic understanding of Aminta's dilemma, has not yet assumed the "patient unemotional watchfulness" of Meredith-ian critical intelligence. His moralizing and disapproval, in fact, bring him perilously close to priggishness (here and at various other points in the novel), while the narrator's insistence that we also understand the pain of Ormont's compressed roar warns against the oversimplifications brought on by a partisan spirit.

If we consider the fair-minded patient watchfulness fostered in the reader toward such blatantly flawed late heroes as Victor Radnor, Ormont, and Fleetwood, we can appreciate the way in which Meredith in his final years of novel writing actively pursued the precept of humane disinterestedness that was always central to his theoretical position. The impatience, anger, and contempt ruled out in the *Essay*—but so evident in Meredith's narrative treatment of earlier figures from Shibli Bagarag to Willoughby Pat-terne—are scrupulously kept to a minimum in these late novels. Ormont, as we have seen, is portrayed as diligently engineering his own public execution, while the reader is provided a model of "un-solicitous observation . . . without any fluttering eagerness" (*Essay* 23:89) in the "sane and solid mind" of a narrator who "would not . . . hurt the foolish, but merely demonstrate their foolishness" (*Essay*, 23:91). On the other hand, Meredith's model here is not a "view from nowhere"—not a claim to infallible objectivity—but an appeal to open-mindedness and even inconclusiveness that Wey-burn's developing judgments of Ormont are still far from encom-passing.[6]

2

Another important view of Ormont is provided by Lady Charlotte. Early in the novel we hear her make a statement, in regard to an Ormont duel, that epitomizes her position: " 'I hate duelling, but I side with my brother' " (18:27). We find in her a strong component of humane intelligence that must accommodate itself to her in-tense sisterly and class loyalty. When she intercepts a second Or-montian blast at the press, we see the same combination at work: "She laid [the letter] in her desk, understanding well that it was a laugh lost to the world. Poets could reasonably feign it to shake the desk inclosing it. She had a strong sense of humour; her mind re-verted to the desk in a way to make her lips shut grimly. She sided with her brother" (18:29).

Lady Charlotte is another in a line of older aristocratic Meredithian women, stretching back to Lady Blandish in *Richard Feverel* and Lady Emily Jocelyn in *Evan Harrington*, who show an instinctive good sense that counters inherited class prejudice. The terms used to describe Lady Charlotte repeatedly remind one of various aspects of the comic spirit: "She could be humane, even sisterly, with women whose conduct or prattle did not outrage plain sense . . . ; she read men minutely . . . [as] creatures of importunate appetites, humorous objects. . . . She knew how much stronger than ordinary men the woman who can put them in motion" (18:30) and so on. She is described as thoughtful rather than tender, and is refreshingly heterodox in her religious views: she prefers chapel to church (18:167) and has sent a check " 'to a poor man punished for blasphemy. The man,' " she says, " 'had the right to his opinions, and he had the courage of his opinions.' " " 'Honest sinners,' " she pronounces, " 'have no fear' " before God because " 'they don't deceive themselves' " (18:45). On the subject of sex, she shows herself to be well ahead of her time: "Sex she saw at play everywhere, dogging the conduct of affairs, directing them at times; she saw it as the animation of nature, senselessly stigmatized, hypocritically concealed, active in our thoughts where not in our deeds; and the declining of the decorous to see it, or admit the sight" brings from her "a grimly melancholy shrug over the cruelties resulting—cruelties chiefly affecting women" (18:47).

Lady Charlotte is vigorous in supporting " 'things females can do. That is, when they stand for their rights' " (18:158), as is evident in her battle with her neighbor, Mr. Addicote, in a hot dispute over property lines. She is also vigorous in her condemnation of the indignities of old age. Her doctor has told her that it is time to " 'renounce the saddle. He says it's time. Not if I've got work for horseback!' she nicked her head emphatically: 'I hate old age. They sha'nt dismount me till a blow comes. Hate it!' " (18:160). Later, we find that she has finally given up riding and is glad her ailment is heart disease since death " 'was likely to be quick; no doctors, no nurses and daily bulletins for inquirers' " (18:205).

However, in spite of her tough unconventionality, her insistence on fidelity to what she perceives as the truth, and her strong sympathy for women of sound sense who find themselves entrapped in life's circumstances, Lady Charlotte persists for most of the novel in viewing Aminta as she is defined by society—as Lady Doubtful, "an impudent, underbred, ambitious young slut" (18:183) who has temporarily captured Ormont's attentions. When Ormont tells his sister to go to Madrid, where the wedding has taken place, for proof, Lady Charlotte's response delightfully sums up her inability even to consider Aminta's legitimacy as Countess of Ormont: " 'Married in Madrid! Who's ever married in Madrid!' " (18:268). Matey Weyburn quietly persists in telling Lady Charlotte that her view of Aminta would change if the two women were to meet—and from our knowledge of them we are made aware that this is undoubtedly true—but the meeting never takes place. Ironically, Lady Charlotte's refusal to refer to Aminta as Lady Ormont ends only after Aminta herself has renounced the title late in the novel. Earlier, Lady Charlotte denies selfhood to Aminta by defining her as " 'a woman springing up out of nothing' " (18:166) or simply " 'this young person' " (18:161) or " 'the young woman' " (18:65).

Semiotics, then, is a matter of special concern in this novel. As Marjorie Goss has pointed out, "Names and nicknames are used . . . not only to characterize, but to pinpoint significant developments in the novel's narrative."[7] Both Ormont and Lady Charlotte, for example, are in a sense right in refusing to acknowledge Aminta as Countess of Ormont since she herself is shown to be increasingly uneasy about the implications of that title and its implied identity. Further, the sexual tension evoked in a number of scenes between Weyburn and Aminta simply over how to address one another— "Browny" (her school name), "Aminta," "Lady Ormont," or "Matey," "Matthew," "Mr. Weyburn"—nicely pinpoints the questions of identity and relationship with which the novel concerns itself. Even Lady Charlotte, when Weyburn tells her Aminta's name for the first time, is instantly reminded of her own youth when Ormont (Rowsley) called her by another name and she seemed to be another person: " 'I read poetry then. You wouldn't have imagined that. I did, and liked it. I hate old age. It changes you so. None of my children know me as I was when I had life in me and was myself, and my brother Rowsley called me Cooey. They think me a hard old woman. I was Cooey through the woods and over the meadows and down stream to Rowsley' " (18:163). She wishes to visit Steignton, the Ormont estate where she grew up, one more time in order to recapture something of that past when she was Cooey—somehow a more essential version of herself: " 'No place on earth is equal to Steignton for me,' " she tells Matey. " 'Here at Olmer I'm a mother and a grandmother—the 'devil of an old woman' my neighbors take me to be' " (18:163).

In similar fashion we are made to see Aminta awakening to the painfulness of her own mutability: as Lady Ormont she finds an identity imposed upon her—that of leisured matron in seclusion— which does violence both to the lively schoolgirl of the past and the potentially creative woman of the future. Like Dorothea Brooke, Gwendolyn Harleth, and a host of other nineteenth-century female protagonists, Aminta discovers that the Victorian ideal of leisured womanhood has little to do with what Matthew Arnold called the genuine self. *Lord Ormont* traces in its central plot the emergence of Aminta's buried stream as she gradually moves to assert an identity premised, not on the social perquisites and court presentation she initially envisions as Lady Ormont, but rather on a simple declaration of the potential of Aminta Farrell: "'I, too, can work'" (18:180). Her eventual break from Lord Ormont, then, is not simply a revolt against neglect—he is, in fact, readying Steignton for her presentation to society when Aminta, no longer interested in such things, leaves him. Her revolt expands from unhappiness at a loveless marriage to rejection of an entire style of life and the definition of self that accompanies it; it is a revolt in which Aminta moves from object to subject, from an identity premised on leisured gentility and subservience to the work ethic premised on purposeful activity that haunted the imagination of so many aspiring Victorian heroines.[8] Although the novel is set in the twenties and thirties, its approving treatment of a "runaway" wife[9]—one who achieves fulfillment in an extramarital relationship centered in the world of work—is clearly reflective of the increasingly radical spirit of the nineties. On the other hand, it would be a mistake to overstress Meredith's sense of his audience's readiness for this theme—he did not, for example, attempt to dramatize the success of Weyburn's and Aminta's joint career in Britain. The fact that they must travel to the land of John Calvin to achieve this end has both its appropriateness and its ironies. And perhaps it is not surprising that in portraying such a resolution Meredith runs into his most serious aesthetic difficulties. Before looking at the resolution, however, I wish to examine the novel's real center of interest— Meredith's treatment of Aminta's slow process of awakening to a sense of mental freedom and genuine selfhood.

3

When we first see Aminta as Lady Ormont through Matey Weyburn's eyes, she is distant and cold, seeking safety in the definition

implied by the title, Countess of Ormont. In an amusing sequence
in Chapter 4 (18:60–67), Weyburn is unnerved as he recognizes
the eyes, then the voice of "this tall and stately lady of the proud
reserve" (18:67); he is trying to persuade himself that Lady Ormont could not be Aminta when she breaks the spell by asking
about a mutual school friend. The school friend and Weyburn, it
turns out, are planning to establish a progressive school in Switzerland, but at this point Aminta, as Countess of Ormont, "clearly . . .
could not understand enthusiasm for the schoolmaster's career"
(18:69). Weyburn's response to this narrowness is characteristic of
him at his best: "He admired her for not concealing her disdain of
the aspirant schoolmaster, quite comprehending, by sympathy, why
the woman should reproach the girl who had worshipped heroes, if
this was a full-grown specimen. . . . He spared the girl, but he
laughed at the woman he commended, laughed at himself"
(18:80).

Such a passage suggests, even at this relatively early point in the
text, that Matey has his moments of being an agent for the spirit of
critical intelligence. But like other Meredithian *raisonneur* figures
he tends to come on a bit stiffly, partly because we see very little of
his having to win his right-thinking through experience; also, aspirant schoolmaster that he is, he does have a tendency to lecture at
times. Aminta is clearly the more interesting and central figure as
we see her contending with her extraordinarily difficult position
and moving in the direction of emancipation. As the novel progresses, Weyburn in effect becomes her schoolmaster while her
changing attitudes toward teaching and school, appropriately
enough, provide strategic markers to her development. However,
this aspect of her relations with Matey also has its disturbing qualities and, as I will discuss shortly, helps to explain much of the un-
easiness one experiences with Meredith's handling of the novel's
resolution.

Through the first half of *Lord Ormont* terms like "toneless,"
"languor," and "stupefaction" are used to characterize Aminta's
state of mind in the present, while her dreams of the past are
"abodes of bloom and briny vigour." She daydreams in Chapter 6,
"In a Mood of Languor," setting a pattern of mental escape that is
to be repeated several times. Sea imagery associated with Aminta's
love of swimming and boating is combined with memories of school
and Matey's "godlike figure of young manhood"; "Memory had of
late been paying visits to a droopy plant in the golden summer

drought on a gorgeous mid-sea island, and had taken her on board to refresh her with voyages, always bearing down full sail on a couple of blissful schools" (18:89–90). The thought of Weyburn in the present, as secretary and aspirant schoolmaster, by contrast, "involved her in the burlesque of the transformation" and causes her "to quench memory. She was, therefore, having smothered a good part of herself, accountably languid" (18:90). "Lady Ormont," then, is directly at odds with the more essential self connected with school and Weyburn. Conscious quenching and smothering, like Matey's mental attempt to "stop the dance," is no match for the force of the subconscious that Meredith here is intent on dramatizing as an intuitive source of wisdom—in Aminta's case, as an escape from stupefaction.

When Matey and Aminta meet again much later, after Aminta has nursed Weyburn's mother on her deathbed, we find Aminta's intuitive sense growing stronger under Mrs. Weyburn's influence. When Matey refers to his mother's views on " 'men and women. . . . and about marriage' "—views on women's rights to divorce and equality that are clearly Meredithian—"Aminta shook herself out of a sudden stupor." She notes that Mrs. Weyburn, like herself, had " 'regretted his not being a soldier. . . . Then she learned to think he could do more for the world as the schoolmaster' " (18:176). The next step is Aminta's longing " 'to talk over the future school with you' " and to " 'be the friends we—You will not be formal with me?—not from this day?' " With this appeal for *tutoiement*, Aminta tentatively attempts escape from the confines of her identity as Lady Ormont, but at such close quarters the vision of escape and its attendant water imagery necessarily suggests peril rather than comfort: "Their hands fell apart. They looked. The old schooltime was in each mind. They saw it as a shore-bank in grey outline across morning mist. Years were between; and there was a division of circumstance, more repelling than an abyss or the rush of deep wild waters" (18:177).

From this point on we see Aminta's mind at work, following out the implications of intuitions that will no longer bear suppression. Ormont is recognized both as "her masterful lord" and "a gilt weather cock" (18:178) and the fact that "she had changed. . . . gave her full view of the compliant coward she had been" (18:179). But in another sense—that of Aminta's essential self—it is not change but continuity that is significant: Browny is Aminta, Matey is Weyburn. In a striking mental sequence suggesting this revelation, Aminta is described in a moment of similtaneity, past and present, girl and woman:

> she turned a corner, on a sudden, in her mind, and ran against a mirror, wherein a small figure running up to meet her, grew large and nodded, with the laugh and eyes of Browny. So little had she changed! The steadfast experienced woman rebuked that volatile, and some might say, faithless girl. But the girl had her answer: she declared they were one and the same, affirmed that the years between were a bad night's dream, that her heart had been faithful, that he who conjures visions of romance in a young girl's bosom must always have her heart, as a crisis will reveal it to her. She had the volubility of the mettled Browny of old, and was lectured. When she insisted on shouting 'Matey! Matey!' she was angrily spurned and silenced. (18:179–80)

The woman's resistance to the child gradually gives way to embrace as she begins to openly resist her subservience to and absorption in Ormont: "Aminta's pride of being chafed at the yoke of marriage" (18:196). A few pages later this recognition of an emerging self takes the form of a daydream sequence which, moving in and out of narrated monologue, renders Aminta's mental stream as she throws off the remnants of the Countess of Ormont:

> She would take the girls, Matthew Weyburn the boys. She had lessons to give to girls, she had sympathy, pity, anticipation. That would be a life of happy service. . . . Aminta was launching a dream of a lass she had seen in a field, near a white hawthorn, standing upright. . . . [with] stately air, gallant ease, and splendour of pose. Matthew Weyburn would have admired the girl. Aminta did better than envy, she cast off the last vestiges of her bitter ambition to be a fine lady, and winged into the bosom of the girl, and not shyly said "yes" to Matthew Weyburn, and to herself, deep in herself: "A maid has no need to be shy." Hardly blushing, she walks on into the new life beside him, and hears him say: "I in my way, you in yours; we are equals, the stronger for being equals," and she quite agrees, and she gives him the fuller heart for his not requiring her to be absorbed—she is the braver mate for him. . . .
> Reason whispered a reminder of facts to her.
> "But I am not the Countess of Ormont!" she said. She felt herself the girl, her sensations were so intensely simple. (18:201–2)

Here in explicit form is the position towards which Meredith had been moving since the beginning of his literary career. The stress on equality between the sexes and maintenance of individual identity—"herself, deep in herself"—also anticipates what were to be some of the primary concerns of D. H. Lawrence. But just as in Lawrence, the dramatization may work out somewhat differently from the declared precept, creating, to borrow from Jacques Derrida, a "*différance*" produced by critical reading that can be both disturbing and illuminating. Rupert Birkin in *Women in Love* goes on at length about his desire for equality between man and woman, "a pure balance of two single beings,"[10] but the relationship we see developing between Birkin and Ursula Brangwen may be read as suggesting that some are more equal than others. The degree to which Lawrence "commands . . . [or] does not command" this disjunction between "declaration" and "description"[11] is, of course, impossible to define precisely. In the case of *Lord Ormont*, however, one may make the point about *différance* even more emphatically. One sees, first, that the contrast between Ormont and Weyburn is established in black and white in Aminta's eyes. Weyburn's "was the larger view. Her lord's view appeared similar to that of her aunt's 'throned Ottoman Turk on his divan.' Matthew Weyburn believed in the bettering of the world; Lord Ormont had no belief like it" (18:201). Aminta's turning from Ormont to Weyburn, then, is a turning away from absorption in Ormont's aristocratic identity and the self-serving male standards of the past as she moves to embrace a relationship premised on equality, fulfillment of individual identity, and a vision of a better future. So much for the declaration. The description or, better, dramatization—what we see acted out in the last third of *Lord Ormont* as Aminta and Weyburn move together—cannot be summed up quite so neatly.

4

On her own, Aminta is shown to have substantial courage and a firm sense of newfound independence. It is important, for example, that she writes Ormont about her leaving him before she meets Matey in the famous "Marine Duet" scene that precedes "The Plighting" (Chapter 28). The sentimentality I have previously mentioned tends to arise in its most problematic form when the two lovers are together. An image occurring during the long chase sequence in which Weyburn rescues her from various dangers begins to suggest the problem: "Aminta was passive as a water-weed in the sway of the tide" (18:242). This passivity before Weyburn's expertise—whether in evading pursuing coaches or in making pronouncements about progressive curricula and right conduct—becomes more than a bit exasperating to the twenty-first-century reader who would like to see more of Aminta's awakening intelligence asserted in Weyburn's presence. This response might be inappropriate if Meredith did not make us anticipate precisely such qualities in Aminta's dream sequences and in her extraordinarily brave decision to leave Ormont, with or without Weyburn. But what we have with Weyburn and Aminta together is something very like the male hero-worship that the novel initially seems to set out to criticize.

Barbara Hardy makes an interesting point when she speculates that our liking of Meredith may not be

> because he is really less sentimental . . . than Dickens and George Eliot, but because he is sentimental about different things. His is the sentimentality of the 1890s, which still has a certain appealing, if diminishing, affinity with our own: it tends to be strongly affirmative about youth rather than babies, about sex rather than true love, about the right relationship rather than the perfect marriage, about nature rather than God, feminism rather than womanliness, discovery of identity rather than the moral change of heart. We might want to say that Meredith's beliefs are progressive, or *avant-garde* in the double sense that implies both courage and progress, but his ninetyish *avant-garde* sentimentality is still sentimentality. He can become as ludicrously ecstatic, soft and blurred on the subjects of feminism, England and co-education as Dickens could on the subjects of womanly virtue, religion and child-death. It is this sentimentality which marks Meredith at his worst, and whose triumphant absence marks him at his best.[12]

Most of the Meredithian values Hardy mentions are also Weyburn's values. These values are not inherently sentimental, of course; it is the treatment that creates the tone, and the tone becomes most sentimental exactly when Aminta is most uncritically subservient to Weyburn. The damaging point, then, is that Aminta trades one kind of subservience for another. Her adulation of Weyburn is no doubt immensely preferable to her adulation of Ormont. And we may feel drawn to Weyburn's ideas and admire his translation of progressivism into action, but the problem of sentimental tone linked with Aminta's Matey-worship, especially in the novel's denouement, remains a seriously damaging one, a distinct source of our uneasy critical awareness of *"différance."*

A late scene, occurring before Aminta takes her leave of Ormont, will illustrate the kind of tone I refer to. In Chapter 24, Matey and Aminta spend "a day of sheer gold" (18:292) on and by the upper reaches of the Thames. The scene is reminiscent of the Ferdinand and Miranda sequence in *Richard Feverel*, both in its use of natural imagery to evoke an aura of romance—"Thames played round them on his pastoral pipes," etc. (18:285)—and in its stylistic excesses. The water imagery links the scene with the earlier treatments of the Matey-Aminta relationship, and it also contributes directly to the evocation of sentimental hero-worship:

> Love . . . was teaching her to know the good and bad of herself. Women [are] educated to embrace principles. . . . [and] the principles depend much on the beloved. . . . [If he is] a man whose contact with the world has given him understanding of life's laws, and can hold him firm to the right course in the strain and whirling of a torrent, they cling to him, deeply they worship. . . . Her faith in his guidance was equal to her dependence. The retrospect of a recent journey told her how he had been tried.
> She could gaze tenderly, betray her heart, and be certain of safety. Can wine match that for joy? She had no schemes, no hopes, but simply the desire to bestow, the capacity to believe. Any wish to be enfolded by him was shapeless and unlighted, unborn. (18:281–82)

The operative word here is "dependence," while we have been schooled by the novel so far to view Aminta's awakening to positive identity as a break from dependence. Indeed, all of Weyburn's theorizing on equal relationships between boys and girls seems bent in the direction of fostering independence.

As the passage goes on matters get worse: "Intellectually, morally, she had to bow humbly. Nor had she, nor could she do more than lean on and catch example from, his prompt spiritual valiancy. It shone out from him, and a crisis fulfilled the promise. Who could be his mate for cheerful courage, for skill, the ready mind, easy adroitness, and for self-command? To imitate was a woman's utmost" (18:283). We are reassured two pages later that Weyburn "is the brother of women" because "he is neither sentimentalist nor devourer" (18:285), and this may, to a degree, be demonstrably true from the text. What is equally true, however, is that such a narrative declaration inevitably increases our discomfort with what is, precisely, an "ecstatic, soft and blurred" vision of Matey. We are told, in a typical sentimental oversimplification, that "he is just—he is Justice," while Ormont "was unjust—he was Injustice" (18:285), even though the text is already showing Ormont's growth in fair-mindedness (e.g. 18:252). The argument might be made that these "arrows of thoughts [that] . . . shot over . . . Aminta's mind" (18:286) are intended to have ironical effect, showing how far she has yet to go in reaching mature and fulfilled identity, but the approving tone of the text simply does not support this reading. The implied author, as far as we can tell, stands squarely with Aminta's effusions; our sense of *"différance,"* then, joins in this case with our sense that the narrative is out of control.

When we move to a scene in which Weyburn and Aminta discuss the very point at issue—equality between the sexes—the sentimental tone again enters to suggest something quite different from egalitarianism. Matey lectures on "education in common," while Aminta asks appropriate questions:

> "Would [education in common] increase their mutual respect? . . . ."
> "In time, under management; catching and grouping them young. A boy who sees a girl do what he can't, and would like to do, won't take refuge in his muscular superiority—which, by the way, would be lessened."
> "You suppose their capacities are equal?"
> "Things are not equal. I suppose their excellencies to make a pretty near equal sum in the end. But we're not weighing them each. The question concerns the advantage of both."
> "That seems just!"
> Aminta threw no voice into the word "just." It was the word of the heavens assuaging earth's thirst, and she was earth to him. Her soul yearned to the man whose mind conceived it. (18:288)

One might contrast this entire scene with Jane Austen's handling of the Box Hill episode in *Emma* (III, 7): Emma Woodhouse and Frank Churchill are made to discuss "self-command" at the same time Austen brilliantly dramatizes the gradual loss of self-command that finally allows Emma to insult Miss Bates. The tension created between what the characters say and what their tone and actions show allows the reader to see Emma's moral dilemma—her misreadings of Churchill, herself, her entire society—with extraordinary clarity. This scene, in fact, could be taken as an example of what Edward Said has described as a text whose "deconstruction has already been begun self-consciously by the novelist and by the novel . . . ; the text commands and indeed permits, invents, . . .

its misinterpretations and misreadings, which are functions of the text."[13] In the just quoted scene between Matey and Aminta, however, the opposite is true. The tension is there: Aminta subscribes to Matey's egalitarian precepts and, at the same time, "bows humbly" and "imitates" his male superiority, but the dramatic irony works to obscure rather than to clarify. And the obfuscation does not stop there. The last paragraph of this passage also strongly suggests a recurrent problem directly connected with Meredithian indulgence in sentiment—turgidity of style: here the water imagery gushes a bit out of control. The paragraph, moreover, with its echo of the Song of Songs, sounds like certain passages in *The Rainbow* and reminds us again of Meredith's strong—and not always positive—influence on Lawrence, who was also given to stylistic excesses in moments of unguarded enthusiasm.

5

Sentiment, then, is at odds with Meredithian critical intelligence in *Lord Ormont* in what appear to be both intended and unintended ways. The development of the identity theme, so central to the novel's strengths, is blurred when sentiment takes over. But Meredith does sporadically reassert control over his materials as *Lord Ormont* moves to its close. "A Marine Duet" (Chapter 27), in which the lovers swim together and perform a mock marriage ceremony before Triton, effectively recapitulates the novel's water imagery and links the significance of names with the assertion of positive adult identity. Reestablishing their connection with the past, the pair address one another as Matey and Browny, and then, discarding the childhood names, for the first time they call one another by their "proper Christian names," Matthew and Aminta (18:324). Further, Meredith shows us that these two, unlike Victor Radnor and Nataly Dreighton, clearly confront together the implications of their decision and acknowledge full responsibility for their actions. Critical intelligence, as a tempered balance of Meredithian blood, brain, and spirit, is for the moment in the ascendent: "Rationally and irrationally, the mixed passion and reason in two clear heads and urgent hearts discussed the stand they made before a world defied" (18:332–33).

The oversimplifications and ambiguities associated with the novel's sentimentality, however, continue to reappear to the very end.

Almost the last thing we hear Aminta say to Weyburn, for example, occurs at their Swiss school during a brief exchange in French: " 'Je suis, comme toujours, aux ordres de Monsieur' " (18:353). Her statement sums up the subservient side of her character and allows it to dominate our final impression. More damaging, however, to use Barbara Hardy's term, is the "blurred" quality of Meredith's attempts to suggest the physical side of the relationship. We have already seen in Chapter 24 that Aminta's thoughts about what the narrator calls "enfolding" are "shapeless and unlighted, unborn" (18:282). In the swimming scene in Chapter 27, the two dive together and we are coyly told, in a Fieldingesque aside, that "there is no history of events below the surface" (18:324). But it is in the novel's last pages that the "unlighted" quality of these asides becomes problematic—problematic because the narrator seems to try to tell us more at the same time the sentimental diction, by its indirection, obscures the effort. After Aminta has watched from the window of her home at the school as Weyburn and Ormont converse for the first time in seven years, she sees Ormont leave; then "her arm was pressed by a hand. Weyburn longed to enfold her and she desired it, and her soul praised him for refraining. Both had that delicacy" (18:352). One is prompted to ask, perhaps with some indelicacy, what is the nature of this "delicacy"? Does it merely suggest Ormont's unexpected visit has caused them to keep separate for the moment? (We are told, incidentally, that "a series of geometrical figures [were] shooting across her brain, mystically expressive of the situation, not communicably. The most vivid and persistent was a triangle. Interpret who may" [18:351–52].) Or does this "delicacy" mean that for seven years Weyburn and Aminta, conscious of their triangular situation, have lived together without "enfolding"? "Interpret who may" indeed!

When the magnanimous letter from Ormont arrives, enrolling his grandnephew in the school and, by implication, forgiving all, we are exposed to more of the same kind of evasive rhetoric and ambiguity:

Weyburn and Aminta were strolling to the playground, thinking in common, as they usually did. They read the letter together. . . .

The two raised eyes on one another, pained in their deep joy by the religion of the restraint upon their hearts, to keep down the passion to embrace.

"I thank heaven we know him to be one of the true noble men," said

Aminta, now breathing, and thanking Lord Ormont for the free breath she drew. (18:353)

This is the kind of passage for which the term "literary abomination" might come to mind, and for a number of important reasons. We not only have to contend with the lovers "thinking in common" and reading in common, but also with the absolute nobility of all parties, including the transmogrified Ormont. But the most vexing aspect, once again, is the nature of that "religion of the restraint upon their hearts" that brings both pain and "deep joy." What kind of lovers are these? The question is posed by yet another "gap in the text," a blank that could bring about the clarifying mental "activity required of the reader as he produces the meaning of the novel,"[14] but which in this case grows larger the more one examines it, the result being the production of obscurity rather than meaning. If the "restraint" is a temporary gesture due to Ormont's proximity, such restraint is difficult to explain after his departure. If, on the other hand, the restraint is of seven years' duration, then a very complicated aspect of the relationship is being passed off as noble and uncomplicated.[15] The overall effect of this final scene becomes one of sentimental reduction and the full-dimensional quality of Aminta's character one encounters earlier in the novel— especially in the daydream sequences—is lost.

All this is to say that Meredith is indeed occasionally "at his worst" in *Lord Ormont* precisely at the times when he is most sentimental. But I would also maintain that this novel allows us to understand the perils of Meredithian sentimentalism more clearly—both as novelistic subject and as authorial self-indulgence; in addition, we see Meredith for the first time struggling to develop a portrait of a young woman who asserts her hidden self through a clear break from a bad marriage. It is not a full portrait of such a process, however, principally because, as we have seen, Meredith lapses into the kind of sentimentalism that allows Aminta to trade one form of subservience for another, or that blurs the implications of adultery by the rhetoric of a "religion of restraint." For a more satisfying treatment of a similar process of feminine assertion of subjectivity through marital revolt, we must turn to the portrait of Carinthia Kirby in Meredith's last completed novel, *The Amazing Marriage*.

7

The Amazing Marriage and the Construction of Feminine Identity

Wᴴɪʟᴇ MEREDITH'S PORTRAIT OF AMINTA FARRELL'S PROGRESS TOWARD fulfillment in *Lord Ormont and His Aminta* remains somewhat problematic, the history of Carinthia Kirby in *The Amazing Marriage* (1895) moves considerably further in the direction of a full portrait of feminine self-determination. The central concern of this last completed novel, set for the most part in the 1830s, is to depict the struggles involved in the successful establishment of a strong, assertive, self-reliant feminine subject. Like Aminta, Carinthia is depicted as being charmed into marriage at an early age by an experienced man of the world who proves to be the embodiment of Meredithian egoism. Also like Aminta, Carinthia's growing sense of her need to break from this marriage acts as an index to the development of her identity. Where Carinthia moves beyond Aminta and other Meredithian female protagonists is in the degree to which she is ready, by the second half of the novel, to make her own decisions. And yet it is also in this area that we again see a tension at work: in Carinthia's relation to her brother Chillon there are elements of the same kind of reverential deference to the towering male one finds, finally, in all of Meredith's—and most Victorian—heroines. As in *Lord Ormont*, we see marital revolt translated at times into the substitution of one male authority figure for another. When Carinthia leaves Fleetwood, it is to follow her brother in the ill-fated British Auxiliary Legion expedition to the Carlist wars in Spain (fall, 1835). But Meredith is also much less insistent here about this kind of feminine deference than he is in his earlier fiction, and at the novel's end Carinthia has become the most fully integrated and self-possessed young woman in the canon, a female hero whose gradual understanding and subsequent rejection of the possessive implications of Victorian marriage are made to signal her coming into her own.

Meredith's stress early in *The Amazing Marriage* is on Carinthia's pastoral innocence. She has been brought up by her expatriate English parents in the eastern Austrian Alps—her name, in fact, acts as a reminder throughout the novel of this origin and its Meredithian associations of rural freedom and openness. We are told, further, that "England, though [Carinthia] was of British blood, was a foreign place to her, not alluring" (19:33). And this foreignness—her role as "pastoral outsider,"[1] as Barbara Hardy has put it—remains central to our understanding of Carinthia's progress in Britain as she has to learn and evaluate the intricacies of English convention. Henrietta Fakenham, the society woman who eventually marries Chillon, sums up Carinthia's anomalous position in relation to society succinctly: " 'It's impossible to dislike her. Oh! she is wild! She knows absolutely nothing of the world. She can do everything we can't—or don't dare to try.' " And the response of Henrietta's cousin, Livia, adds to our sense of Carinthia's displacement of ordinary society values: " 'Carinthia! She's well fitted with her name. What with her name and her hair and her build and her singular style of attire, one wonders at her coming into civilized parts. She's utterly unlike Chillon' " (19:115). Carinthia's "uncivilized" qualities, then, help to explain her charm—her fresh lack of conventional responses—*and* her vulnerability in a society which her very different brother navigates with skillful conventionality.

We first encounter Carinthia and Chillon in Chapter 4 as they set out for England after the death of their parents. Carinthia's future is a recurrent topic between them, and she strikes the keynote of her personality when she tells her brother, " 'I hate anything that robs me of my will' " (19:40); he counters a little later with *his* view of her proper role—she should " 'marry, and be a blessing to a husband' "(19:47). As we shall see, the novel is full of males who wish to construct their own versions of Carinthia's identity, and in this case Chillon's notion of her future role as beatific subordination to a husband has a clear purpose: not only to save her from the parsimonious inattention of their maternal uncle and her guardian, Lord Levellier, but also to take her off Chillon's hands. Maintaining her vague but intent wish for freedom, Carinthia proposes a nursing career as an alternative to conventional marital domesticity, saying, " 'a plain girl should think of work to earn independence' "(19:52). Chillon characteristically laughs at this idea, although by the novel's end he is ready to accept it when it suits his own plans. At this early point, Carinthia's nursing ambitions are linked with her wish to "be near her brother [who is a soldier] to

nurse him in case of wounds. . . . That was her meaning, involved
with the hazy project of earning an independence; but she could
not explain it, and Chillon set her down for one of the inexplicable
sex, which the simple adventurous girl had not previously seemed
to be" (19:52–53). The conflict between Chillon's conventionality
and Carinthia's innocent freedom from conventionality, then, is
well established here, along with Carinthia's clear need to develop
her powers of analysis—to link critical intelligence with her intu-
itional strengths.[2]

All this is dramatized in interesting fashion when brother and sister meet a fellow-countryman on their alpine path—Gower Woodseer, modeled in part on Meredith's friend and fellow nature
enthusiast, Robert Louis Stevenson. Temporarily disabled by a fall,
Woodseer is the first of many figures in the novel to whom Carinthia instinctively "was the Samaritan," while Chillon, especially
after hearing that Woodseer's father is a bootmaker, carefully keeps
his distance. When they separate, she "frankly extend[s] her open
hand" to Woodseer and refers to him as a "gentleman." Chillon
is prompted by this openness to instruct Carinthia in some of the
rudiments of Anglo-Saxon reserve: " 'Don't give your hand when
you are meeting or parting with people: it's not done' "(19:61); further, "he would have liked to inform her, for the sake of educating
her in the customs of the world she was going to enter, that the
word 'gentleman' conveys in English a special signification" and,
finally, she is told that " 'you meet people of your own class; you
don't meet others' "(19:63). Convention, then, is a set of arbitrary
rules, linguistic and otherwise, that must be assimilated by Carinthia in order to divest herself of her "foreignness"—the "wild" and
"uncivilized" qualities that allow her to respond warmly and directly to Woodseer and his difficulties. Not surprisingly, the degree
to which Carinthia is able to continue her "foreign" directness and
humanity in response to the demands of convention will be a mark
of the maintenance and development of her integrity as the novel
proceeds.

Meredith has come up with an effective strategy here: Carinthia's English/non-English status allows him to dramatize her adult
development as substantially more autonomous than that of her
predecessors. Her questioning of any convention that seems irrational or inhumane grows quite plausibly out of this special status,
which also includes the early influence of her highly unorthodox
expatriot parents, who are the subject of "Dame Gossip's" exuber-

ant monologue in the opening three chapters. All this prepares for Meredith's central preoccupation in *The Amazing Marriage*—the process by which its female hero may develop a strong, independent sense of feminine identity in the Britain of the 1830s, a problem that was, of course, much more topical in 1879 when Meredith began the novel and especially so in 1895 when he finished it. The way in which he developed this question was to explore Carinthia's confrontation with British society, particularly as embodied in the person of the Earl of Fleetwood. Fleetwood functions in social terms much as Victor Radnor and Lord Ormont do in that he represents society and its limitations at the same time he is socially alienated; this sense of alienation draws Fleetwood to Carinthia and prompts the abrupt, and later regretted, proposal of marriage which she, equally abruptly and unconventionally, accepts. It is this "amazing marriage" that provides the true testing ground for Carinthia's character.

2

The testing is prepared for early in the novel when Fleetwood also encounters Gower Woodseer in his alpine wanderings and, ignoring class distinctions, takes him on as a traveling companion. Fleetwood's unconventional behavior, however, is shown to be in large part a function of his enormous wealth—he can afford to indulge in the "eccentrics" and "heterodox ideas" that Chillon's "soldierly and social training opposed" (19:62). But the matter of real significance here is the way in which both Woodseer and Fleetwood initially respond to Carinthia. No less than Chillon, they too attempt to impose on her their own constructions of her essence. Fleetwood's introduction to Carinthia is through Woodseer's entries in his hiking notebook where she is self-consciously described in oxymoronic terms—"beautiful Gorgon, haggard Venus"—or as a manifestation of nature—"the rock that loses the sun at night and reddens in the morning" (19:79). And this reduction of "Carinthia to an abstract enthusiasm" is precisely what appeals to the world- (and woman-) weary Fleetwood: " 'You have done what I thought impossible—fused a woman's face and grand scenery. . . . I should think her sacred' "(19:79).

When Fleetwood later sees Carinthia for the first time, he does not know who she is, but instinctively defines her as "a sort of Carinthia—a sister, cousin, one of the family" (19:122). As he watches her skillfully climbing the forest trail above him, he experiences his own brand of abstract enthusiasm and produces a stream of definitions, some of which have a basis in fact, others of which are wildly off the mark:

> She was a German girl, apparently. . . . Her face and bearing might really be taken to symbolize the forest life . . . , a noble daughter of the woods. . . .
>
> Fleetwood recalled the strange girl's face. There was in it a savage poignancy in serenity unexampled among women—or modern women. One might imagine an apotheosis of a militant young princess of Goths or Vandals, the glow of blessedness awakening her martial ardours through the languor of the grave:—Woodseer would comprehend and hit on the exact image to portray her in a moment, Fleetwood thought, and longed for that fellow. (19:121–22)

While both men sense Carinthia's extraordinary qualities, including her remarkable affinity to the natural scene, they use her primarily as a departure point for romantic and "poetic" effusions that have only marginal connection with Carinthia herself. In other words, both play apparently harmless mental and linguistic games with Carinthia's identity, games of the same sort we find "Dame Gossip" playing with various characters, including Fleetwood himself, in her romantic and sentimental sections of the narrative. Joseph Warren Beach notes that while the "Modern Novelist" "wishes to analyze the motives of the Earl of Fleetwood and lay bare the spring of his perverse actions, 'Dame Gossip prefers to ejaculate, Young men are mysteries! and bowl us onward. No one ever did comprehend the Earl of Fleetwood, she says'" (19:295). Beach goes on to say that "these are the cajoleries of sentimentalism, the willful blindness of a lazy mind. These are the delusions that make men ludicrous if not vicious. Lord Fleetwood has the same easy way of disposing of his motives."[3] But as the novel proceeds, the viciousness inherent in Fleetwood's sentimental obscurantism becomes increasingly evident, as does the inadequacy of any single narrative—or reader's—view that refuses the opportunities for understanding "motives" provided by Fleetwood's self-serving and -absorbed career. While making Dame Gossip's method of non-analytical story telling attractive (as Lionel Stevenson has noted, the text "succeeded marvelously in imitating the intonation of a garrulous old woman"[4]), Meredith's dual narrative in *The Amazing*

Marriage always maintains our edgy awareness that complexity and indeterminacy are an inevitable part of what this novel has to offer us—in this case including the tensions inevitably created between traditional and "modern" modes of reading the world.[5]

Perhaps the most revealing part of the scene I have just mentioned is found in Meredith's description of Fleetwood's parting glimpse of Carinthia as she displays a formidable bit of mountain-climbing sangfroid. This moment is significant partly because it sets the pattern for a series of later scenes in which Carinthia handles a difficult situation—a mad dog, an injured child, a lamb trapped dangerously out of reach—with assured self-command, while Fleetwood plays the essentially passive role of awestruck onlooker. The pattern is rather like that developed by Jane Austen in *Persuasion*, where Anne Elliot is shown in several awkward or dangerous moments—culminating in the famous scene on the Cobb at Lyme Regis—to have a commendably cool head when others, including Frederick Wentworth, are more or less inert. The main point is that both heroines demonstrate remarkable competence in situations that are found to be incapacitating by their male counterparts. In the scene at hand, Carinthia is viewed at a distance by Fleetwood:

> She was tempted to adventure by a projected forked head of a sturdy blunted and twisted little rock-fostered forest tree pushing horizontally for growth about thirty feet above the lower ground. She looked on it, and took a step down to the stem soon after. . . .
>
> And now a shameful spasm of terror seized him at sight of a girl doing what he would have dreaded to attempt. She footed coolly, well-balanced, upright. She seated herself. (120–21)

Meredith and Austen, in their own ways, play on the paradox of how admiration of this sort may also lead to prolonged, pain-inducing neglect. Both Wentworth and Fleetwood, of course, eventually realize the errors of their inattention, but while Austen directs her characters to her invariable rationally romantic and marital resolution, Meredith proceeds in just the opposite direction. Late in the novel he dramatizes Carinthia's hard-earned maturity through her rejection of Fleetwood, his mistreatment of her, and their marriage—at the very time his admiration is finally taking a more substantial form and curing neglect.

As we have seen, Fleetwood's early view of Carinthia is filtered through a self-consciously literary and "artistic" mode of perception which, along with his restless and directionless bearing, the "Modern Novelist" alerts us to view critically from early on. Fleetwood's sentimental idealization of Carinthia as a symbol of nature or as a militant tribal princess, his spasm of terror and dread— suggestive of a carefully cultivated sense of the sublime—are all part of a self-regarding response that shows him far more interested in himself than in her. Such solipsism is shown to become problematic, however, only when Fleetwood afterward proposes marriage; it is then that we may begin to see fully how his increasing inability to come to terms with Carinthia's quotidian reality is specifically prepared for by this early scene.

The physical arrangement of Carinthia and Fleetwood in this first encounter is also significant: standing alone and below, he admires her performance, shudders, and indulges in fantasies from a safe distance, seeing her as he chooses—larger than life and without contradiction. In this respect Meredith is portraying the attractions and perils of the romanticizing imagination in some of the same ways that Walter Scott does. Scott's first novel, for example, is a work primarily about the disabilities induced by an overly literary and romantic sensibility. The connection is particularly clear in a scene that occurs one-third of the way through *Waverley* in which Edward Waverley is shown as an awed spectator of feminine agility in a way strikingly similar to Fleetwood's vision of Carinthia's casual mountain expertise. In the scene in question, Waverley has recently been introduced into the north and is still unaccustomed to his Highland surroundings. He is looking for Flora MacIvor, whom he has already identified as the woman of his dreams. He then sees a pair of pine trees laid across a chasm forming a narrow bridge high above him:

> While gazing at this pass of peril, which crossed, like a single black line, the small portion of blue sky not intercepted by the projecting rocks on either side, it was with a sensation of horror that Waverley beheld Flora and her attendant appear, like inhabitants of another region, propped, as it were, in mid air, upon this trembling structure. She stopped upon observing him below, and, with an air of graceful ease which made him shudder, waved her handkerchief to him by way of signal. He was unable, from the sense of dizziness which her situation conveyed, to return the salute; and was never more relieved than when the fair apparition passed on from the precarious eminence which she seemed to occupy with so much indifference, and disappeared on the other side.[6]

The primary contrast in both scenes is between purposeful feminine agility and masculine passivity, a contrast that highlights essentials in the characters of all four figures. Waverley and Fleetwood are both without real direction or purpose, while the controlled movements of both women suggest the skilled possession of these qualities. The actual situation in both cases is, of course, more complicated. Flora's chosen direction is with the Jacobite Rebellion of 1745, which she knows to be doomed, while Carinthia's direction early in the novel is more theoretical than concrete. But both women, within the limits of their circumstances, are models in whom their wavering male counterparts discover qualities they themselves not only lack, but also willfully misinterpret. For much of Scott's novel, Waverley's confused romanticizing results in his failure to comprehend the social, political—even chronological—complexities represented by Flora and her brother Fergus, while Fleetwood also continues to prefer his daydream vision of Carinthia, especially as opposed to the more difficult facts of marital existence that soon replace it. Both novelists, then, highlight the dangerous escapism of their male protagonists in contrast to female heroes who are repeatedly shown to have great competence in dealing with life's realities.

But just as revealing as the similarities between Scott's and Meredith's treatment of this contrast are the differences: Scott shows the very qualities in Flora that attract Waverley—her independence, her capacity for political activism, her fearlessness, her alien nature—hopelessly mired in a political and social cause that is trying to reinvent the past, a past that is at once attractive and, finally, forbidden in Scott's nineteenth-century Unionist context. Meredith shows these same qualities in Carinthia with contrasting effect: her instinctive good sense compels her in the end to disencumber herself from the cause (her marriage) that mires her in the past. As with Aminta, she "is absolved of all duty toward a husband too egoistic to accept her as an equal partner."[7] Scott, on the other hand, condemns Flora to end her heterodox career in religious retirement; in Meredith's novel this is, precisely, the end reserved for Fleetwood after he has failed in his efforts to preserve patriarchal authority. While there are some striking parallels between Scott's and Meredith's female protagonists, then, their careers lead them, finally, in exactly opposite directions. And while Scott's resolution focuses on preservation of the Union of England and Scotland in the marriage of Waverley and Rose Bradwardine,

Meredith's resolution provides the radical model of a broken contract of unsatisfactory marriage as the essential means to a fulfilling future for his assertive heroine.

3

As *The Amazing Marriage* progresses, Fleetwood's initial misunderstanding of Carinthia is expanded upon in a number of interesting ways that center on his and her uses of convention—in particular, their uses of language. In his view of language, Fleetwood is shown to be a literalist, much more interested in the letter than in the spirit. While still in Baden, for example, he gives his word that he will attend a ball, then decides that he detests the idea of going. Nonetheless, "he was the prisoner of his word;—rather like the donkeys known as married men. . . . At half-past eleven, the prisoner of his word entered under the Schloss portico, having vowed to himself on the way that he would satisfy the formulas to gain release by a deferential bow to the great personages, and straight-way slip out into the heavenly starlight"(19:122; 124). As it turns out, Fleetwood does not escape before encountering Carinthia's charms at close quarters and, "during their third dance," proposing marriage—all this in spite of his abhorrence of the words "wife," "engaged," and "husband." The disjunction between Fleetwood's sense of language and the significance of his actions lies at the center of his problematic character: he speaks and acts impulsively at one moment, wants to recant the next, and then, with a compulsive reflex of will, forces himself to act just to the point where speech becomes literal truth—"to satisfy the formulas." "His word," once spoken, "binds him" (19:126); "he was renowned and unrivalled as the man of stainless honour: the one living man of his word. He had never broken it—never would. There was his distinction among the herd" (19:153).

Fleetwood, then, is at once conventional, in his reverence for the spoken word as rule of conduct, and unconventional, in the license with which he departs from the word in anything but its literal enactment. The conflict that results from these unprobed and opposed impulses accounts for much of Fleetwood's anguish; his is the unexamined—in Meredith's terms, the "unread"—life. And as Judith Wilt has so well pointed out, what Meredith "wants to make of us all is *readers*, in the comprehensive, tough-souled sense in which he uses the word. . . . For Meredith, reading is the name, not really the metaphor, for the primary human act of mind."[8] Fleetwood's egoism, impulsiveness, and refusal to examine his motives and actions all contribute to an essential illiteracy of the same sort that Dame Gossip prizes in her urge for rapid narration without Meredithian reflection. And it is finally Carinthia who begins to dispel this illiteracy, to challenge him into some semblance of dialogical thinking. She bears "the blame for forcing him to an examination of his conduct at this point and that" (19:297).[9] This last completed novel is no exception to the pattern we have noted from the beginning in *The Shaving of Shagpat*—Meredith's women repeatedly act as the prime movers for the forces of common sense.

Fleetwood's problems with language are most centrally illuminated by his proposal and marriage to Carinthia. "Mad in his impulses, mad in his reading of honour," he sees her as having "ensnared his word. . . . How had it leaped from his mouth? . . .—he was bound. . . . for a slip of his tongue" to "the subjection of a partnership" (19:151). Carinthia, on the other hand, views the linkage between language and action as natural and straightforward: " 'I am bound if I say yes,' " she comments, without any of Fleetwood's self-congratulatory heroics and, we are told, "she is ready to have the fullest faith in the sincerity of his offer" (19:128). Thus Carinthia's relation to convention—and specifically, to "reading" and language—is worked out by Meredith as a positive complement to Fleetwood's failures in literacy. And Carinthia's primary task in dealing with her new experience in England is to become more sophisticated in recognizing the problematic nature of the relationship between language and its referents—specifically, to recognize that her linguistic sincerity is not matched by Fleetwood.

Ironically, it is his sense of Carinthia's difficulties with English idiom and custom that most irritates Fleetwood on the day of their marriage. Forms of address in particular produce results maddening to him—and amusing to the reader. Carinthia, following the logic of a direct connection between signifier and signified, several times calls Fleetwood "my husband," while Fleetwood finds such directness agonizing—even in its absence:

> She did not this time say "my husband," still it flicked a whip at his ears.
> She had made it more offensive, by so richly toning the official title just won from him as to ring it on the nerves; one had to block it or

be invaded. An anticipation that it would certainly recur haunted every opening of her mouth.

Now that it did not, he felt the gap, relieved, and yet pricked to imagine a mimicry of her tones, for the odd foreignness of the word and the sound. . . . "My husband" was a manner of saying "my fish."

He spoke very civilly. "Oblige me by telling me what name you are accustomed to answer to."

She seemed unaware of an Arctic husband, and replied: "My father called me Carin—short for Carinthia. My mother called me Janey; my second name is Jane. My brother Chillon says both." (19:153–54)

For Carinthia, then, naming and language in general are a direct expression of honesty and one's sense of self. When she assumes the same is true for Fleetwood, as here, she puts herself in a vulnerable position; at the same time, his cavalier attempts at irony are made to miss the mark altogether and rebound on himself.

Fleetwood's irritation at "her baby English" does begin to have its effect on Carinthia's alert mind, however: "a curious imitation, gathered she knew not whence, of the word 'husband' on a young wife's lips as being a foreign sound in England, advised her to withhold it. *His behavior was instructing her*" (19:155—italics added). As Carin adapts moment by moment to English custom and the peculiarities of her husband's manner, she proves herself an apt student, recognizing more and more that Fleetwood is not one in whom to confide. When he submits her, immediately after their marriage ceremony, to the utterly confusing spectacle of an English prizefight, she has already learned not to ask him questions, "though the unanswered of her inquisitive ignorance in the strange land pricked painfully at her bosom" (19:166). What she also learns is to direct questions to more willing confidants, such as her new friends Madge Winch, Gower Woodseer, and Owain Wythan, the sympathetic Welshman whom she is to marry at the novel's end.

Further, we learn that her fluency literally extends far beyond Fleetwood's own limits. She speaks not only German and English but also French: " 'I will talk French if you like, for, I think, German you do not speak. I may speak English better than French; but I am afraid of my English with you'" (19:156). By the novel's end, Carinthia is adding Welsh and Spanish to her dialogic repertoire, extending still further her ability to comprehend life's polyphony. Fleetwood, on the other hand, remains linguistically restricted, hearing Welsh, for example, only as "caged monkey lingo" (19:342). It is, in fact, his inability to "read" his Welsh colliers that finally plunges him into the crisis of a strike in his mines, but this dilemma simply provides a backdrop to the novel's more central problem, that posed by his repeated misreadings of his wife.

The remainder of *The Amazing Marriage* depicts the gradual strengthening of Carinthia's sense of identity and self-worth as she deals with the conventions of her new world and contends with prolonged abandonment and mistreatment by Fleetwood. By mid-way we learn that she has ceased to call him "husband" altogether (19:267), recognizing her insistence that he link the word and meaning to have been " 'a madness in me. Now it has gone, I see all round. I see straight, too' " (19:317). Fleetwood, whom Dame Gossip chooses to term "the unreadable earl" (19:284), has by this time become quite readable to the eye of Carinthia's developing critical intelligence. As for the earl himself, he has begun to regret his literal reading of marriage as the most minimally binding of contracts: " 'It is my husband,' " we overhear him thinking, is a "bit of simplicity [that] would bear repeating once. . . . In the grasp of her character, one inclines, and her husband inclines, to become her advocate" (19:320–21).

In chapters 32 and 33, Meredith brings the two together after prolonged separation, producing a central scene that nicely drama-tizes the essential positions reached by each. The scene is set in the Welsh mining village near Fleetwood's estate. Gower Woodseer is Fleetwood's guest, but by this point Gower has progressed beyond his early stages as a youthful seeker of an abstract ideal of the pic-turesque and sublime to a passionate but accurate observer of the concrete in nature—both scenic and human. Fleetwood's charac-teristic response when confronted by concrete reality that disturbs his sense of the ideal has been to turn to escape—nowhere more than in his aborted relations with Carinthia and their child. " 'Such animals these women are!' " he says when Gower presses Carin-thia's case as wife and mother, to which Gower—true Meredithian that he is—responds, " 'You speak that of women and pretend to love Nature. . . . You hate Nature unless you have it served on a dish by your own cook. . . . Women are in and of Nature. I've stud-ied them' " (19:325–26). He has Carinthia specifically in mind, having become her enthusiastic partisan, as he delicately puts it, " 'during her time of endurance' " (19:326). Fleetwood, however, in the narrator's refraction of his mental stream, would like to turn

away from all this: "Petty domestic dissensions are . . . poor webs
to the man pulling single-handed at ropes with his revolted miners.
On the topic of wages, too, he was Gower's master, and could hold
forth: by which he taught himself to feel that practical affairs are
the proper business of men, women and infants being remotely sec-
ondary" (19:330).

But "practical affairs," like domestic affairs, hold Fleetwood's
shifting attention only briefly. In the next breath he announces that
he is off for a yachting trip to the Hebrides, only to lament that because of the voyage he cannot go hiking with Gower through the
Malvern Hills—"'We're never free to do as we like'"—and then,
about to leave, he announces to his foreman, "'If the mines are
closed, more's the pity: but I'm not responsible. You can let them
know if you like, before I drive off; it doesn't matter to me'"
(19:331). Precisely at this point of moral self-revelation on Fleetwood's part, Carinthia, and the baby he has never seen, make their
appearance.

Chapter 32, in which these events take place, displays Carinthia
in her full powers, providing a series of strong contrasts to Fleetwood's nervous, divided consciousness. And Meredith emphasizes
these contrasts throughout the chapter by again using a strategically important narrative device: we see Carinthia through Fleetwood's eyes as we move in and out of narrated monologue, a
technique that makes us aware not only of her development but
also of his fragmentary, biased perception of that development
as he begins to read beyond his preconceived notions of who Carinthia is:

Carinthia came on at her bold mountain stride to within hail of him.
Met by Gower, she talked, smiled, patted her donkey, clutched his ear,
lifted a silken covering to show the child asleep; entirely at her ease and
unhurried. These women get an aid from their pride of maternity. And
when they can boast a parson behind them, they are indecorous up to
insolent to their ostentation of it.
    She resumed her advance, with a slight abatement of her challenging
march, sedately; very collectedly erect; changed in the fullness of her
figure and her poised calm bearing. . . .
    She stood before him. There was on his part an insular representa-
tion of old French court salute to the lady, and she replied to it in the
exactest measure, as if an instructed proficient. . . .
    Her face was not the chalk-quarry or the rosed rock; it was oddly in-
dividual, and, in a way, alluring, with some gentle contraction of her

eyelids. But evidently she stood in full repose, mistress of herself. (19:332–33)

Beyond Carinthia's self-possession as woman and mother—her ability to counter Fleetwood's attempts at stylistic intimidation "in the exactest measure"—perhaps the most striking effect of this scene is our sense of Fleetwood's seeing Carinthia herself for the first time. She is "oddly individual," maternally fuller in figure than recollected and unlike either extreme of his often repeated abstract mental word-plays, neither the abomination of chalk-quarry nor the quintessential beauty of sun-reddened rock.

Instead, Fleetwood stands confronted by a specific woman who is both alluring and disconcertingly without need of his protection, even indifferent to his presence. And, as he tries to convince Carinthia—and himself—of his own importance by managerial bustle, the scene is again rendered largely through his challenged perspective:

> He hardened. "We have had to settle business here," he said, speaking resonantly, to cover his gazing [at the baby] discomposedly, all but furtively.
> The child was shown, still asleep. A cunning infant: not a cry in him to excuse a father for preferring concord or silence or the bachelor's exemption.
> "He is a strong boy," the mother said. "Our doctor promises he will ride over all the illnesses."
> Fleetwood's answer set off with an alarum of the throat, and dwindled to "We'll hope so. Seems to sleep well." (19:333)

4

Repeatedly in this novel, Fleetwood's efforts to assert his masculine and aristocratic superiority are turned harmlessly aside by Carinthia's directness and simplicity. A point of crisis is reached between them, however, when this directness is extended to a petition for a yearly stipend in order to "live where I please" (19:335), rather than as he would wish her—captive in one of his country residences. Here Fleetwood balks, the issue clearly being not simply whether she will "have control of some money" (19:336), as she puts it, but also whether she will have control of herself and their child, free of husbandly jurisdiction. This, of course, was a lively topic, both during the historical period of the novel, when the Honorable Caroline Norton was having her well-publicized difficulties with her husband, and in the 1890s, when later Victorian Britain was adjusting to the effects of the Married Women's Property Acts and their challenge to the common law. Especially challenged was the age-old legal doctrine of spousal unity that viewed a wife apart from her husband as a nonentity, a view summed up in the popular saying, "in law husband and wife are one person, and the husband is that person."[10] *The Amazing Marriage* challenges this tradition directly; of all Meredith's heroines, including Mrs. Norton's fictional counterpart, Diana Warwick, Carinthia becomes the most assertive and independent, the most fully competent in conducting herself without any deference to a husband's guidance. And this is nowhere more graphically illustrated than in the event that suddenly interrupts Carinthia and Fleetwood's sparring in Chapter 32.

Meredith uses the appearance of a rabid dog among some village children to dramatize much of what I have been discussing. The focus is mainly on Carinthia and her quick response to the situation, but we are also made fully aware of Fleetwood's ineffectual role—as we were in the early scene in Baden forest—on the margins, "hover[ing] helpless as a leaf on a bough" (19:337). In contrast to Fleetwood, not only does Carinthia know what to do—she diverts the mongrel with her skirts and raised arms—she is also able to warn the children and order them indoors "with such warning Welsh as she had on the top of her mountain cry" (19:336). The point of view is still primarily Fleetwood's as he once again witnesses her remarkable sangfroid, but this time with attention to accurate detail, largely omitting his Baden romanticizing and abstraction or his more recent attempts at patriarchal one-upmanship:

> Her arms were straight above her head; her figure overhanging, on a bend of the knees. Right and left, the fury of the slavering fangs shook her loose droop of gown; and a dull, prolonged growl, like the clamour of a far body of insurrectionary marching men, told of the rage. . . .
> 'Back, I pray,' she said to him, and motioned it, her arms at high stretch.
> He held no weapon. The sweat of his forehead half blinded him. And she waved him behind her, beckoned to the crowd to keep wide way, used her lifted hands as flappers; *she had all her wits.* (Italics added; 19:336–37)

This scene acts as a paradigm of Carinthia's development, adaptation, and maintenance of integrity: she has literally translated her alpine training to meet the demands of her new situation rather than in any way being overwhelmed. Fleetwood, on the other hand, bound by conventions at once social, linguistic, and economic, has failed, both in his domestic relations and in his public role as mine owner (we are particularly reminded of this last in the reference to striking colliers in the simile of "insurrectionary marching men"). Further, in the next chapter when Carinthia turns her attention to the plight of the child who has been bitten, Fleetwood finds himself willingly taking orders from her, thus openly acknowledging this state of affairs: "The earl spun round, sensible of the novelty of his being commanded and submitting; but no sooner had he turned than he fell into her view of the urgency, and he went, much like the boy we see at school, with a strong hand on his collar running him in" (19:340).

Fleetwood shows his own capacity for development under stress soon afterward when he abruptly turns to his foreman and instructs him to settle the strike. Progress for Fleetwood is always mixed, however: he soon reverts to an attempt to assert husbandly prerogatives, telling Carinthia, "'I wish you to leave,'" to which she responds simply that she "'must not be commanded'" (19:342). Fleetwood soon admits, rather gratuitously, that "'I can neither command nor influence'" (19:343), but, the now detached narrative voice goes on, "courage to grapple with his pride and open his heart was wanting in him. Had that been done, even to the hint of it, instead of the lordly indifference shown, Gower might have ventured on a suggestion that the priceless woman he could call wife was fast slipping away from him and withering in her allegiance" (19:344).

The scene closes as Fleetwood rides away in his carriage, "feeling small" and "requiring a rapid transportation from these parts for him to regain his proper stature." The narration once again runs with his mental stream: "Had he misconducted himself at the moment of danger? It is a ghastly thought, that the craven impulse may overcome us. But no, he could reassure his repute for manliness. He had done as much as a man could do in such a situation. At the same time, he had done less than the woman" (19:344). In this frame of mind, Fleetwood's great fear is "violation of his dignity," "[e]clipsed behind the skirts of a woman waving her upraised hands, with, 'Back, pray!'—no, that ignominy is too horribly abominable!" At the same time he imagines himself "seized, besides admiring her character, with a taste for her person! Why, then, he would have to impress his own mysteriously deep character on her portion of understanding" (19:346–47).

Echoing other overbearing husbands of later Victorian fiction like Henleigh Grandcourt and Gilbert Osmond, and anticipating a host of D. H. Lawrence's self-destructive characters, Fleetwood sees his relations with Carinthia increasingly as a conflict of wills— "the battle for domination would then begin." And following a pattern that by this time had become quintessentially Meredithian, the male protagonist blocks his own better impulses in the supreme effort to protect his ego from the dangers he imagines to be posed by an assertive woman—"she will usurp the lead; she will play the man. . . . Anticipation of the possibility of it hewed division between the young man's pride of being and his warmer feelings. Had he been free of the dread of subjection, he would have sunk to kiss the feet of the statuesque young woman, arms in air, firm-fronted over the hideous death that tore at her skirts" (19:347).

5

Barbara Hardy has pointed out that "the tragic aspect of [this] novel lies in the missed affinities."[11] Fleetwood seeks and "feels wildness, impulse, solitude, integrity, courage, unconventionality, and the stroke that makes this a great love-story is his deep and long-denied recognition that all these things are to be found in Carinthia."[12] As *The Amazing Marriage* moves toward its close, Meredith shows the linked pride and "dread of subjection" that afflict Fleetwood impeding his progress in "reading" just enough to block the affinities between himself and Carinthia that might otherwise have drawn them finally together.

Meredith's repeated use of the term "reading" through this section invokes the same values of critical/emotional intelligence—of fair-mindedness and capacity for open respect towards others— that we have seen in his work from the outset. And it is precisely this capacity that Fleetwood cannot quite muster here; consequently, his participation in what Judith Wilt has called the "community of literacy"[13] is only fitful and finally unproductive for him in his relations with Carinthia. Instead of pursuing direct communication, expanded understanding, and the "warmer feelings" that would result from such "reading," Fleetwood reverts, as we have seen, to obscurantism—"to impress [on her] his own mysteriously deep character" (19:347)—and Lovelacean fantasies of repeating the exercise of male power that marked his one sexual encounter with Carinthia: "His old road [up] the ladder appeared to Fleetwood an excellent one for obviating explanations and effecting the reconcilement without any temporary seeming forfeit of the native male superiority" (19:365).

Fleetwood's predominant wish in his weak moments, then, is simply a desire to escape the implications of direct communication and dialogic openness central to the exercise of Meredithian common sense. When he later tells Carinthia, "Pray, speak, speak out," he in fact wants nothing of the sort. We are shown that his actual intent is still premised on a battle of wills: "He was for inducing her to deliver her mind, that the mountain girl's feebleness in speech might reinstate him" (19:387). The irony by this point (Chapter 37) is unmistakable since Carinthia's capacities for reading and speech are no longer in question—an irony that becomes even clearer later when, as she prepares to leave for her mission as nurse in the Carlist wars, Fleetwood cannot get beyond "the stammered beginning of his appeal to her" (19:440).

The most interesting late dramatization of Carinthia's assertive competence and Fleetwood's increasing sense of how that competence highlights his own inadequacy occurs in their final meeting. Once again, Meredith uses the device of refracting our perception of Carinthia through Fleetwood's eyes and, briefly, Fleetwood through her eyes, and thereby gives us a view that illuminates both husband and wife:

> She stood calmly discoursing, with a tempered smile: no longer a novice in the social manner. An equal whom he had injured waited for his remarks, gave ready replies; and he, bowing to the visible equality, chafed at a sense of inferiority following his acknowledgement of it. He was alone with her, and next to dumb; she froze a full heart. As for his heart, it could not speak at all, it was a swinging lump. The rational view of the situation was exposed to her; and she listened to that favourably, or at least attentively; but with an edge to her civil smile when he hinted of entertainments, voyages, travels, an excursion to her native mountain land. . . . He ventured to say that the child was a link uniting them; and she looked at him. He blinked rapidly as she had seen him do of late, but kept his eyes on her through the nervous flutter of the lids; his pride making a determined stand for physical mastery, though her look

was but a look. Had there been reproach in it, he would have found the voice to speak out. Her look was a cold sky above a hungering man. She froze his heart from the marble of her own. (19:492–93)

Fleetwood's habitual uses of convention—his fluency and superiority in civilized banter along with his legalistic pride in his "word"—all now act as disabilities: he cannot speak his heart when he most needs to. Instead he utters banalities—"the rational view" divorced from feeling—that do not touch on the reality of his betrayal of Carinthia's trust nor of his sense of awakened tenderness for her. A truer reading—a giving way to "a desire seizing him to make sacrifice of the demon he had been, offer him up hideously naked to her mercy" (19:495)—Meredith's Novelist seems to suggest, is the only way Fleetwood could begin to overcome the distance between himself and his wife. And by this late point he is schooled enough by Carinthia's example to be drawn to such directness; moreover, the reorientation he has undergone in acknowledging to himself that she is "an equal whom he had injured" impels him further. But, like other Meredithian egoists before him, he fears the nakedness of self-revelation above all else. Fleetwood, then, chooses to miss this final opportunity to read both himself and Carinthia more openly and thereby is shown to doom himself to solitude and silence.

As for Carinthia, several critics have complained that, by the end of *The Amazing Marriage*, her characterization has changed in ways suggesting a falling off of Meredith's creative energies. Gillian Beer sees Carinthia as having "stiffened into an emblematic figure remote from the eager girl of the mountain opening,"[14] and Jack Lindsay finds the ending "blurred" because we do not see her "realise the shallow selfishness of her brother and discover with renewed depth of meaning what her going back to Wales with Owain [Wythan] means."[15] Meredith himself wrote to Richard Le Gallienne that "the latter part has worn me,"[16] but I think it a mistake to assume that he would have wished to render his denouement differently. In the passage we have just examined, for example, Carinthia is remote, but it is a remoteness entirely consistent with her recognition that Fleetwood is still unwilling to change in essentials. The narrative refraction of his view—"she froze his heart from the marble of her own"—creates two significant effects: first, our sense of his attempt to shift responsibility from himself to her, and second, seen *through* Fleetwood's guilt-tripping mental gymnastics,

our recognition of Carinthia as a woman who sees clearly and refuses to be duped again by romantic expostulations. In the very last
pages of the novel, in a context that does not require her to assume
a self-defensive posture, we find Carinthia's old eagerness and
warmth in her response to Henrietta after the latter's disfiguring
accident: "Never had she loved Henrietta, never shown her so
much love, as [now]. . . . Her sisterly warmth surprised the woeful
spotted beauty with a reflection that this martial Janey was after all
a woman of feeling, one whom her husband, if he came to know it
and the depth of it, the rich sound of it, would mourn in sackcloth
to have lost" (19:507).[17]

What is most important, however, is that the Carinthia we see
here *has* significantly changed through adversity from the ingénue
of Chapter 4 to a woman of articulate strength and true independence of mind at the novel's close. *The Amazing Marriage* traces
her rapid and skilled adaptation to the complexities of British convention without any compromise to her integrity. And this point is
nowhere better illustrated than in her final scene with Fleetwood
where she is described at ease in "the social manner" and absolutely in control of the exchange, confronting her husband in his
own world and "calmly discoursing" in his own language.[18] What
she has done, of course, is to make both world and language her
own. And as a result I do not find myself, as Gillian Beer suggests I
might, feeling rebuffed along with Fleetwood at the novel's end.[19]
Rather, I experience something of the same kind of exhilaration I
feel when Elizabeth Bennet, in a scene I have already discussed,[20]
successfully confronts Lady Catherine de Bourgh, meeting and
turning aside a fusillade of self-serving arguments through skillful
use of the very language of "honour, decorum, prudence, nay, interest"[21] with which Lady Catherine attempts to intimidate and
manipulate her. It is quite true, as Beer argues, that we experience
an "emotional and grammatical intimacy"[22] with Fleetwood due to
Meredith's frequent use of his point of view in narration, but this
does not alter the fact that we are allowed all the more by such a
technique to see not only Fleetwood's advances, but also his continued failures in hermeneutics that are, finally, directly related to
the permanent division between husband and wife.

It is tempting to see such narrative "intimacy" with a central
character's thinking errors as another index of Meredith's modernist mode—shades of John Dowell!—but it is also useful to remember that this is precisely the technique we find brilliantly at work in

Austen's *Emma*: "*She* would notice her; she would improve her; she would detach her from her bad acquaintance and introduce her into good society; she would form her opinions and her manners. It would be an interesting and certainly a very kind undertaking, highly becoming her own situation in life, her leisure, and powers."[23] The comment I cited earlier by Richard Poirier—that the "features thought to be unique to literary modernism are to be found . . . nearly everywhere in English literature"[24]—is well worth keeping in mind.

Jack Lindsay's brief summation may most clearly articulate where we find ourselves at the end of *The Amazing Marriage*: "No doubt, tired, [Meredith] feels that his long book cannot be made any longer, and that he has shown enough of Carinthia's inner drive to convince us that she will go on struggling through any veils, lies, class-distortions to the naked human truth."[25] This statement also directs us back to some of the central concerns with which I have been preoccupied throughout this study of the experimental impulse in Meredith's fiction. Carinthia comes to represent the values associated with the innovative and questioning edge of Meredithian common sense more fully and more effectively, I think, than any of his other major figures. And she does so precisely because her pursuit of an elusive "naked human truth" is shown to be at once clear-sighted and humane. As Meredith reminds us in a now familiar line from the *Essay on Comedy*, heroines are "not necessarily heartless from being clear-sighted: they seem so to the sentimentally-reared only for the reason that they use their wits, and are not wandering vessels crying for a captain or a pilot" (*Essay* 23:29).

Carinthia uses her wits and, as she is described joining the mild-mannered Owain Wythan in Wales, one is given reason to suspect that she is well beyond need of a pilot of any sort, including her brother Chillon. If we are to believe any of Dame Gossip's mythologizing in the novel's last paragraphs, a significant alteration of roles has taken place when Carinthia, by means of her diplomatic expertise and, presumably, her recently acquired fluency in Spanish, rescues a wounded Chillon from the clutches of Don Carlos, no mean feat, given that the historical Don Carlos decreed in 1835 that the Eliot Convention forbidding execution of prisoners did not apply to foreign troops. She confronts the Pretender, we are told, in his very tent with her petition for Chillon's release, a petition that is granted "in acknowledgement of her 'renowned humanity to both conflicting armies'" (19:510). Meredith leads us, then, to see a Carinthia at the novel's end who will indeed continue to use her hard-won critical and emotional intelligence to contend with a world full of "veils, lies, [and] class distortions," just as she will continue to respond to those around her with the fully developed sense of feminine identity that prompted her to save a child from a rabid dog and herself from the sophistic words of Fleetwood.

Conclusion:
George Meredith in the
Twentieth Century and After

1

Meredith stood to us in those days as the wholly novel example of the intellectual novelist into whose introspective and riddling story-telling one had to mine for treasure. Meredith's stylized obscurity, his *boutades* at the expense of the English character and the conventions of English society, and what long afterwards I have seen characterized in him as "oracular allusiveness" all seemed to me to have some equivalent in what I was reading of Joyce. Anyway, Joyce did not seem to think so.

Constantine Curran[1]

ALMOST A CENTURY AFTER HIS DEATH, GEORGE MEREDITH REMAINS A "riddling" figure in the history of the English novel. Writing in 1971 about Meredith's reputation, John Lucas summed up his profoundly ambivalent assessment as follows: "Meredith is badly flawed, often infuriating, sometimes downright silly and vulgar. But he is also—or he ought to be—of permanent interest, and at his best he is probably a master."[2] More recently, John Sutherland has pronounced Meredith to be "to all intents and purposes a literary corpse—a well-remembered and abstractly revered corpse but apparently beyond critical exhumation."[3] And even more recently James Francken has provided another literary epitaph, ominously succinct: "No one reads George Meredith any more."[4]

The position I have developed in this study of Meredith's experimental impulse is that his fiction is very much alive today—of permanent interest and well worth reading, if not revering—precisely because he is a riddling storyteller whose discomfort with his own age prompted him to write in ways that both annoy and delight, thus creating the sense of indebtedness suggested by the appropriately hedging term, "probably a master." And because I argue, as Virginia Woolf and others have done, that Meredith's extensive experimentation makes him especially interesting as a precursor of modernism, it is important to emphasize that his questioning of Victorian values and realist literary techniques also identifies him as quintessentially Victorian. George Levine has noted that in "even the most conservative of the classic novels of the nineteenth century, we find continuing experiments with forms, styles, modes of valuing. Those experiments are not aberrations from some realistic norm, but intrinsic to its nature." Meredith, in his uneasy relation to Victorian values and the realist tradition, provides a striking example of Levine's view that realism, a "dangerously multivalent" term, "is itself intimately and authoritatively connected to the modernist position."[5]

To put this another way, when one argues that the presence of competing narrative voices or the depiction of disintegrating subjectivity in Meredith's work is compelling evidence of his proto-modernity, it is also salutary to bear in mind that such a canonical early Victorian novelist as Emily Brontë, for example, can provide equally interesting constructions of competing narrative voices (suggesting, at the least, a distrust of conventional views of truth and identity) as well as disturbing portraits of disintegrating subjectivity. Hillis Miller, while inviting comparison of *Wuthering Heights* with *Lord Jim*, also reminds us that "[e]ach technical device contributing to the celebrated complexity of narration in *Wuthering Heights* has its precedents in modern fictional practice from Cervantes down to novelists contemporary with Brontë."[6] Modernism, once again, "is not so modern as it seems."[7]

Nevertheless, in Meredith we do find a career of novel writing uniquely rich in what we can now see as its anticipations of attitudes, preoccupations, and techniques we conventionally associate with twentieth-century modernism. Not unexpectedly, what we find in the major practitioners of the modernist novel themselves, vis-à-vis Meredith, is ambivalence—a combination of outright Edwardian and Georgian rejection of the Victorian sage Meredith had become in his final years, along with explicit or implicit signs of admiration, in some cases conveyed through veiled or not-so-veiled emulation. We have, in other words, a series of interesting examples, some much more striking than others, of what Harold Bloom has famously theorized as the "anxiety of influence." As Bloom suggests in his most recent formulation, this "'influence' is a metaphor, one that implicates a matrix of relationships—imagistic, temporal, spiritual, psychological—all of them ultimately defensive in their nature."[8] And defensiveness is what we repeatedly encounter in modernist responses to, and evasions of, George Meredith,[9] both "in what their work is compelled to manifest"[10] and in what they literally say about his impact—or lack of it—on their writing.

In 1904, when Joyce was hard at work on *Stephen Hero*, he circulated the manuscript among various acquaintances, including Constantine Curran, who expressed warm admiration for the text. Curran noted the lyricism of the early (now lost) chapters and later commented, apparently in an effort to flatter Joyce, on George Meredith as "one of its models." This, Richard Ellmann tells us, "made Joyce's eyes assume a look of 'indignant wonder.' He was more pleased by Curran's perception of his 'desperate hunger for truth.'"[11]

This amusing memory of Joycean body language captures an attitude toward Meredithian influence that could be taken as representative of any number of emerging early twentieth-century novelists writing in, or in exile from, Britain—representative, that is, in its ambivalence and ambiguity. Does Joyce's facial expression indicate, as Ellmann and Curran both seem to interpret it, outright rejection of the Meredithian inference—"Joyce did not seem to think so"—or is Brian Caraher closer to the mark when he suggests that Joyce was probably "taken aback at a connection which might detract from his own originality or purportedly *sui generis* effort"?[12] A Bloomian reading would no doubt argue that both are right, the indignant rejection of the allegation of influence covering the uneasy awareness of "agonistic misprision performed upon [a] powerful forerunner."[13]

Stanislaus Joyce's comments on this issue are of considerable interest. Remarking on his brother's laconically tepid assessment of Meredith in a brief 1902 review (Meredith's novels "have no value as epical art . . . , [b]ut they have a distinct value as philosophical essays"[14]), Stanislaus, in a decidedly pre-Bloomian analysis, finds the review to be

a strange appreciation of a novelist whose influence, after all, was predominant in the first draft of *A Portrait of the Artist*. There is no mention of Meredith's wit or humour, or of those passionate glowing passages of a poet writing prose, which are Meredith's most characteristic contribution to the novel. Yet I know that my brother liked them and

imitated them in various places—for example, at the end of the fourth
chapter of *A Portrait*. In Trieste, when making a pupil a present of *The
Ordeal of Richard Feverel*, he accompanied the gift with a letter advancing many reservations as to the author's merits, but he would not have
chosen that book if he had not liked it.[15]

Exactly. But the "many reservations" are also telling, perhaps representative of Joyce's looking back at his youthful enthusiasm for
Meredithian lyricism with the same critical impulse that caused
him to rein in what he came to view as the lyrical excesses of *Stephen Hero*.

Nevertheless, the rhythm, diction, and ebullient theme of youthful sexuality conveyed in the famous purple passage at the end of
Chapter 4 of *A Portrait* ("He was alone. He was unheeded, happy,
and near to the wild heart of life . . .") has a distinctly Meredithian
quality to it, as Stanislaus suggests, and may perhaps be most
profitably compared with the prelude to the "Ferdinand and Miranda" chapter of *Richard Feverel* ("Above green-flashing plunges
of a weir, and shaken by the thunder below . . ."[16]). As Donald
Fanger has noted in making this comparison, "both passages carry
a charge of impassioned vision through a diction which strains
toward the poetic, and swelling, incantatory rhythms which weave
the observed detail into a whole more felt than seen." This is the
"lyrical intensity" in Meredith that Woolf responds to with strong
affinity, but it is also a familiar danger zone, as I have discussed in
Chapter 2, a zone Fanger acknowledges when he notes that "[l]yri-
cism represented a temptation which Meredith could not always
control"[17] while, he later goes on, "Joyce characteristically found
ways to *discipline* his verbal energy, to give it plausible forms—as
Meredith never could."[18]

What is most striking, however, when one thinks of Joyce in a
Meredithian context, is how both novelists are preeminently and
self-consciously writing in an experimental mode from the beginning of their careers, and how the Meredithian experiment, for
Joyce, provided a strong precursor, as Bloom would put it, from
which Joyce necessarily swerved away. Brian Caraher argues that
the Meredithian model is still a strong presence for Joyce later in
his career, suggesting the "Proteus" episode in *Ulysses* as another
example "of Joyce's moments of 'visionary intensity' which would
seem to have clear precedents in similar lyrical incantations in
Meredith."[19] Caraher goes so far as to propose that in the "Telema-

chus" episode we find "the expectation that a Meredithean sort of novel is in the process of unfolding," and he goes on to such specific expectations as "the undermining of plot in favor of the development of disjunct but finely drawn scenes, the use of moments of interior monologue, the focusing on the consciousness of one character, and the irruption of lyrical moments within that character's consciousness."[20] One must add, however, that while all these qualities are recognizably "Meredithian," it is abundantly clear that some of them are equally recognizable in other strong precursors like Henry James or Newman and Pater.[21]

In some ways Caraher's most interesting point about the uneasy presence of Meredith in Joyce's work is that the Meredithian model helps prepare for the "generic experiments and rhetorical profusion" of *Ulysses*. Keeping in mind that Joyce particularly admired *The Ordeal of Richard Feverel* and *The Tragic Comedians*,[22] it is not difficult to see the connection between Meredith's departures from traditional notions of genre, and the "rhetorical profusion" that accompanied it, and Joyce's own generic experimentation in *Ulysses*. Caraher quotes A. Walton Litz's argument that "[m]ost of our difficulties with the genre of *Ulysses* fall away when we cease to fret about a single 'model' for the work and concentrate upon the experience of reading, which involves the constant use of familiar genres and types."[23] As I have already argued in Chapter 2, much the same could be said of *Richard Feverel* (and *The Tragic Comedians* is a logical addition), that is, these texts, by nature experimental and genre-challenging, to some degree become *sui generis* and thus, in Litz's words, "[n]o extrinsic notion of what the novel or fiction should be can be taken as an ideal model, and we must allow the work to establish its own intrinsic genre as we read it."[24] The relative success or failure of a work in establishing "intrinsic genre," of course, is a much different question. In the case of Meredith—and especially in the shadow cast back on him by Joyce—the novels are most interesting, I think, when viewed as vital, flawed precursors to a possible solution to the problem of intrinsic genre, rather than as the solution itself.

2

We have to hate our immediate predecessors to get free from their authority.

D. H. Lawrence[25]

When Lawrence wrote these words to Edward Garnett in early 1913, Meredith was clearly one of those authoritative figures from the previous generation whom he loved to hate. Meredith appears from time to time in Lawrence's early letters as an influence that is the occasion for more than a little anxiety or "horror of contamination."[26] As a poet he does best—"Love in the Valley," "The Woods of Westermain," and "Modern Love" are all "very fine indeed"— while as a novelist he characteristically provokes some Lawrentian ambivalence: "I am reading Meredith's *Tragic Comedians*," he wrote to Louisa Burrows in 1911, "which is wonderfully clever: not a work of art, too turgid," or, again writing to Burrows a few months earlier, "I have not the beautiful pristine fervour of a young Feverel to meet you with."[27] Indeed, perhaps the most obvious connection here is that turgidity and fervor are two elements not uncharacteristic of Lawrence's own style, sometimes occurring—as we've seen in Meredith—discordantly together.

But there is, I think, a more productive way of perceiving an essential connection between Lawrence and Meredith, and that is in their shared "modernist" distrust of an overemphasis on rationality and a stress on the corollary need for what I have termed, borrowing from the work of Peter Salovey, John Mayer, and Daniel Goleman, emotional intelligence. In Lawrence this recurrent expression of distrust and need can perhaps be most clearly seen in *Women in Love*, where the "struggle for verbal consciousness," *"the passionate struggle into conscious being"* that "should not be left out in art," is at once intellectual and anti-intellectual. Rupert Birkin's quest for release from traditional patriarchal rationality seems to move toward something like a Meredithian balance of blood, brain, and spirit, and it is characteristic of Lawrence that he expresses this quest in metaphors of natural growth—"New unfoldings struggle up in torment in him, as buds struggle forth from the midst of a plant."[28]

The famous scene in which Hermione Roddice beats Birkin over the head with her elegant lapis lazuli paperweight certainly leads to a desire for escape from an old form of living—from Hermione's warmed-over hyper-rational version of Birkin's own theorizing— but this event also leads to Birkin's attempted realignment with nature and natural feeling in the subsequent scene in which he experiences the texture of primroses, fir trees, and hyacinths next to his skin. The sequence is quintessentially Lawrentian, especially in its insistence on Hermione's demonic will to power and Birkin's discovery of the wonders of nakedness in nature, but it is also very reminiscent of natural scenes in Meredith—the prelude to "Ferdinand and Miranda" and the "Ferdinand and Miranda" chapter itself with its luxuriant, lyrical evocation of nature as the setting for adolescent sexual attraction, or the depiction of Richard Feverel's epiphanic response to nature in the Rhineland forest ("he had a sense of purification so sweet he shuddered again and again"[29]) or Harry Richmond and Princess Ottilia communing under the overturned boat in the driving rain as they gaze out on the tumultuous natural scene, for example. And what makes such Meredithian scenes especially characteristic is that they are poised in contrast to—and as a release from—the dementedly "rational" scheming of figures like Richard himself, Sir Austin, and Richmond Roy. Lawrence establishes his own very characteristic tone, but he shares with Meredith a recoil from what they both saw as an unbalanced and excessive faith in rationality—"'all that Lady of Shalott business,'" as Birkin puts it to Hermione; "'You've got that mirror, your own fixed will, your immortal understanding, your own tight conscious world, and there is nothing beyond it.'"[30]

Part of the impulse shared by Meredith and Lawrence, then, is their drive to get "beyond" a purely "conscious world" to the more balanced state implied by the term emotional intelligence and by the images of the individual communing with nature they both characteristically turn to in their poetry and fiction. These images also suggest, of course, how both are indebted to the heritage of Romanticism, looking back to the possibility of a natural mode of living premised on what amounts to an escape from modernity. This impulse is repeatedly expressed in Lawrence through inconclusive endings that depict his characters indulging their desire to seek an atavistic "silence in the empty spaces" in escape from the "whole clockwork"[31] of the modern world, or, in Meredith, in the Swiss or Welsh mountain retreats to which his heroes and heroines instinctively turn as an alternative to the complexities of contemporary life in England.

Both writers, however, are "modern" in their emphasis on the importance of a state of becoming rather than of static being. Lawrence's insistence on the inclusion of the "struggle for verbal consciousness" in his art may be taken as a gloss on his famous admonition to Edward Garnett not to look in his fiction "for the old stable ego of the character. There is another ego, according to whose action the individual is unrecognizable, and passes through, as it were, allotropic states which it needs a deeper sense than any we've been used to exercise, to discover are states of the same single radically–unchanged element."[32] Robert Kiely is no doubt correct when he suggests that, "[i]n part, Lawrence is trying to answer the criticisms aimed at the ideological inconsistencies of some of his characters and of his own authorial persona"[33] here, but that very capacity for inconsistency with a past self may be the most characteristic mark of the Lawrentian protagonist, like Rupert Birkin or Louise Witt or Ursula Brangwen in *The Rainbow*, whose "same single radically–unchanged element" may be best defined by its potential for further allotropic differentiation. And if one thinks of similar capacity for differentiation in the Meredith canon, it is clearly the female protagonists, and especially those of the later novels, who embody this "modern" capacity for escape from "the old stable ego," with Carinthia Kirby providing the preeminent example.

3

[Meredith] will never be the spiritual power he was about the year 1900.
E. M. Forster[34]

Joseph Conrad seems to have had a much less complicated relation to George Meredith than either Joyce or Lawrence. Conrad had some fellow feeling for Meredith in that both were eternally seeking that elusive wider reading audience their experimental fiction simultaneously drove away. But even Meredith, after the publication of *Diana of the Crossways*, saw some commercial success and his reputation gradually rose to a peak at about the turn of the century, which is the period when Constantine Curran observed his popularity among Joyce's Dublin contemporaries and E. M. Forster reported that "much of the universe and all Cambridge trembled" at "the great name."[35] Conrad, in a letter written at this time, commented with more envy than anxiety that "[s]ome day I too shall put out my 'Diana of the Crossways'—be it said without instituting comparisons," and a few years later he struck a similar ironical note in regard to Meredith's modest success: "But even Meredith ended by getting his sales. Now, I haven't Meredith's delicacy and that's a point in my favour."[36]

Ford Madox Ford, like Conrad, seems to have regarded Meredith not so much as a forefather in a literary family romance as a commanding figure in the distance, one who, Ford being Ford, was appealing especially as a source for literary anecdotes, as in the following recollection from the early days of *The English Review*:

> I think that only one contributor to my first two numbers did not tell me that the *Review* was ruined by the inclusion of all the other contributors. James said: "Poor old Meredith, he writes these mysterious nonsenses and heaven alone knows what they all mean." Meredith had contributed merely a very short account of his dislike for Rossetti's breakfast manners. It was quite as comprehensible as a seedsman's catalogue.
>
> Meredith said on looking at James's *Jolly Corner* which led off the prose of the review:
>
> "Poor old James. He sets down on paper these mysterious rumblings in his bowels—but who could be expected to understand them?" So they went on.[37]

James and Meredith, as Ford's (no doubt partially manufactured) story suggests, had a more complicated literary relationship, though on a personal level they were formally cordial with one another from the time of their first meeting in 1878. At the age of seventeen, James had read *Evan Harrington* as it appeared serially and experienced a catalytic effect, as Lionel Stevenson puts it, on "his own nascent impulse to be a writer."[38] This early indebtedness, however, later turned increasingly to irritation at what James saw as Meredith's stylistic excesses. The essential Jamesean criticism becomes clear, I think, in "The Lesson of Balzac," where James distinguishes between the "lyrical instinct" of the poet and its complete absence in Balzac, Scott, Thackeray, and Dickens—"which is precisely why they are so essentially novelists, so almost exclusively lovers of the image of life." By contrast, the "lyrical element. . . . is considerable in that bright particular genius of our own day, George Meredith, who so strikes us as hitching winged horses to the chariot of his prose—steeds who prance and dance and caracole, who strain the traces, attempt to quit the ground, and yearn for the upper air."[39] Clearly, James looks for—and does not find—the novelist's image of life in Meredith, while the winged horses of the prose chariot remain on the ground, in spite of straining and prancing, still at some distance from the upper air.

James's relative civility in this public statement was entirely overcome in his (now famous) private outburst to Edmund Gosse on "the unspeakable *Lord Ormont*, which . . . . fills me with a critical rage, an artistic fury. . . . [N]ot a difficulty met, not a figure presented, not a scene constituted—not a dim shadow condensing once either into audible or into visible reality—making you hear for an instant the tap of its feet on the earth."[40] James's rage at the absence of audible and visible reality—in a word, the "scenic consistency"[41] of his own work—in *Lord Ormont* is matched by Meredith's own dismay at the lack of lyrical finesse in the Jamesean search for the last nuance and beyond in *The American Scene*:

> At each sentence I receive electric shocks. Our Henry is generally full-charged. He has the enlivening sparks from head to heel in this vast book; they fly at me from his ten fingers, his ten toes, his brows, eyes, lips; and I have to share his pangs of delivery, and once more his partial hits, renewals of effort, misses, and finally some conclusion—but what? For he is uncertain. And so the electrification continues.[42]

If we see a mutual swerving away from a strong precursor/contemporary in James and Meredith, it is equally possible to see a similar process at work in E. M. Forster's relation to Meredith. Early in Forster's career he paid Meredith—especially the Meredith of *The Egoist*—the compliment of direct imitation in his portrayals of English egoism receiving its just deserts. As Frederick Crews has suggested, in Forster's Italian novels, egotistical "error is always punished with ironic appropriateness." In fact, as Crews goes on to say, Forster follows the precepts of the *Essay on Comedy* more closely than Meredith the novelist does, Forster's comic spirit marked by a "gentleness and impartiality"[43] that, as we have already seen in Chapter 4, is not Meredith's way in *The Egoist* in his relentless satiric exposure of Willoughby Patterne's self-absorption.

Forster's debt to Meredith is probably clearest in *A Room with a View*, in which the love plot of Cecil Vyse and Lucy Honeychurch provides an obvious parallel to that of Willoughby and Clara—so much so that we have the spectacle of Cecil confidently referring to Meredith's comments on comedy at the same time his lack of self-knowledge is rapidly propelling him toward the demolition of his own love plot. While this irony is rather like Willoughby's telling Clara the story of an egoist to get her attention at the dinner table, one can also see an emerging critique of Meredith here, blended with Forster's Cantabrigian admiration. As Lionel Trilling has observed in regard to Cecil, "even as [Forster] uses the Meredithian spirit he dissociates himself from it."[44] When, writing a few years later, Forster had the lamentable Leonard Bast blurt out to the Schlegel sisters, "'Yes, but I want—I wanted—have you ever read *The Ordeal of Richard Feverel?* . . . It's a beautiful book. I wanted to get back to the earth, don't you see, like Richard does in the end. Or have you ever read Stevenson's *Prince Otto?*,'"[45] Meredith had clearly become a vulnerable figure in Forster's pantheon.

By 1927, when he delivered the Clark lectures at Trinity College, Cambridge, Forster's early admiration for Meredith had been gradually replaced by something much more like contemptuous pity as he offered the devastating critique which, in the last lines below, has become the single most quoted comment[46] on Meredith in the years since:

> Meredith is not the great name he was twenty or thirty years ago. . . . His philosophy has not worn well. His heavy attacks on sentimentality—they bore the present generation. . . . When he gets serious and noble-minded there is a strident overtone, a bullying that becomes distressing. . . . What with the faking, what with the preaching, which was never agreeable and is now said to be hollow, and what with the home counties posing as the universe, it is no wonder Meredith now lies in the trough.[47]

If, as Daniel Mark Fogel sums up Harold Bloom's argument, "poets must in some sense murder their poetic fathers in order to come into their own, to achieve their own identities and authority,"[48] then this act of literary patricide follows the oedipal prescription with gusto and can be read, in part, as Forster's acknowledgement of his later-regretted susceptibility to Meredith's "spiritual power" during and after his days as a King's undergraduate. But this rejection of a strong precursor may also be read more simply in terms of changing tastes: work seen at the beginning of the century as strikingly liberating, inspiriting, and avant garde had become, some decades later, so familiar to Forster and his contemporaries as to become commonplace.

4

[T]he effort is prodigious, and the confusion often chaotic. But the failure arises from the enormous scope of his ambition. Let us suppose that he has to describe a tea party; he will begin by destroying everything by which it is easy to recognise a tea party—chairs, tables, cups, and the rest; he will represent the scene merely by a ring on a finger and a plume passing the window. But into the ring and the plume he puts such passion and character and such penetrating rays of vision play about the denuded room that we seem to be in possession of all the details as if a painstaking realist had described each one of them separately. . . . That is the way, as one trusts at such moments, that the art of fiction will develop.

Virginia Woolf[49]

Virginia Woolf's well-articulated ambivalence about the experience of reading George Meredith provides, in my view, the most intriguing of the modernist responses to the experimental impulse in his fiction. Her first extended treatment of Meredith appeared in the *Times Literary Supplement* in 1918, and in this essay she strikes an initial note that sounds rather like Forster's dismissive utterances nine years later: on re-reading Meredith "[s]ome readers, to judge from our own case, will feel a momentary qualm, as at meeting after the lapse of years some hero so ardently admired once that his eccentricities and foibles are now scarcely tolerable; they seem to preserve too well the faults of our own youth."[50] We have here the same self-chastisement for early enthusiasm combined with self-regard for later mature rejection. Woolf takes the additional step of willingly identifying her/our youthful indiscretions with Meredith's eccentricities as a useful means to understanding the emotional force of the later rejection of the "scarcely tolerable," thus providing a Bloomian deconstruction as she proceeds.

However, just as Daniel Mark Fogel observes of Woolf in agonistic relation to Henry James, repeatedly "an attack . . . is mounted and then, characteristically, retracted"[51] in her discussions of Meredith. The passage quoted above from later in her 1918 essay provides an interesting example. As Woolf analyzes Meredith's challenge to traditional realism, prodigious effort and ambition begin by leaving confusion, chaos, and failure in their wake; then, as she begins to reverse field, we have Meredith's destruction of the recognizable accoutrements of conventional scene painting (the audible and visible reality that James seeks but does not find in *Lord Ormont*). Next, images of a ring on a finger and a plume passing the window miraculously evoke passion and character as penetrating rays play about the once-empty room to provide all the details we need and, *mirabile dictu*, we find ourselves witness to a new mode of novel writing that points "the way . . . the art of fiction will develop." More than attack and retraction, this single paragraph tracks a transition from literary disaster to avant garde triumph and discovery of the way to the future of the novel.

What Woolf has done here, through metaphors characteristic of both her and Meredith, is to develop a shorthand of extremes to convey something of the powerful but mixed effect reading Meredith has on her. Ten years later, when she wrote the more familiar essay on "The Novels of George Meredith" that I briefly discuss in the Introduction, she returns to the same transgressive issues raised in the 1918 essay and follows a similar pattern of oscillation between celebration of experimental triumph and acknowledgement of disastrous error, and then back again to another manifestation of brilliance: *Richard Feverel* is distinguished by Meredith's "keen sense . . . of the splendour of a scene. One after another. . . . [w]e are galloped to [such scenes] over every obstacle on the pounding hoofs of rhapsodical prose," but the novel is also "cracked through and through with those fissures which come when the author seems to be of twenty minds at the same time. Yet it succeeds in holding miraculously together, not certainly by the depths and originality of its character drawing, but by the vigour of its intellectual power and by its lyrical intensity."[52]

The qualities of intellectual power and lyrical intensity—the latter the same characteristic in Meredith we have already seen driving James to distraction—repeatedly provide Woolf with the means to articulate Meredith's achievement and help explain her own ambivalent affinity for his writing. In a draft of another essay also written in 1928, she notes how young writers are influenced by "the r[h]ythm of the sentences first; then by the actual words" of "highly mannered"[53] writers like James and Meredith. This observation applies equally to the effects of strong idiosyncratic styles on Woolf herself and, again, her position vis-à-vis Meredith invites Bloomian exegesis: we can see traces or "tokens of recognition"[54]—some repressed, others less so—of the strong precursor's uses of rhythm and diction as they contribute to her own remarkable lyrical intensity. But this formulation also runs the danger of exercising a kind of tunnel vision, missing the obvious fact that at any moment Woolf, like any novelist of rank, is operating within an impossibly complex matrix of imaginative impulse and multiple influence. Nevertheless, if we bear in mind the dangers of oversimplification, a move to intertextual specifics can be illuminating, and thus I will conclude by placing Meredithian and Woolfian texts—each characterized by a strong experimental impulse—side by side.

We have already briefly examined the following quotation from *One of Our Conquerors* in Chapter 5; it depicts Nataly Dreighton's struggle with her impossible social position after discovering Victor's grandiose Lakelands plan:

> He sang: he never acknowledged a trouble, he dispersed it; and in her present wrestle with the scheme of a large country estate involving new intimacies, anxieties, the courtship of rival magnates, followed by the wretched old cloud, and the imposition upon them to bear it in silence though they knew they could plead a case, at least before charitable and discerning creatures or before heaven, the despondent lady could have asked whether he was perfectly sane.
>
> Who half so brilliantly!—Depreciation of him, fetched up at a stroke the glittering armies of her enthusiasm (17:50–51)

For comparison, we'll go to a familiar passage from the beginning of *Mrs. Dalloway*:

> How fresh, how calm, stiller than this of course, the air was in the early morning; like the flap of a wave; the kiss of a wave; chill and sharp and yet (for a girl of eighteen as she then was) solemn, feeling as she did, standing there at the open window, that something awful was about to happen; looking at the flowers, at the trees with the smoke winding off them and the rooks rising, falling; standing and looking until Peter Walsh said, "Musing among the vegetables?"—was that it—"I prefer men to cauliflowers"—was that it?[55]

In spite of the obvious differences of theme and context, one is struck by the syntactical similarities—the extended sentences that, phrase upon qualifying phrase, rhythmically, sometimes abruptly, build the psycho-narration of Nataly's and Clarissa's sense of dread in relation to the male figure who, in each case, is the focus of intense, only partially understood ambivalence, an ambivalence punctuated by questioning, fragmentary utterances. Woolf is clearly innovating brilliantly with her own characteristic lyrical style, but Meredith may be glimpsed at the margins, here and elsewhere, as a forerunner whose work, I would argue, is essential to understanding the modernist translation of realism into new formal, thematic, and psychological realms.

Notes

INTRODUCTION

1. George Meredith, *The Letters of George Meredith,* ed. C. L. Cline (Oxford: Clarendon Press, 1970), 1:32.

2. Abel Chevalley, *Le Roman anglais de notre temps* (London: Humphrey Milford, 1921), 55 (my translation).

3. Woolf characteristically ranked Meredith and James as the two most influential practitioners of the English novel from her parents' generation. They appear, for example, in "On Re-Reading Novels" (1922) on her short list of the great nineteenth-century "masters—Tolstoy and Flaubert, and Dickens, and Henry James, and Meredith" (*The Essays of Virginia Woolf*, 3, ed. Andrew McNeillie [New York: Harcourt Brace Jovanovich, 1988], 342). And as Daniel Mark Fogel has pointed out, her comment on the power of their joint influence in a draft of her 1929 essay, "Phases of Fiction," is most revealing in its Bloomian metaphor of inescapable contagion: "some writers are far more infectious than others. They [sic] young can hardly read Henry James or Mere[d]ith without copying them" (*Covert Relations: James Joyce, Virginia Woolf, and Henry James* [Charlottesville: University of Virginia Press, 1990], 70; 115). Fogel's aim is to extend our knowledge of the extent and depth of what has long been a critical commonplace—James's influence on and participation in the founding of modernism; full recognition of Meredith's role, needless to say, is a more problematic issue.

4. Virginia Woolf, "The Novels of George Meredith," *The Second Common Reader* (New York: Harcourt, 1932), 206.

5. Ibid., 211–12.

6. Ibid., 207. Joan Bennett begins *Virginia Woolf: Her Art as a Novelist* (Cambridge: Cambridge University Press, 1964) by observing the parallel lyrical/experimental impulses that link Woolf and Meredith.

7. Richard Poirier, *The Renewal of Literature* (New York: Random House, 1987), 95. The recognition of continuity within discontinuity in literary history appears often and in interesting variety in contemporary theoretical writing, as in Gerald Graff's observation that a "logical evolution . . . connects the romantic and post-romantic cult of the creative self to the cult of the disintegrated, disseminated, dispersed self and of the decentered, undecidable, indeterminate text. . . . [P]ostmodern literature extends rather than overturns the premises of romanticism and modernism" (*Literature Against Itself: Literary Ideas in Modern Society* [Chicago: University of Chicago Press, 1979], 51; 52). More recently, Michael McKeon has succinctly summed up his dialectical method in *The Origins of the English Novel, 1600–1740* (Baltimore: The Johns Hopkins University Press, 1987) as a way to contend with exactly this issue—to allow us to "come closer to conceiv-

ing how change occurs: how the past can persist into the present, and help to mediate the establishment of difference through the perpetuation of similarity" (*Theory of the Novel: A Historical Approach*, ed. Michael McKeon [Baltimore: The Johns Hopkins University Press, 2000], 384).

8. See Ian Duncan's *Modern Romance and Transformations of the Novel: The Gothic, Scott, Dickens* (Cambridge: Cambridge University Press, 1992) for a brilliant exposition of this innovative process in late eighteenth- and early nineteenth-century British fiction.

9. Neil Roberts, *Meredith and the Novel* (New York: St. Martin's Press, 1997), 7. On the other hand, Roberts takes a position very close to that of Chevalley when speaking of the innovative quality of *Richard Feverel* in which Meredith "overleaped realism before it had consummated itself in Eliot's later work" (18).

10. Suzanne Keen, *Victorian Renovations of the Novel: Narrative Annexes and the Boundaries of Representation* (Cambridge: Cambridge University Press, 1998), 1–2.

11. Ibid., 181; 185.

12. It should be clear that I will be using this term much as Woolf does, to convey an intensively innovative, questioning approach to novelistic tradition—that is, in the way the term is often applied to Woolf, her contemporaries, and postmodern fiction—rather than as anything remotely programmatic or "scientific" in the style of *Le Roman experimental* of Émile Zola, about which Meredith had severe reservations. At the same time, I do not wish to make the claim that Meredith stands alone or even preeminently as a Victorian practitioner of experimental fiction. One can see innovative writing everywhere in nineteenth-century Britain—as in, for example, the development of popular romance (taking romance to signify the remarkable variety of nineteenth-century hybrid narratives that explored alternatives to domestic realism) produced by a diversity of writers from Walter Scott through Edward Bulwer-Lytton to Wilkie Collins, Marie Corelli, Henry Rider Haggard, Bram Stoker, and others. And of course Henry James is often viewed as the premier canonical practitioner of experimental fiction in English in the later part of the century, as in Sergio Perosa's argument in *Henry James and the Experimental Novel* (Charlottesville: University Press of Virginia, 1978). What I do want to claim for Meredith is to some degree similar to what Perosa, Fogel, and many others have claimed for James—a very significant impact on modernist writing, seeing him (to adapt Fogel's comment on James) "as a leading symptom of the pervasive patriarchy by which Woolf [among others] knew herself to be both oppressed and obsessed" (*Covert Relations*, 2). Unlike Fogel's useful method of treating Joyce, Woolf, and James together, however, the emphasis of my approach will fall where I think it is most needed—in analysis of Meredith as a brilliant and challenging precursor of modernism, with some brief commentary along the way and in the conclusion on his aftermath.

13. Protagonists, respectively, in *Richard Feverel, The Adventures of Harry Richmond* (1871), *The Egoist* (1879), *One of Our Conquerors* (1891), and *The Amazing Marriage* (1895).

14. Lyn Pykett, *Engendering Fictions: The English Novel in the Early Twentieth Century* (London: Edward Arnold, 1995), 3. I am also much indebted here to Eugene Lunn's *Marxism and Modernism: An Historical Study of Lukács, Brecht, Benjamin, and Adorno* (Berkeley: University of California Press, 1982), especially

pp. 34–37, and Astradur Eysteinsson, *The Concept of Modernism* (Ithaca: Cornell University Press, 1990).

15. Meredith's nineteenth-century feminism is in many respects the quality that makes him at once most attractive to our age and most vulnerable to late twentieth-/early twenty-first-century misinterpretation. Throughout this study, when I refer to Meredith's feminism, I will be implying the nineteenth-century qualifier. To judge (and dismiss) him by the standards of our own gender consciousness, rather than seeing him in his nineteenth-century context, is to miss much of what is truly innovative in Meredith's thinking about gender issues. A useful treatment of Meredith as a radical questioner of Victorian gender roles can be found in Barbara Leah Harman's excellent chapter on *Diana of the Crossways* in *The Feminine Political Novel in Victorian England* (Charlottesville: University Press of Virginia, 1998), 76–112. Harman analyzes in *Diana* what may be seen to be a leitmotif in Meredith's fiction from *Richard Feverel* to *The Amazing Marriage*—his exposure of "domestic privacy as a violation rather than a preserve of personal liberty. . . ; he saw the confinement of women to domestic life as impeding their essential growth and their development toward full citizenship" (79).

16. Eysteinsson, *The Concept of Modernism,* 150.

17. Mohammad Shaheen, *George Meredith: A Reappraisal of the Novels* (Totowa: Barnes and Noble, 1981), 4.

18. *An Essay on Comedy and the Uses of the Comic Spirit* in *The Works of George Meredith*, 29 vols. (New York: Scribner's Sons, 1909–1912), 23:42. With the exception of *The Ordeal of Richard Feverel* (for which I use a modern edition of the original 1859 version), all quotations from Meredith's prose texts will be from the Scribner's edition.

Cf. Judith Wilt, *The Readable People of George Meredith* (Princeton: Princeton University Press, 1975), 179, where she notes that "The Imps in [*The Egoist*] represent the original sin of comedy; they are the Luciferian side of the Comic Spirit."

19. Woolf, "The Novels of George Meredith," 209.

20. Joseph Moses, *The Novelist as Comedian: George Meredith and the Ironic Sensibility* (New York: Schocken Books, 1983), 7.

21. David Howard, "*Rhoda Fleming*: Meredith in the Margin," *Meredith Now: Some Critical Essays,* ed. Ian Fletcher (New York: Barnes & Noble, 1971), 131.

22. Donald David Stone, "Meredith and Bakhtin: Polyphony and *Bildung,*" *Studies in English Literature* 28 (fall 1988): 693–712, David McWhirter, "Imagining a Distance: Feminism and Comedy in Meredith's *The Egoist,*" *Genre* 22 [fall 1989], Susan Payne, *Difficult Discourse: George Meredith's Experimental Fiction* (Pisa: Edizioni ETS, 1995), and Neil Roberts, *Meredith and the Novel.*

23. Woolf, "The Novels of George Meredith," 206.

24. M. M. Bakhtin, *The Dialogic Imagination*, ed. Michael Holquist, trans. Caryl Emerson and Michael Holquist (Austin: University of Texas Press, 1981), 7.

25. Susan Morgan, *Sisters in Time: Imagining Gender in Nineteenth-Century British Fiction* (Oxford: Oxford University Press, 1989), 164. Morgan goes on to stress the importance of the relations of the sexes in Meredith, a point that will be borne out in every chapter of this book: "What is special about Meredith's work, and finally what is appealing and energizing about reading his novels, is that they assume that whether one is male or female matters, and not in the insignificant

sense of being a matter of biology but in the significant sense of being a matter of culture" (165).

26. I am in accord here with Walter F. Wright when he says that Meredith is "loath, indeed too loath, to relinquish [*Richard Feverel*'s] witty commentary as the narrative plunges toward its tragic end" (*Art and Substance in George Meredith* [Lincoln: University of Nebraska Press, 1953], 148).

27. In *Richard Feverel*, *Rhoda Fleming* (1865), and *One of Our Conquerors* respectively.

28. I am indebted in my use of this term to Norman Kelvin who, in *A Troubled Eden: Nature and Society in the Works of George Meredith* (Stanford, Calif.: Stanford University Press, 1961), suggests that "what Meredith really meant by 'common sense' was critical intelligence" (103).

29. "The Woods of Westermain," IV, 170, *The Poems of George Meredith*, ed. Phyllis B. Bartlett (New Haven: Yale University Press, 1978), 1:217.

30. The term "emotional intelligence" is gaining considerable currency as a result of work by such psychologists as Howard Gardner at Harvard, Peter Salovey at Yale, and John Mayer at the University of New Hampshire. Psychologist Daniel Goleman, who reports on the behavioral and brain sciences for *The New York Times*, defines the term as applying to those who excel in, among other things, "rapport, empathy, cooperation, persuasion and the ability to build consensus. . . . [and] to read one's own feelings" ("Ideas and Trends: The Decline of the Nice-Guy Quotient," *The New York Times*, 10 September 1995, E6). Goleman's book, *Emotional Intelligence* (New York: Bantam, 1995), provides an extended treatment of the subject, centered on the joint principles of emotional self-awareness and empathy—the very qualities of emotional literacy Meredith repeatedly shows to be supremely deficient in his egoist-protagonists from Sir Austin Feverel through Sir Willoughby Patterne to the Earl of Fleetwood.

31. Hillis Miller, *Fiction and Repetition* (Cambridge, Mass.: Harvard University Press, 1982), 19.

CHAPTER 1: *AN ESSAY ON COMEDY*

1. Joseph Warren Beach, *The Comic Spirit in George Meredith* (New York: Longmans, Green, 1911), 3.

2. Even in the case of *The Egoist*, however, seeing Meredith's world as "essentially comic" has raised some interesting and problematic questions, especially in regard to his feminism. These questions, including those raised thirty-plus years ago by Kate Millet about what she claims to be Meredith's endorsement of, among other things, the "feudal character of patriarchal marriage" (*Sexual Politics* [New York: Doubleday, 1970], 139), have been summed up by David McWhirter as founded on the "suspicion that comedy is, structurally and ideologically, an inherently androcentric genre." McWhirter argues persuasively, however, that Meredith "is acutely aware of the conservative and androcentric implications of the comic form he employs" and, further, that he "was led, in part by his feminist politics, to a striking enactment [in *The Egoist*] of the process Bakhtin describes as 'the novelization of other genres'" (Mikhail Bakhtin, *The Dialogic Imagination*, 6; David McWhirter, "Imagining a Distance: Feminism and Comedy in Meredith's

The Egoist," 266; 271). As Donald Stone has put it in his illuminating essay linking Bakhtin and Meredith, "[c]omedy, for Bakhtin and Meredith, rejects all forms
of authoritarianism . . . ; it rejects stasis and celebrates a world of 'becoming,
change, and renewal' " (Mikhail Bakhtin, *Rabelais and His World,* trans. Helene
Iswolsky [Bloomington: Indiana University Press, 1984], 10; Donald D. Stone,
"Meredith and Bakhtin: Polyphony and *Bildung,"* 702).

3. I. M. Williams, "The Organic Structure of *The Ordeal of Richard Feverel,"
Review of English Studies* 18 (1967): 18.

4. Walter Wright's comments upon the problems of a generic approach to
Meredith are still most apropos: "As life usually consists [in] a mixture of tragedy,
romance, and comedy, Meredith would test his artistic skill by encompassing all
three in the same canvas. It is this determination which accounts for his major
originality—the exploration of the tragicomic—but also for the diffuseness which
disturbs those who think of Aeschylus and Sophocles as the standards of unity"
(*Art and Substance in George Meredith,* 127).

5. Lewis Horne, without mentioning Beach, argues precisely the opposite position. He notes that "the potential for tragedy looms" in Sir Austin's willingness
"to sacrifice the mortal for the System," which he compares with Agamemnon's
sacrifice of Iphigenia ("Sir Austin, His Devil, and the Well-Designed World," *Studies in the Novel* 24 [1992]: 38; 41).

6. J. B. Priestly, *George Meredith* (New York: Macmillan, 1926), 145.

7. Joseph C. Landis, "George Meredith's Comedy," *Boston University Studies
in English* 2 (1956): 27; 29.

8. John W. Morris, "Inherent Principles of Order in *Richard Feverel,"* PMLA
78 (1963): 335.

9. Williams, "Organic Structure," 29.

10. Roger Henkle, *Comedy and Culture* (Princeton: Princeton University Press,
1980), 241.

11. Richard Keller Simon, *The Labyrinth of the Comic: Theory and Practice
from Fielding to Freud* (Tallahassee: Florida State University Press, 1985), 168.
Stuart Pratt Sherman was one of the earliest of Meredith's contemporaries to recognize the significance of "tragi-comedy" in his work. See Sherman's obituary
essay on Meredith in *Nation* 88 (3 June 1909), reprinted in *Meredith: The Critical
Heritage,* ed. Ioan Williams (London: Routledge & Kegan Paul, 1971), 488–96.

12. Robert Martin, "Notes Toward a Comic Fiction," *The Theory of the Novel:
New Essays,* ed. John Halperin (New York: Oxford University Press, 1974), 76.

13. Daniel Smirlock, "The Models of *Richard Feverel,"* *The Journal of Narrative Technique* 11 (spring 1981): 102; 104.

14. Robert Scholes and Robert Kellogg, *The Nature of Narrative* (Oxford University Press, 1966), 230–31.

15. Joseph Moses, *The Novelist as Comedian: George Meredith and the Ironic
Sensibility,* 216. Although Moses's title would seem to place him in the camp of
those who see Meredith as an essentially comic writer, his book, as this quotation
indicates, develops a more comprehensive view. Moses wants to minimize generic
distinctions, to show "Meredith's peculiar enforcement of an intimacy between
comedy and tragedy" (214). While I am sometimes in disagreement with how far
he carries this notion of generic "intimacy," I find Moses's central point comple-
mentary to my own argument as to just how essential the innovative and experi-

mental impulse is in Meredith, and a useful articulation of the characteristic Meredithian ironic sensibility: Meredith shows "a need for traditional structures of form and statement," which is then "threatened and frequently toppled by a countervailing impulse to assail such structures" (39). *Richard Feverel*, with its nervous changes of generic orientation, is a particularly good demonstration of such "countervailing impulses."

16. Gillian Beer, *Meredith: A Change of Masks* (London: Athlone Press, 1970), 16. Moses's "countervailing impulse" suggests a less controlled process, but is nonetheless similar to Beer's notion of "counterpoint."

17. Donald D. Stone, "Meredith and Bakhtin," 694. Stone's central point is to link Meredith and Bakhtin in the homage they both pay to Goethe in their emphasis on "Polyphony (the recognition and celebration of multiple voices and perspectives) and *Bildung* (the need for development, both of the individual and his society)."

18. Neil Roberts, *Meredith and the Novel*, 5. Carlos Fuentes, in a review of Edith Grossman's new translation of *Don Quixote,* reminds us of a major source of the kind of generic scrutiny and questioning Roberts sees Meredith promoting: "Cervantes inaugurates the modern novel through the impurity, the *mestizaje* of all known genres. . . . The modern novel is born as both an encounter of genres and a refusal of [generic] purity" ("Tilt," *The New York Times Book Review* [2 November 2003]: 15).

19. Fredric Jameson, *The Political Unconscious: Narrative as a Socially Symbolic Act* (Ithaca: Cornell University Press, 1981), 145.

20. Ramon Fernandez, *Messages*, première série (Paris: Librairie Gallimard, 1926), 128; translation, Montgomery Belgion, *Messages* (New York: Harcourt, 1927), 166.

21. Robert Martin, *The Triumph of Wit* (Oxford: Oxford University Press, 1974), 90.

22. James Gindin, *Harvest of a Quiet Eye: The Novel of Compassion* (Bloomington: Indiana University Press, 1971), 59.

23. Northrop Frye, *Anatomy of Criticism* (New York: Atheneum, 1968), 163. As I have already suggested, the emphasis on reason and common sense in the *Essay* often has an eighteenth-century ring to it. Fielding and Johnson come to mind at once, for example, in their characteristic preoccupation with the Horatian linkage of the pleasurable and corrective functions of literature. Fielding's famous summary definition of the moral role of the fictional "biographer" brings us close to the role of the comic dramatist implied in the *Essay*: "to hold the glass to thousands in their closets, that they may contemplate their deformity and endeavor to reduce it" (*Joseph Andrews*, III, i [Boston: Houghton Mifflin, 1961], 159). For our purposes, perhaps the most interesting point about Fielding's expression of this notion of the private self-corrective function of literature is that it echoes the summary statement of Uranie on the same subject in the sixth scene of *La Critique de L'École des femmes*: "Let us take advantage of the lesson, if we can, without appearing to notice that it is we who are being addressed. All of these ridiculous depictions presented on stage . . . are public mirrors in which one never has to admit that one sees oneself" (*Oeuvres complètes de Molière*, ed. René Bray and Jacques Scherer [Paris: Le Club du meilleur livre, 1954] 1:927, my translation). Molière's significance in the comic tradition Meredith was looking back upon in the *Essay* cannot be too strongly emphasized.

24. For arguments in favor of Molière's authorship, see Robert Ren, "Les Commentaires de première main sur les chefs-d'oeuvre de Molière," *Revue des sciences humaines* 81 (1956): 19–49. For arguments against Molière's authorship, see J. D. Hubert, *Molière and the Comedy of Intellect* (Berkeley: University of California Press, 1962), 106–8.

25. "Lettre sur la comèdie de L'Imposteur," *Oeuvres complètes de Molière*, 2:1249, my translation.

26. Paul Lauter, *Theories of Comedy* (Garden City, N.Y.: Doubleday, 1964), 143–44.

27. "Lettre sur la comèdie de L'Imposteur," 2:1253, my translation.

28. Plato, *Philebus*, 48, trans. Seth Benardete (Chicago: University of Chicago Press, 1993), 57–58.

29. For discussion of the *raisonneur* in Molière, see G. Michaut, *Les Luttes de Molière* (Paris: Librairie Hachette, 1925), 227–29 and W. G. Moore, *Molière: A New Criticism* (London: Oxford University Press, 1964), 143–44.

30. Henkle, *Comedy and Culture*, 11–12.

31. Priestly, *George Meredith*, 123.

32. Moore, *Molière*, 74.

33. Susan Bordo, *The Flight to Objectivity: Essays on Cartesianism and Culture* (Albany: State University of New York Press, 1987), 97.

34. Maura Ives puts the point this way: "Meredith shows that certain valorized traits traditionally assigned to men—objectivity, 'clear-sightedness,' and 'common sense'—are more likely to be achieved by women and . . . marginalized men" ("Introduction," *George Meredith's Essay On Comedy and Other New Quarterly Magazine Publications* [Lewisburg, Pa.: Bucknell University Press, 1998], 21).

35. See note 2 above.

36. Wilt, *The Readable People of George Meredith*, 173–74; McWhirter, "Imagining a Distance," 282).

37. McWhirter, "Imagining a Distance," 282–83.

38. Priestly, to give him credit, does note later, in another context, that "woman is the ally of the Comic Spirit" (*George Meredith*, 129).

39. McWhirter, "Imagining a Distance," 268.

40. Ibid., 278; 280; 278.

CHAPTER 2: *THE ORDEAL OF RICHARD FEVEREL*

1. George Meredith, *The Ordeal of Richard Feverel*, ed. Edward Mendelson (London: Penquin Books, 1998). This edition presents the original 1859 version of the novel and is the one to which page references will refer throughout my discussion of *Richard Feverel*.

2. Virginia Woolf, "The Novels of George Meredith," 206.

3. As Sven-Johan Spånberg has pointed out, however, in adopting the parodic mode in *Richard Feverel*, Meredith "conforms to an established practice in fiction." Spånberg goes on to paraphrase Harry Levin, noting that "it is part of the very essence of realism continually to distinguish between fact and fiction and to vindicate truth by repudiating falsehood. To attain this end, a surprising number of novelists have resorted to parody" (*The Ordeal of Richard Feverel and the Tradi-*

tion of Realism [Uppsala: Acta Universitatis Upsaliensis, 1974], 16). Sir Austin, then, in Spånberg's terms, is a parody of an "eighteenth-century ideal of rational, impassive virtue." Like Richardson's Sir Charles Grandison, Sir Austin wishes to be an embodiment of prudence and self-control, but "whereas Sir Charles's perfection is presented as genuine, Meredith makes it clear that Sir Austin's moral excellence is in part only a successful mask. When he tries to maintain not only that he struggles to be good but that he is good without a struggle, he becomes an imposter" (22). Thus, once again, Meredithian critical intelligence is seen coming down hard on a claim to a purely rationalist position: Sir Austin is a parody of self-assured masculine rationality with his "pompous complacency, his exaggerated faith in reason, and his Puritanical fear of passion and impulse" (25). I shall deal with the specific problem of implied objectivity claims in Sir Austin's "science" in the next section.

4. See L. T. Hergenhan, "Meredith's Use of Revision: A Consideration of the Revisions of *Richard Feverel* and *Evan Harrington*," *Modern Language Review* 59 (1964): 539–44.

5. Donald David Stone, *Novelists in a Changing World* (Cambridge, Mass.: Harvard University Press, 1972), 102.

6. Meredith to Samuel Lucas, 7 July 1859, *The Letters of George Meredith*, 1:40. Also see L. T. Hergenhan, "The Reception of George Meredith's Early Novels," *Nineteenth Century Fiction* 19 (1964): 220.

7. Thomas Nagel, *The View from Nowhere* (New York: Oxford University Press, 1986), 8–9; David McWhirter, "Imagining a Distance: Feminism and Comedy in Meredith's *The Egoist*," 269–70.

8. William E. Buckler, "The Artistic Unity of Richard Feverel: Chapter XXXIII," *Nineteenth Century Fiction* 7 (1952): 123.

9. Walter Wright, *Art and Substance in George Meredith*, 155. I am indebted here and at points in the previous paragraph to Wright's discussion of *Richard Feverel*.

10. I am adopting Dorrit Cohn's term for *style indirect libre* or *erlebte Rede*. Here, the narrated monologue characteristically slides into and out of what Cohn terms "psycho-narration," indirect discourse that combines "mental verbs" with "the tense system and third-person reference" of narrated monologue (*Transparent Minds: Narrative Modes for Presenting Consciousness in Fiction* (Princeton: Princeton University Press, 1978), 104–5.

11. George Meredith, *The Poems of George Meredith*, ed. Phyllis B. Bartlett (New Haven: Yale University Press, 1978), 1:217, lines 170–80.

12. Meredith to Augustus Jessopp, 8 April 1873, *The Letters of George Meredith*, 1:478.

13. "Ye" was omitted and "spiritual" changed to "sentimental" in the first revision—surprising modifications in that they show Meredith tinkering with the passage without altering its essential incongruity.

14. For an amusing about-face from the views expressed in *George Meredith and the Comic Spirit*, see Joseph Warren Beach's denunciation of Meredith's stylistic exuberance in "Ferdinand and Miranda" in *The Twentieth-Century Novel* (New York: Appleton-Century-Crofts, 1932), 42–44.

15. Jacques Derrida, *Of Grammatology*, trans. Gayatri Chakravorty Spivak (Baltimore: The Johns Hopkins University Press, 1976), 157–58; 218; see Michael

Sprinker, "'The Intricate Evasions of As': Meredith's Theory of Figure," *Victorian Newsletter* 53 (spring 1978): 9–12, for a brief discussion of *"différance"* in Meredith. For convenience, I am using part of Sprinker's definition of *"différance"* here.

16. Janet Horowitz Murray, *Courtship and the English Novel: Feminist Readings in the Fiction of George Meredith* (New York: Garland, 1987), 79–80.

17. Gary Handwerk, *Irony and Ethics in Narrative: From Schlegel to Lacan* (New Haven: Yale University Press, 1985), 114–15.

18. See especially Gladys W. Ekeberg, "*The Ordeal of Richard Feverel* as Tragedy," *College English* 7 (1946): 387–93; William E. Buckler, "The Artistic Unity of Richard Feverel: Chapter XXXIII"; Phyllis Bartlett, "Richard Feverel, Knight-Errant," *Bulletin of the New York Public Library* 63 (1959): 329–40; Charles J. Hill, "Introduction," *The Ordeal of Richard Feverel* (New York: Holt, Rinehart and Winston, 1964); David E. Foster, "Rhetorical Strategy in *Richard Feverel*," *Nineteenth-Century Fiction* 26 (1971): 185–95; U. C. Knoepflmacher, *Laughter and Despair* (Berkeley: University of California Press, 1971), 118–28; Jerome Hamilton Buckley, *Season of Youth* (Cambridge, Mass.: Harvard University Press, 1974), 63–82; Sven-Johan Spånberg, *The Ordeal of Richard Feverel* and the Traditions of Realism, especially 75–85; Mohammad Shaheen, *George Meredith: A Reappraisal of the Novels*, 27–29; Janet Horowitz Murray, *Courtship and the English Novel*, 39–82; Debra Stoner Barker, "Richard Feverel's Passage to Knighthood," *American Notes and Queries* 3 (October 1990): 168–71; Lewis Horne, "Sir Austin, His Devil, and the Well-Designed World," 35–47.

19. Knoepflmacher, *Laughter and Despair,* 124.

20. Priestly, *George Meredith,* 145.

21. Foster, "Rhetorical Strategy in *Richard Feverel*," 195.

22. Jacob Korg, "Expressive Styles in *The Ordeal of Richard Feverel*," *Nineteenth-Century Fiction* 27 (1972): 260.

23. Renate Muendel, *George Meredith* (Boston: Twayne, 1986), 61.

24. "Have you noticed the expression in the eyes of blind men? That is just how Richard looks, as he lies there silent in his bed—striving to image her on his brain."

25. Buckler, "Artistic Unity," 120.

26. Judith Wilt links Mrs. Berry in this respect with other minor figures like Frank Skepsey in *One of Our Conquerors* or Madge Winch in *The Amazing Marriage*: their efforts "usually allow these minor characters to win through to the truths, to image the realities, to see wholly or philosophically, before the central characters in the book do" (*The Readable People of George Meredith*, 84).

27. Thomas Campbell, "Adrian's Shrug: A Note on the 'Wise Youth,'" *Victorian Newsletter* 66 (spring 1982): 20.

28. Mohammad Shaheen, *George Meredith,* 20.

29. See Frank Curtin's essay, "Adrian Harley: The Limits of Meredith's Comedy," *Nineteenth-Century Fiction* 7 (1953): 272–82, for an examination of Adrian's role in *Richard Feverel* as the novel's prime representative of the comic spirit. My quarrel with Curtin's position is that it fails to recognize adequately how the fact that Adrian "has no heart" makes his lucidity deeply perverse in Meredith's view and hence a parody, not a representation, of the comic spirit. As I have already argued, Lucy Desborough, in spite of her lapses into yielding sentimentality,

seems to me to be the most important and interesting touchstone of common sense in the novel. In addition, as Gillian Beer has observed, Lucy is distinguished in an essential way from figures like Adrian or the rather pedestrian *raisonneur*, Austin Wentworth: "In a book where the characters are persistently subjected to irony, [Lucy] is the one character who has remained unsatirized: an ideal being, gentle and strong" (*Meredith: A Change of Masks*, 14).

30. Robert Scholes and Robert Kellogg, *The Nature of Narrative*, 231.

CHAPTER 3: *THE ADVENTURES OF HARRY RICHMOND*

1. Allon White, *The Uses of Obscurity: The Fiction of Early Modernism* (London: Routledge & Kegan Paul, 1981), 26.

2. These tensions show up in Meredithian narrative throughout his career, right down to *The Amazing Marriage* (1895), where he again created two explicit narrative voices (Dame Gossip and the Modern Novelist) that reveal many of the same tensions between popular tale-spinning and analytical commentary. Gillian Beer and Judith Wilt provide especially useful commentary on these narrative strategies.

3. *Richard Feverel* and *The Egoist* are the two Meredith novels with which one may assume a fair number of readers are familiar. In discussing other texts in the Meredith canon, then, I will provide somewhat more in the way of plot and context in order to orient the reader, whom I also direct to the useful appendix of plot summaries in Mervyn Jones's *The Amazing Victorian: A Life of George Meredith* (London: Constable, 1999), 249–86.

4. L. T. Hergenhan, ed., "Introduction," *The Adventures of Harry Richmond* (Lincoln: University of Nebraska Press, 1970), xvi.

5. For a treatment of Dickensian and Goethean Bildungsroman elements in *Harry Richmond*, see Mohammad Shaheen, *George Meredith: A Reappraisal of the Novels*, 30–52.

6. Paul Armstrong, *The Challenge of Bewilderment: Understanding and Representation in James, Conrad, and Ford* (Ithaca: Cornell University Press, 1987), 267.

7. The treatment of this theme in the preceding passage is typical: Meredith is careful throughout the novel to veil Roy's pretensions in obscurity. As Lionel Stevenson has remarked, "in the heyday of Victoria's reign it would have been highly impolitic, if not positively treasonable, to base a novel openly upon a challenge to her tenure of the monarchy" (*The Ordeal of George Meredith* [New York: Scribner's Sons, 1953], 182). Nevertheless, it does eventually become clear that Roy's pretensions are founded on the belief that his actress mother had been secretly married to a Royal Personage and hence his eternal "Case" against the government for recognition and compensation.

8. Anyone who discusses imagery—and especially imagery of fire—in *Harry Richmond* is inevitably indebted to Barbara Hardy's superb essay, "The Structure of Imagery: George Meredith's *Harry Richmond*," originally published in *Essays in Criticism* and republished in *The Appropriate Form* (London: Athlone Press, 1964), 83–104. As will be evident, however, I do take issue with Hardy's contention that the fire at the Bench "has little to do with ordeal or aggression" and is

merely "another wild adventure for Harry Richmond" (96). See also Margaret Tarratt's discussion of fire imagery in *"The Adventures of Harry Richmond— Bildungsroman* and Historical Novel" in *Meredith Now: Some Critical Essays*, ed. Ian Fletcher, 182–86.

9. Tarratt, *"The Adventures of Harry Richmond,"* 171.

10. The practical explanation for Roy's posing as a bronze equestrian soon becomes clear—he is in league with the prince's sister, the margravine, who has bet the prince that she could produce the statue within a period of eight days.

11. Barbara Hardy, "The Structure of Imagery," 99. See also L. T. Hergenhan's reading of this scene, especially his treatment of its death motif, in "Introduction," *The Adventures of Harry Richmond*, xxi–xxiii.

12. Jerome Hamilton Buckley, *Season of Youth*, 90.

13. Diane Johnson, *Lesser Lives* (New York: Alfred A. Knopf, 1972), 79.

14. Allon White, in *The Uses of Obscurity*, takes this episode in Meredith's life as the source of an intense preoccupation with shame throughout his career. White makes the interesting, if perhaps overstated, point that "Meredith's major achievement was to write more sensitively and extensively of shame than any other English writer despite [the] intense pressure which shame exerts to remain unarticulated" (106).

15. One finds the same pattern in Walter Scott where essentially domestic heroines, for example, Rose or Rowena in *Waverley* and *Ivanhoe*, supplant the more exotic and forbidden romantic heroines, Flora and Rebecca.

16. The marriage occurs only after Harry is suitably chastened by a lonely year of voyaging and Janet's close escape from a loveless marriage to Lord Edbury.

17. An annual income, plus a mysterious gift of £25,000, have been interpreted by Roy as hush money from the government. The money, in fact, has come from Harry's aunt Dorothy.

18. See Allon White's interesting discussion of the recurrent "nightmare of public nudity" in Meredith's fiction: *The Uses of Obscurity*, 100–102.

19. Paul Armstrong, *The Challenge of Bewilderment*, 267.

20. Allon White, *The Uses of Obscurity*, 26; 49.

21. Hardy, "The Structure of Imagery," 92.

22. Ibid., 94.

CHAPTER 4: *THE EGOIST*

1. I use the term "female hero" in this chapter to lay stress on the more active, self-determining role Meredith gives his central women characters in the later fiction.

2. Susan Morgan, *Sisters in Time*, 172.

3. Carol Christ, "Aggresssion and Providential Death in George Eliot's Fiction," *Novel*, 9 (1975): 130–40.

4. George Levine, "Isabel, Gwendolen and Dorothea," *English Literary History* 30 (September 1963): 256.

5. Henry James, *The Wings of the Dove* (New York: Charles Scribner's Sons, 1909) 2:298.

6. Robert Polhemus, *Comic Faith: The Great Tradition from Austen to Joyce*

(Chicago: University of Chicago Press, 1980), 211.

7. Dorrit Cohn, *Transparent Minds*, 117.

8. Ibid., 115.

9. Wayne Booth, *The Rhetoric of Fiction* (Chicago: University of Chicago Press, 1961), 247.

10. The phrase was coined by Robert Louis Stevenson.

11. William Ernest Henley, Review of *The Egoist* in *The Academy* 394 (22 November 1879): 369. Reprinted in Maurice Buxton Forman, ed., *George Meredith: Some Early Appreciations* (New York: Charles Scribner's Sons, 1909), 191–93.

12. Abel Chevalley, *Le Roman anglais de notre temps*, 55 (my translation).

13. Booth, *Rhetoric of Fiction*, 199.

14. Jonathan Smith, in " 'The Cock of Lordly Plume': Sexual Selection and *The Egoist*" in *Nineteenth-Century Literature* 50 (June 1995), provides a useful exegesis of how Meredith's novel explores "the controversial topics of evolutionary theory and the rights of women. . . . In its depictions of courtship it both exploits and challenges Darwin's theories about sexual selection" (51; 52). Smith argues persuasively that "Meredith's view of sexual selection among humans is more critical than Darwin's, more interested in exposing the tensions that Darwin suppresses. . . . Meredith joins [John Stuart] Mill [in *The Subjection of Women* (1869)] in rejecting the notion of female intellectual inferiority and in blaming the condition of women on men" (70; 74).

15. These two critical extremes may be represented by René Galland and Lionel Stevenson. Galland, in *George Meredith: Les cinquante premières années* (Paris: Les Presses Françaises, 1923), laments Laetitia's fate as follows: "Her weariness and her feebleness do not allow her to resist forever. We pity this wife of Willoughby with all our hearts" (390; my translation). Stevenson, on the other hand, notes in *The Ordeal of George Meredith* that "in maintaining the suspense of [the novel's denouement], the author failed to make Laetitia's behavior convincing" (232). Laetitia's treatment by the critics may be explained at least in part by the way in which Meredith introduces her as a "shy violet" and contrasts her apparent passivity to the energies of Clara, Mrs. Mountstuart Jenkinson, and the absent Constantia. By the final act of the comedy, however, when Laetitia asserts an imposing tough-mindedness in beginning to bring Willoughby under control, the reader—and Willoughby—may plainly see in her a true strength of character.

16. The comic spirit in *The Egoist* has been associated with Vernon Whitford (see Stevenson, *Ordeal*, 231, and Norman Kelvin, *A Troubled Eden*, 108–09) as well as with Clara Middleton (see Gillian Beer, *Meredith*, 133, S. R. Swaminathan, "Meredith's Pictures of the Comic Muse and Clara Middleton," *Notes and Queries* 11 (1964): 228–29, Robert S. Baker, "Faun and Satyr: Meredith's Theory of Comedy and *The Egoist*," *Mosaic* 9 (1976): 193, and Maaja A. Stewart and Elvira Casal, "Clara Middleton: Wit and Pattern in *The Egoist*," *Studies in the Novel* 12 (1980): 211). Baker, Stewart and Casal, and Gary Handwerk (*Irony and Ethics in Narrative*), however, all caution against the oversimplification, in Handwerk's words, of "*equating* Clara, or anyone else, with the corrective Comic Spirit" (emphasis added). Handwerk goes on to note that "Individuals are at most the occasional agents of it for others" (95) and, taking a position relatively close to the one I will take in the argument that follows, he singles out Laetitia as the most important of these "agents": she is the character "who emerges as the most skilled reader as

the text advances, and who is most successful in restoring a measure of hermeneutic integrity to the situation" (105).

17. Stevenson, *Ordeal*, 227.

18. Donald R. Swanson, in *Three Conquerors: Character and Method in the Mature Works of George Meredith* (The Hague: Mouton, 1969), notes that "the fact that her father has a private income at all suggests that they are not so poor as Laetitia makes out" (48). But Laetitia here is anticipating what her life is to be *after* her father's death, when the outlook is bleak indeed.

19. Jane Austen, *Pride and Prejudice*, ed. Donald Gray (New York: Norton Critical Edition, 2001), 1:22:83.

20. Susan Payne effectively sums up the function of these characters: "Mrs. Mountstuart, a development of a series of dowagers in nineteenth-century literature, is, like her forebears, a protective figure for young heroines only if they fit into the social scheme . . . ; the ladies Busshe and Culmer. . . . [b]acked by Mrs. Mountstuart Jenkinson and counterpointed by Willoughby's aunts Isobel and Eleanor . . . provide the comic chorus in the novel. They are above all gimlet-eyed observers of the state of affairs at Patterne and are not to be deceived" (*Difficult Discourse*, 144; 158).

21. Here again we encounter the theme that Allon White so effectively develops in relation to Meredith's fiction in *The Uses of Obscurity*.

22. Henry James, *The Portrait of a Lady* (New York: Charles Scribner's Sons, 1908), 2:79. Dorothy Van Ghent in *The English Novel* (New York: Rinehart, 1953) suggests some other interesting parallels between Osmond and Willoughby (190–92).

23. Randall Craig, "Promising Marriage: *The Egoist*, Don Juan, and the Problem of Language," *English Literary History* 56 (1989): 898.

24. Ibid., 913.

25. Robert Polhemus's description of the typical form of Willoughby's speech: "the verbal wrappings of his egoism unwind until the naked shrieking 'I' is laid bare upon the page" (*Comic Faith*, 244).

26. See Sophie Gilmartin's illuminating discussion of how nineteenth-century accounts of suttee (Sanskrit "sati," literally "good woman") display an "admiration for the Hindu widow (especially the young and attractive widow) who sacrifices herself, [an admiration that] has parallels with what I would argue is a sentimentalization of the young widow in English culture. In entreating Clara to be 'true to [his] dust, true to [his] name!' Willoughby sentimentalizes his fiancée in her imagined future role as his faithful 'relict'" (*Ancestry and Narrative in Nineteenth-Century British Literature* [Cambridge: Cambridge University Press, 1998], 188).

27. Neil Roberts usefully defines "monologist" in relation to this same exchange "in the sense that [Willoughby's] word is designed to repel or divert the word of the other. In the most literal sense, he does not enter into dialogue. . . . Like his generic models in Molière, Willoughby is largely the creation of his own discourse" (*Meredith and the Novel*, 160).

28. Robert Polhemus notes in this extended conversation in Chapter 6 "the clear pattern of the book as a whole: Willoughby makes a self-defeating attempt to absorb the soul and individuality of a woman and in doing so teaches her the necessity of her independence for self preservation" (*Comic Faith*, 214).

29. Roberts, *Meredith and the Novel*, 161.

30. George Eliot, *Middlemarch* (New York: Norton Critical Edition, 2000) 20:125; 126.

31. Payne, *Difficult Discourse*, 136.

32. Gary Handwerk suggests that this epithet, like those of Mrs. Mountstuart Jenkinson, also involves dangers: Clara "sees more by employing it, but also less, due to the hermeneutic overconfidence it engenders" (*Irony and Ethics in Narrative*, 99).

33. Janet Horowitz Murray, *Courtship and the English Novel*, 91.

34. Charles J. Hill, "Theme and Image in *The Egoist*," *University of Kansas City Review* 20 (1954): 282. Hill provides a hair-raising catalogue of "the imagery of devouring" in the novel, and Judith Wilt also discusses the novel's imagery of violence, but points out that there is only "one act of direct physical brutality in the book"—Willoughby's collaring of Crossjay just after Clara and De Craye return from the railway station (*The Readable People of George Meredith*, 165–69).

35. Smith, "'The Cock of Lordly Plume,'" 76; 51; 76.

36. "That he might ease *her* heart of its charitable love," which is a misprint, has been emended to read "*his*," as in the first edition.

37. Stephanie Green has put the point effectively: "Willoughby's role as the English cavalier is revealed as a disguise for his rather more sinister incarnation as the domesticated Gothic patriarch who preys upon women and children" ("'Nature Was Strong in Him': Spoiling the Empire Boy in George Meredith's *The Egoist*," *Australasian Victorian Studies Annual*, 5:89).

38. Handwerk, *Irony and Ethics in Narrative*, 104.

39. Alanna Kathleen Brown, "The Self and the Other: George Meredith's *The Egoist*," in *Women and Violence in Literature: An Essay Collection*, ed. Katherine Anne Ackley (Garland: New York, 1990), 110.

40. J. Hillis Miller, "'Herself Against Herself': The Clarification of Clara Middleton," *The Representation of Women in Fiction*, eds. Carolyn G. Heilbrun and Margaret R. Higonnet (Baltimore: Johns Hopkins University Press, 1981), 106.

41. Miller, "'Herself Against Herself,'" 102; 104; 106.

42. Handwerk, *Irony and Ethics in Narrative*, 126.

43. Gary Handwerk, "Irony as Intersubjectivity: Lacan on Psychoanalysis and Literature," *Comparative Criticism: A Yearbook* 7 (1985): 123.

44. Handwerk, *Irony and Ethics in Narrative*, 127.

45. See above, Chapter 1, section 3. As I have also noted in Chapter 1, it is quite possible to see a regressive side to Meredith's feminism—some, for example, will see Meredith's use of the traditional comic marriage resolution to Laetitia's and Clara's plots as regressive. What I am arguing here is not that Meredith's plots will provide a "satisfactory" post-modern resolution for his female heroes, but that he is developing what, for the 1870s, was an avant-garde position. For an overview of progressive and regressive aspects of Meredith's position in this novel, including the problems raised by the narrative tone of patriarchal benevolence, see Carolyn Williams, "Unbroken Patternes: Gender, Culture, and Voice in *The Egoist*," *Browning Institute Studies*, 13 (1985): 45–70, and David McWhirter, "Imagining a Distance: Feminism and Comedy in Meredith's *The Egoist*, 263–85.

46. Donald Swanson notes that by the novel's end, Laetitia is able "partially to change, herself, but only at the expense of a disillusionment that makes love, at

least in [her] earlier, sentimental sense, no longer possible" (*Three Conquerors*, 48). This statement strikes me as a variation on the unwarranted "lament" I have mentioned previously (above, note 15). Laetitia's "disillusionment" is central to what I see as Meredith's purposes: in all his fiction the demise of sentimental—that is, self-deluded—love is critical if anything approaching a healthy marital relationship is to become possible. Whether or not the impending marriage of Willoughby and Laetitia could begin to generate such "health" is highly problematic, but Meredith is at the least indicating the necessary first steps. (I am indebted here to Gary Handwerk [*Irony and Ethics in Narrative*, 211], who suggests, I now feel correctly, that an earlier, rather different published version of this argument, in which I was somewhat more sanguine about the possibilities of the Willoughby-Laetitia marriage, was overstated.)

47. For my use of this term, see note 29 of the Introduction.

48. Carolyn Williams seems to miss this reforming aspect of "the ever-waiting Laetitia Dale," whom she groups with the "female voices upholding and reinforcing the traditional Patterne of male dominance" ("Unbroken Patternes," 52). But in a note Williams makes it clear that she sees this reinforcement coming to an end in the novel's last chapters as she points to the precise aspect of Laetitia's role I am discussing here: "By the time [Willoughby] engages to marry her, she is older, wiser, and less subservient and doting. By the novel's closure *she is a figure of potential change*" (my emphasis). Williams adds an important caveat when she notes that "actual change is projected by implication only, beyond the novel's closing frame" (69).

49. In "Natural Selection and Narrative Form in *The Egoist*," (*Victorian Studies* 27 [autumn 1983]: 53–79), Carolyn Williams suggests that Laetitia's sickliness is an indication that she "has become too weak to echo and reflect" Willoughby, which may be taken both in the sense of Laetitia as ego-satisfying mirror and as the potential mother of his children. Thus, "having pronounced others extinct, he ends in danger of extinction himself." While I do not question that the text supports this admonition, I find it most interesting that Williams goes directly on to suggest a rather different reading, one which highlights the *strength* of Laetitia's new status of disillusionment in relation to Willoughby: "If he is to have a bride at all, he must have her on her own terms, breaking the sterility of his isolation by permitting difference from his pattern" (75).

50. An additional piece of evidence that a new way of life at Patterne Hall may have indeed begun at the novel's end is Laetitia's insistence that Willoughby restore Adam Flitch to his household staff. In a note on "The Functions of Flitch in *The Egoist*," *Nineteenth-Century Fiction* 24 (1969): 234, Michael C. Sundell mentions in a footnote that "Flitch's name would have recalled to Victorian readers the 'Dunmow Flitch,' a side of bacon traditionally awarded at Dunmow in Essex to any married couple who could prove that they had lived in conjugal harmony for a year and a day." While Sundell reads Laetitia's success in reinstating Flitch as an intensification of Meredith's irony, I would argue that Willoughby's yielding to Laetitia's demand can, on the contrary, be seen in a different light—as an indication of some possibilities for positive change at Patterne Hall.

51. See Roger B. Wilkenfeld's essay, "Hands Around: Image and Theme in *The Egoist*," *English Literary History* 34 (1967): 367–79, for an interesting exegesis of the ways in which "the image of the hand . . . is carried along through an elabo-

rate series of associations until, at the climax of the fable, it is fully translated into action and becomes the pivot upon which the denouement turns" (369).

CHAPTER 5: *ONE OF OUR CONQUERORS*

1. Meredith to Lady Ulricha Duncombe, 19 April 1902, *The Letters of George Meredith*, 3:1438.
2. Barbara Hardy, *"Lord Ormont and his Aminta* and *The Amazing Marriage,"* in *Meredith Now*, ed. Ian Fletcher, 308.
3. For an interesting feminist reading of *Diana*, see Jane Marcus, "'Clio in Calliope': History and Myth in Meredith's *Diana of the Crossways"* in *Art and Anger: Reading Like a Woman* (Columbus: Ohio State University Press, 1988), 20–48.
4. See Elizabeth Langland's *Nobody's Angels: Middle-Class Women and Domestic Ideology in Victorian Culture* (Ithaca: Cornell University Press, 1995) for an extended treatment of this issue, including a useful analysis of the "persistent myth" of the idle middle-class woman in her separate sphere, a sphere Langland persuasively shows to be much less separate than has been popularly supposed. It is precisely this myth of domestic refuge—so dominant in Victor's thinking—that Meredith is at pains to demolish in his portrait of the Radnor ménage.
5. Donald Stone provides a serviceable summary of the situation: "As a young man [Victor] married an elderly woman for her money; for twenty years he lived with another woman, Nataly, waiting for Mrs. Burman to die. Meredith is not concerned with the lawlessness of Victor's action, but with Victor's inability to face the consequences of his act" (*Novelists in a Changing World*, 160).
6. Walter Wright, Susan Payne, and Gayla McGlamery all note the prefiguring qualities of Victor's fall: *Art and Substance in George Meredith* (188), *Difficult Discourse* (197), and "'The Malady Afflicting England': *One of Our Conquerors* as Cautionary Tale," *Nineteenth-Century Literature* 46 (December 1991): 334.
7. Stone, *Novelists*, 165–66.
8. Ibid., 160.
9. Donald Swanson makes a similar point: "If there is applause for him, he understands; but opposition is inexplicable" (*Three Conquerors*, 124).
10. Fabian Gudas, "George Meredith's *One of Our Conquerors*," in *From Jane Austen to Joseph Conrad*, ed. Robert C. Rathburn and Martin Steinmann, Jr. (Minneapolis: University of Minnesota Press, 1958), 232.
11. Gillian Beer, *"One of Our Conquerors*: Language and Music," *Meredith Now*, ed. Ian Fletcher, 273.
12. Langland, *Nobody's Angels*, 14.
13. Walter E. Houghton, *The Victorian Frame of Mind: 1830–1870* (New Haven: Yale University Press, 1957), 190.
14. From Act 2 of *Lucrezia Borgia*. Meredith's irony is more than a little evident here, since *il segreto* is sung by a character who is about to drink poisoned wine.
15. *The Ordeal of Richard Feverel*, 261.
16. Judith Wilt, *The Readable People of George Meredith*, 194.
17. The phrase is taken from Meredith's 1877 story, "The Case of General Ople

and Lady Camper," in which the eponymous hero is admonished for "nurs[ing] the absurd idea of being one of our conquerors" (21:185).

18. Stendhal, *Le Rouge et le noir* (Paris: Garnier-Flammarion, 1964), 1:24:182.

19. Judith Wilt has effectively summarized Nataly's situation: "Her tragedy is that she has failed the man she loves by failing to challenge *his* obsession with *her* clearer understanding, by failing to support his brain with hers" (*The Readable People of George Meredith*, 193).

20. George Eliot, *Middlemarch*, 20:124.

21. Her full name is Nesta Victoria, but she is most frequently called Fredi by Victor, a nickname in honor of their friend, the prima donna Sanfredini.

22. As reported in the diary of Tolstoy's wife, November 20, 1876. Translated by George Gibian in his edition of *Anna Karenina* (New York: W. W. Norton, 1970), 751.

23. Jane Austen, *Pride and Prejudice*, 3:14:230–234.

24. Northrop Frye, *Anatomy of Criticism*, 169.

25. Austen, *Pride and Prejudice,* 3:19:253.

26. These terms refer to Dartrey, but also accurately describe Nesta at the novel's end.

27. Donald Swanson refers to this and a number of other uses of water imagery in the novel and makes the useful observation that such metaphors are opposed to Meredith's alpine imagery, which "applies to the use of the directed intelligence"; "the image of the sea, in direct contrast, is used to indicate the dominance of sensation" (*Three Conquerors*, 138).

28. Ibid., 132.

29. *The Ordeal of Richard Feverel*, 226. This aphorism may be more familiar to some readers where it surfaces as the telegraph message Stephen Dedalus sends to Buck Mulligan in the "Scylla and Charybdis" chapter of *Ulysses*.

30. Robert Humphrey, *Stream of Consciousness in the Modern Novel* (Berkeley: University of California Press, 1954), 50.

31. Susan Morgan, *Sisters in Time*, 177.

CHAPTER 6: *LORD ORMONT AND HIS AMINTA*

1. E. M. Forster, *Aspects of the Novel* (New York: Harcourt, 1927), 89.

2. An exception is Graham McMaster's essay, "All for Love: the Imperial Moment in *Lord Ormont and His Aminta*," *Shiron*, 30 (1991), 35–55, which analyzes *Lord Ormont* in terms of its linkage of Meredith's liberal-radical critique of Victorian imperialism with its "discourse of liberated sexuality" (35). Useful earlier essays are Barbara Hardy's "*Lord Ormont and His Aminta* and *The Amazing Marriage*" in *Meredith Now*, ed. Ian Fletcher, 295–312, and Marjorie Goss's "Names and the Search for Self in *Lord Ormont and His Aminta*," *Publications of the Missouri Philological Association,* 2 (1977): 39–45.

3. Donald Stone, *Novelists in a Changing World*, 170.

4. Gillian Beer, *A Change of Masks,* 186.

5. Robert Humphrey, *Stream of Consciousness in the Modern Novel*, 2–3.

6. See Chapter 2, section 3 above for a discussion of Sir Austin Feverel's "science" and Meredith's critique of the distorted vision inherent in objectivity claims.

7. Goss, "Names," 39.

8. For an excellent treatment of this subject, see Karla K. Walters, "Ladies of Leisure: Idle Womanhood in the Victorian Novel," (Ph.D. diss., University of Oregon, 1980).

9. George Eliot stresses Gwendolen Harleth's absolute horror of being viewed as "Mrs. Grandcourt run away," a note consistent with the time setting of *Daniel Deronda* in the seventies. As far as Meredith allows us to see, Aminta's development takes her to the point at which she doesn't give a second thought to being viewed as Lady Ormont run away.

10. D. H. Lawrence, *Women in Love* (New York: Penguin Books, 1995), 13:148.

11. Jacques Derrida, *Of Grammatology*, 158; 218.

12. Barbara Hardy, "*Lord Ormont and His Aminta* and *The Amazing Marriage*," in *Meredith Now*, 296–97.

13. Edward W. Said, *The World, the Text, and the Critic* (Cambridge, Mass.: Harvard University Press, 1983),193; 199.

14. Wolfgang Iser, *The Implied Reader* (Baltimore: The Johns Hopkins University Press, 1974), 32.

15. If this is the case, presumably the letter from Lady Charlotte that ends the novel with its announcement of Ormont's death will resolve the issue.

CHAPTER 7: *THE AMAZING MARRIAGE*

1. Barbara Hardy, "*Lord Ormont and His Aminta* and *The Amazing Marriage*" in *Meredith Now*, ed. Ian Fletcher, 305.

2. I am in agreement with Barbara Hardy when she notes that she "cannot quite accept Gillian Beer's view of Carinthia as 'uncivilized, instinctive,' if she really means to imply that this is primitive and under-rational. Carinthia seems to me to acquire the analytic mode without losing anything of instinctive strength" ("*Lord Ormont*," 307). To put this another way, the novel traces Carinthia's development of Meredithian emotional intelligence (see note 30 of the Introduction).

3. Joseph Warren Beach, *The Comic Spirit in George Meredith*, 21.

4. Lionel Stevenson, *The Ordeal of George Meredith*, 320.

5. Judith Wilt discusses the more problematic side of this narrative strategy— the Modern Novelist's "practically unforgivable silence about some major actions on the Dame's battlefield" (*The Readable People of George Meredith*, 224).

6. Sir Walter Scott, *Waverley; or, 'Tis Sixty Years Since*, ed. Claire Lamont (Oxford: Oxford University Press, 1981), 22:105. See Robert Kiely's useful reading of this passage and situation in *The Romantic Novel in England* (Cambridge, Mass.: Harvard University Press, 1972), 144–45.

7. Stevenson, *Ordeal*, 321.

8. Wilt, *Readable People*, 241.

9. Wilt seems to imply that Fleetwood is a "reader" from the outset, though "he allows his contemptuous egoism and his abstract sentimental posturing to interfere with his capacity to read character and situation" (242–43). I would put much more emphasis on Fleetwood's slow and incomplete development, through adversity, of his powers of "reading."

10. The saying is usually attributed to Sir William Blackstone. See Lee Hol-

combe, *Wives and Property: Reform of the Married Women's Property Law in Nineteenth-Century England* (Toronto: University of Toronto Press, 1983), 18.

11. Hardy, *"Lord Ormont,"* 309.

12. Ibid., 308.

13. Wilt, *Readable People*, 243.

14. Gillian Beer, *Meredith: A Change of Masks*, 170.

15. Jack Lindsay, *George Meredith: His Life and Work* (London: The Bodley Head, 1956), 324.

16. Meredith to Richard Le Gallienne, 21 December 1894, *The Letters of George Meredith*, 3:1182.

17. It is immediately after these lines that the narrative shifts for the final time to the voice of Dame Gossip, whose avowed aim from the outset in her treatment of Carinthia's parents is to present character in a romantic, emblematic, non-analytical mode. Gillian Beer and Judith Wilt both provide useful discussions of Meredith's play with these two narrators and the tensions between them.

18. Another good example of Carinthia's assertive maturity is found in the scene in Chapter 37 when she responds to Fleetwood's verbal game-playing with sexual threats by the definitive statement, "'I guard my rooms'" (19:388). See Barbara Hardy's excellent analysis of this section in *"Lord Ormont,"* 310–11.

19. Beer, *Meredith*, 172.

20. See above, Chapter 5, section 8.

21. Jane Austen, *Pride and Prejudice*, 3:14:232.

22. Beer, *Meredith*, 172.

23. Jane Austen, *Emma*, ed. Stephen M. Parrish (New York: Norton Critical Edition, 2000), 1:3:13.

24. Richard Poirier, *The Renewal of Literature*, 95, quoted in Introduction.

25. Lindsay, *George Meredith*, 324.

CONCLUSION

1. Constantine P. Curran, *James Joyce Remembered* (London: Oxford University Press, 1968), 52.

2. John Lucas, "Meredith's Reputation," in *Meredith Now*, ed. Ian Fletcher, 12.

3. John Sutherland, "A Revered Corpse," *Times Literary Supplement*, 5 September 1997 (4927), 5.

4. James Francken, "All Their Dreaming's Done," *London Review of Books,* 8 May 2003, 25:9:37.

5. George Levine, *The Realistic Imagination* (Chicago: University of Chicago Press, 1981), 21; 6; 3.

6. Hillis Miller, *Fiction and Repetition*, 46.

7. Levine, *The Realistic Imagination*, 4.

8. Harold Bloom, *The Anxiety of Influence: A Theory of Poetry*, 2d ed. (New York: Oxford University Press, 1997), xxiii.

9. I am echoing Daniel Mark Fogel here, who describes "the early development of James Joyce from *Stephen Hero* through *A Portrait of the Artist as a Young Man* as a series of responses to, and evasions of, Henry James" (*Covert Relations:*

James Joyce, Virginia Woolf, and Henry James, 3). One of the things I find fascinating about Fogel's excellent study of James's influence on Woolf and Joyce is how often George Meredith's name appears in the process, a name that Fogel appropriately, in his focus on James, largely passes over without comment.

10. Bloom, *Anxiety of Influence*, xxiii.

11. Richard Ellmann, *James Joyce* (Oxford: Oxford University Press, 1959) 168. Curran's comments come from a BBC broadcast, "Portrait of James Joyce" (n.d.). When he wrote down his recollections of this scene much later, Curran simply noted that Joyce "lifted his eyebrows when I said I found Meredith in *Stephen Hero*. When I suggested that some of the sentences in that MS. were as involved and obscure as Meredith's own, he wondered at my obtuseness" (Curran, *James Joyce Remembered*, 30).

12. Brian Caraher, "A Question of Genre: Generic Experimentation, Self-Composition, and the Problem of Egoism in *Ulysses*,"note 12, *English Literary History*, 54 (spring 1987): 212.

13. Bloom, *Anxiety of Influence*, xxiv.

14. James Joyce, *The Critical Writings*, ed. Ellsworth Mason and Richard Ellmann (New York: Viking Press, 1959), 89.

15. Stanislaus Joyce, *My Brother's Keeper* (New York: Viking Press, 1969), 205.

16. *The Ordeal of Richard Feverel*, 127.

17. Donald Fanger, "Joyce and Meredith: A Question of Influence and Tradition," *Modern Fiction Studies*, 6 (summer 1960): 127.

18. Ibid., 130.

19. Caraher, "A Question of Genre," 185. Caraher borrows the term "visionary intensity" from Walter Allen, *The English Novel* (New York: E. P. Dutton and Co., 1954), 275.

20. Ibid., 187.

21. The latter two prose influences were suggested early on by T. S. Eliot (Harry Levin, *James Joyce* [New York: New Directions, 1960], 49). See Daniel Mark Fogel, *Covert Relations*, chapters 2 and 3, for extensive analysis of specific Jamesean presences in Joyce.

22. Ellmann, *James Joyce*, 54; 294.

23. Caraher, "A Question of Genre," 184; A. Walton Litz, "The Genre of *Ulysses*" in *The Theory of the Novel: New Essays*, ed. John Halperin, 116.

24. Litz, "The Genre of *Ulysses*," 115. Litz borrows the term "intrinsic genre" from E. D. Hirsch, Jr., *Validity in Interpretation* (New Haven: Yale University Press, 1967), 78–89.

25. Lawrence to Edward Garnett, 1 Feb 1913, *The Letters of D. H. Lawrence*, ed. James T. Boulton (Cambridge: Cambridge University Press, 1979), 1:509.

26. Bloom, *Anxiety of Influence*, xxiv.

27. Lawrence to Louie Burrows, 27 March 1911, 2 April 1911, 27 Dec 1910, *Letters of D. H. Lawrence*, 1:242; 1:250; 1:214.

28. D. H. Lawrence, "Foreword," *Women in Love*, 485–86.

29. *The Ordeal of Richard Feverel*, 465.

30. Lawrence, *Women in Love*, 3:42. Gerald Crich also functions to represent the dangers of the purely rational view in this novel—for example, in the famous scene in which he insists on riding his terrified mare up close to a loudly clanking train engine ("Coal Dust," 9:110–12) or in his reverence for the rational order

produced by "the great social productive machine" ("The Industrial Magnate," 17:227).

31. D. H. Lawrence, *St. Mawr* (New York: Alfred A. Knoff, 1928), 74; 52.

32. Lawrence to Edward Garnett, 5 June 1914, *The Letters of D. H. Lawrence*, ed. George J. Zytaruk and James T. Boulton (Cambridge: Cambridge University Press, 1981), 2:183.

33. Robert Kiely, *Beyond Egotism: The Fiction of James Joyce, Virginia Woolf, and D. H. Lawrence* (Cambridge, Mass.: Harvard University Press, 1980), 11.

34. E. M. Forster, *Aspects of the Novel*, 89.

35. Ibid.

36. Conrad to J. B. Pinker, 16 June 1901 and 30 July 1907, *The Collected Letters of Joseph Conrad*, ed. Frederick R. Karl and Laurence Davies (Cambridge: Cambridge University Press, 1986; 1988), 2:333; 3:460.

37. Ford Madox Ford, *Return to Yesterday* (New York: Liveright, 1932), 394.

38. Lionel Stevenson, *The Ordeal of George Meredith*, 268.

39. Henry James, "The Lesson of Balzac," in *The Future of the Novel* (New York: Vintage Books, 1956), 105.

40. James to Edmund Gosse, 22 Aug 1894, *Henry James Letters*, ed. Leon Edel (Cambridge, Mass.: Harvard University Press, 1980), 3:485–86. It is interesting, partly as a way to read the "scenic" sensibility in James against the lyrical impulse in Virginia Woolf, to compare her response to *Lord Ormont* in a late diary entry: "I began Lord *Ormont and his Aminta* and found it so rich, so knotted, so alive, and muscular after the pale little fiction I'm used to, that, alas, it made me wish to write fiction again. Meredith underrated. I like his effort to escape plain prose. And he had humour and some insight too—more than they allow him now" (Virginia Woolf, 27 March 1937, *A Writer's Diary*, ed. Leonard Woolf [New York: Harcourt Brace Jovanovich, 1973], 269).

41. Henry James, "Preface to *The Ambassadors*," in *The Art of the Novel* (New York: Scribner's Sons, 1934), 322. See Percy Lubbock's loaded distinction between "scene" and "panorama" in *The Craft of Fiction* (New York: Viking Press, 1957), 66 f., and Sergio Perosa's "Middle Period: (2) Experimental Techniques" in *Henry James and the Experimental Novel*, 45–76.

42. Meredith to Louisa Lawrence, 20 February 1907, *The Letters of George Meredith*, 3:1588.

43. Frederick Crews, *E. M. Forster: The Perils of Humanism* (Princeton: Princeton University Press, 1962), 99; 100.

44. Lionel Trilling, *E. M. Forster* (New York: Harcourt Brace Jovanovich, 1971), 77.

45. E. M. Forster, *Howards End* (New York: Penguin Books, 2000), 100. *Howards End* was published in 1910 and, although published in 1908, much of *A Room with a View* was written in 1903, before the composition of *Where Angels Fear to Tread* (1905) and *The Longest Journey* (1907).

46. James Francken's recent (and inaccurate) summation of Forster's dismissive treatment of Meredith is typical: " 'The Home Counties posing as the universe' was E. M. Forster's first impression on reading Meredith, and for many this slight became the last word" ("All Their Dreaming's Done," *London Review of Books*, 8 May 2003, 25:9:37).

47. Forster, *Aspects of the Novel*, 89–90. This is Virginia Woolf's condensed version of the passage as quoted at the opening of "The Novels of George Meredith."

48. Fogel, *Covert Relations*, 1.

49. Virginia Woolf, "On Re-reading Meredith," *The Essays of Virginia Woolf: 1912–1918*, Vol. 2, ed. Andrew McNeillie (London: The Hogarth Press, 1987), 274–75.

50. Ibid., 273.

51. Fogel, *Covert Relations*, 93.

52. Woolf, "The Novels of George Meredith," 207.

53. Virginia Woolf, Typescript, "Notes of a Day's Walk," quoted in Fogel, *Covert Relations*, 70.

54. Harold Bloom, *Anxiety of Influence*, 14.

55. Virginia Woolf, *Mrs. Dalloway* (New York: Harcourt, Brace & World, 1925), 3–4.

Bibliography

Armstrong, Paul. *The Challenge of Bewilderment: Understanding and Representation in James, Conrad, and Ford.* Ithaca: Cornell University Press, 1987.

Austen, Jane. *Emma.* Ed. Stephen M. Parrish. New York: Norton Critical Edition, 2000.

————. *Pride and Prejudice.* Ed. Donald Gray. New York: Norton Critical Edition, 2001.

Baker, Robert S. "Faun and Satyr: Meredith's Theory of Comedy and *The Egoist.*" *Mosaic* 9 (1976): 173–93.

Bakhtin, M. M. *The Dialogic Imagination.* Ed. Michael Holquist. Trans. Caryl Emerson and Michael Holquist. Austin: University of Texas Press, 1981.

————. *Rabelais and His World.* Trans. Helene Iswolsky. Bloomington: Indiana University Press, 1984.

Barker, Debra Stoner. "Richard Feverel's Passage to Knighthood." *American Notes and Queries* 3 (October 1990): 168–71.

Bartlett, Phyllis. "Richard Feverel, Knight-Errant." *Bulletin of the New York Public Library* 63 (1959): 329–40.

Beach, Joseph Warren. *The Comic Spirit in George Meredith.* New York: Longmans, Green, 1911.

————. *The Twentieth-Century Novel.* New York: Appleton-Century-Crofts, 1932.

Beer, Gillian. *Meredith: A Change of Masks.* London: Athlone Press, 1970.

————. "*One of Our Conquerors*: language and music." In *Meredith Now: Some Critical Essays,* ed. Ian Fletcher. London: Routledge & Kegan Paul, 1971.

Bennett, Joan. *Virginia Woolf: Her Art as a Novelist.* Cambridge: Cambridge University Press, 1964.

Bloom, Harold. *The Anxiety of Influence: A Theory of Poetry.* 2d ed. New York: Oxford University Press, 1997.

Booth, Wayne. *The Rhetoric of Fiction.* Chicago: University of Chicago Press, 1961.

Bordo, Susan. *The Flight to Objectivity: Essays on Cartesianism and Culture.* Albany: State University of New York Press, 1987.

Brown, Alanna Kathleen. "The Self and the Other: George Meredith's *The Egoist.*" In *Women and Violence in Literature: An Essay Collection,* ed. Katherine Anne Ackley. New York: Garland, 1990.

Buckler, William E. "The Artistic Unity of Richard Feverel: Chapter XXXIII." *Nineteenth Century Fiction* 7 (1952): 119–23.

225

Buckley, Jerome Hamilton. *Season of Youth*. Cambridge, Mass.: Harvard University Press, 1974.

Campbell, Thomas. "Adrian's Shrug: A Note on the 'Wise Youth.'" *Victorian Newsletter* 66 (spring 1982): 19–20.

Caraher, Brian. "A Question of Genre: Generic Experimentation, Self-Composition, and the Problem of Egoism in *Ulysses*." *English Literary History* 54 (spring 1987): 183–214.

Chevalley, Abel. *Le Roman anglais de notre temps*. London: Humphrey Milford, 1921.

Christ, Carol. "Aggression and Providential Death in George Eliot's Fiction." *Novel*, 9 (1975): 130–40.

Cohn, Dorrit. *Transparent Minds: Narrative Modes for Presenting Consciousness in Fiction*. Princeton: Princeton University Press, 1978.

Conrad, Joseph. *The Collected Letters of Joseph Conrad*. Vols. 2 and 3. Ed. Frederick R. Karl and Laurence Davies. Cambridge: Cambridge University Press, 1986–1988.

Craig, Randall. "Promising Marriage: *The Egoist*, Don Juan, and the Problem of Language." *English Literary History* 56 (1989): 897–921.

Crews, Frederick. *E. M. Forster: The Perils of Humanism*. Princeton: Princeton University Press, 1962.

Curran, Constantine P. *James Joyce Remembered*. London: Oxford University Press, 1968.

———. "Portrait of James Joyce." B.B.C. broadcast, n.d.

Curtin, Frank. "Adrian Harley: The Limits of Meredith's Comedy." *Nineteenth-Century Fiction* 7 (1953): 272–82.

Derrida, Jacques. *Of Grammatology*. Trans. Gayatri Chakravorty Spivak. Baltimore: The Johns Hopkins University Press, 1976.

Duncan, Ian. *Modern Romance and Transformations of the Novel: The Gothic, Scott, Dickens*. Cambridge: Cambridge University Press, 1992.

Ekeberg, Gladys W. "*The Ordeal of Richard Feverel* as Tragedy." *College English* 7 (1946): 387–93.

Eliot, George. *Middlemarch*. Ed. Bert G. Hornback. New York: Norton Critical Edition, 2000.

Ellmann, Richard. *James Joyce*. Oxford: Oxford University Press, 1959.

Eysteinsson, Astradur. *The Concept of Modernism*. Ithaca: Cornell University Press, 1990.

Fanger, Donald. "Joyce and Meredith: A Question of Influence and Tradition." *Modern Fiction Studies* 6 (summer 1960): 125–30.

Fernandez, Ramon. *Messages*. Première série. Paris: Librairie Gallimard, 1926. Trans. Montgomery Belgion. *Messages*. New York: Harcourt, 1927.

Fielding, Henry. *Joseph Andrews*, Boston: Houghton Mifflin, 1961.

Flaubert, Gustave. *L'Éducation Sentimentale*. Paris: Éditons Garnier Frères, 1961.

———. *Madame Bovary*. Ed. Bernard Ajac. Paris: Garnier Flammarion, 1986.

Fletcher, Ian, ed. *Meredith Now: Some Critical Essays*. London: Routledge & Kegan Paul, 1971.

Fogel, Daniel Mark. *Covert Relations: James Joyce, Virginia Woolf, and Henry James*. Charlottesville: University of Virginia Press, 1990.

Ford, Ford Madox. *Return to Yesterday*. New York: Liveright, 1932.

Forman, Maurice Buxton, ed. *George Meredith: Some Early Appreciations*. New York: Charles Scribner's Sons, 1909.

Forster, E. M. *Aspects of the Novel*. New York: Harcourt, 1927.

———. *Howards End*. New York: Penguin Books, 2000.

———. *A Room with a View*. London: Penguin Books, 1964.

Foster, David E. "Rhetorical Strategy in *Richard Feverel*." *Nineteenth-Century Fiction* 26 (1971): 185–95.

Francken, James. "All Their Dreaming's Done." *London Review of Books*, 8 May 2003, 25:9:37.

Frye, Northrop. *Anatomy of Criticism*. New York: Atheneum, 1968.

Fuentes, Carlos. "Tilt." Review of Edith Grossman's translation of *Don Quixote*. *The New York Times Book Review* (2 November 2003): 15.

Galland, René. *George Meredith: Les cinquante premières années*. Paris: Les Presses Françaises, 1923.

Gilmartin, Sophie. *Ancestry and Narrative in Nineteenth-Century British Literature*. Cambridge University Press: Cambridge, 1998.

Gindin, James. *Harvest of a Quiet Eye: The Novel of Compassion*. Bloomington: Indiana University Press, 1971.

Goleman, Daniel. *Emotional Intelligence*. New York: Bantam, 1995.

———. "Ideas and Trends: The Decline of the Nice-Guy Quotient." *The New York Times*, 10 September 1995, E6.

Goss, Marjorie. "Names and the Search for Self in *Lord Ormont and His Aminta*." *Publications of the Missouri Philological Association*, 2 (1977): 39–45.

Graff, Gerald. *Literature Against Itself: Literary Ideas in Modern Society*. Chicago: University of Chicago Press, 1979.

Green, Stephanie. "'Nature Was Strong in Him': Spoiling the Empire Boy in George Meredith's *The Egoist*." *Australasian Victorian Studies Annual*, 5: 88–95.

Gudas, Fabian. "George Meredith's *One of Our Conquerors*." In *From Jane Austen to Joseph Conrad*, ed. Robert C. Rathburn and Martin Steinmann, Jr. Minneapolis: University of Minnesota Press, 1958.

Halperin, John. *The Theory of the Novel: New Essays*. New York: Oxford University Press, 1974.

Handwerk, Gary. *Irony and Ethics in Narrative: From Schlegel to Lacan*. New Haven: Yale University Press, 1985.

———. "Irony as Intersubjectivity: Lacan on Psychoanalysis and Literature." *Comparative Criticism: A Yearbook* 7 (1985): 105–126.

Hardy, Barbara. "*Lord Ormont and his Aminta* and *The Amazing Marriage*." In

Meredith Now: Some Critical Essays, ed. Ian Fletcher. London: Routledge & Kegan Paul, 1971.

———. "The Structure of Imagery: George Meredith's *Harry Richmond*." In *The Appropriate Form*. London: Athlone Press, 1964.

Harman, Barbara. "Rectitude and Larceny in *Diana of the Crossways*." In *The Feminine Political Novel in Victorian England*. Charlottesville: University Press of Virginia, 1998.

Henkle, Roger. *Comedy and Culture*. Princeton: Princeton University Press, 1980.

Henley, William Ernest. Review of *The Egoist* in *The Academy* 394 (22 Nov. 1879): 369. Reprinted in *George Meredith: Some Early Appreciations*, ed. Maurice Buxton Forman. New York: Charles Scribner's Sons, 1909.

Hergenhan, L. T., ed. "Introduction." *The Adventures of Harry Richmond*. Lincoln: University of Nebraska Press, 1970.

———. "Meredith's Use of Revision: A Consideration of the Revisions of *Richard Feverel* and *Evan Harrington*." *Modern Language Review* 59 (1964): 539–44.

———. "The Reception of George Meredith's Early Novels." *Nineteenth Century Fiction* 19 (1964): 220.

Hill, Charles J., ed. "Introduction." *The Ordeal of Richard Feverel*. New York: Holt, Rinehart and Winston, 1964.

———. "Theme and Image in *The Egoist*." *University of Kansas City Review* 20 (1954): 281–85.

Holcombe, Lee. *Wives and Property: Reform of the Married Women's Property Law in Nineteenth-Century England*. Toronto: University of Toronto Press, 1983.

Horne, Lewis. "Sir Austin, His Devil, and the Well-Designed World." *Studies in the Novel* 24 (1992): 35–47.

Houghton, Walter E. *The Victorian Frame of Mind: 1830–1870*. New Haven: Yale University Press, 1957.

Howard, David. "*Rhoda Fleming*: Meredith in the Margin." In *Meredith Now: Some Critical Essays*, ed. Ian Fletcher. London: Routledge & Kegan Paul, 1971.

Hubert, J. D. *Molière and the Comedy of Intellect*. Berkeley: University of California Press, 1962.

Humphrey, Robert. *Stream of Consciousness in the Modern Novel*. Berkeley: University of California Press, 1954.

Iser, Wolfgang. *The Implied Reader*. Baltimore: The Johns Hopkins University Press, 1974.

Ives, Maura, ed. "Introduction." *George Meredith's Essay On Comedy and Other New Quarterly Magazine Publications*. Lewisburg, Pa.: Bucknell University Press, 1998.

Jameson, Fredric. *The Political Unconscious: Narrative as a Socially Symbolic Act*. Ithaca: Cornell University Press, 1981.

James, Henry. *Henry James Letters*. Vol. 3. Ed. Leon Edel. Cambridge, Mass.: Harvard University Press, 1980.

———. "The Lesson of Balzac." In *The Future of the Novel*. New York: Vintage Books, 1956.

————. *The Portrait of a Lady*. New York: Charles Scribner's Sons, 1908.

————. "Preface to *The Ambassadors*." In *The Art of the Novel*. New York: Scribner's Sons, 1934.

————. *The Wings of the Dove*. New York: Charles Scribner's Sons, 1909.

Johnson, Diane. *Lesser Lives*. New York: Alfred A. Knopf, 1972.

Jones, Mervyn. *The Amazing Victorian: A Life of George Meredith*. London: Constable, 1999.

Joyce, James. *The Critical Writings*. Ed. Ellsworth Mason and Richard Ellmann. New York: Viking Press, 1959.

————. *A Portrait of the Artist as a Young Man*. New York: Penguin Books, 1993.

————. *Ulysses*. Ed. Jeri Johnson. New York: Oxford University Press, 1993.

Joyce, Stanislaus. *My Brother's Keeper*. New York: Viking Press, 1969.

Keen, Suzanne. *Victorian Renovations of the Novel: Narrative Annexes and the Boundaries of Representation*. Cambridge: Cambridge University Press, 1998.

Kelvin, Norman. *A Troubled Eden: Nature and Society in the Works of George Meredith*. Stanford, Calif.: Stanford University Press, 1961.

Kiely, Robert. *Beyond Egotism: The Fiction of James Joyce, Virginia Woolf, and D. H. Lawrence*. Cambridge, Mass.: Harvard University Press, 1980.

————. *The Romantic Novel in England*. Cambridge, Mass.: Harvard University Press, 1972.

Knoepflmacher, U. C. *Laughter and Despair*. Berkeley: University of California Press, 1971.

Korg, Jacob. "Expressive Styles in *The Ordeal of Richard Feverel*." *Nineteenth-Century Fiction* 27 (1972): 260.

Landis, Joseph C. "George Meredith's Comedy." *Boston University Studies in English* 2 (1956): 17–35.

Langland, Elizabeth. *Nobody's Angels: Middle-Class Women and Domestic Ideology in Victorian Culture*. Ithaca: Cornell University Press, 1995.

Lauter, Paul. *Theories of Comedy*. Garden City, N.Y.: Doubleday, 1964.

Lawrence, D. H. *The Letters of D. H. Lawrence*. Vol. 1. Ed. James T. Boulton. Cambridge: Cambridge University Press, 1979.

————. *The Letters of D. H. Lawrence*. Vol. 2. Ed. James T. Boulton and George J. Zytaruk. Cambridge: Cambridge University Press, 1981.

————. *St. Mawr*. New York: Vintage Books, 1928.

————. *Women in Love*. New York: Penguin Books, 1995.

Levin, Harry. *James Joyce*. New York: New Directions, 1960.

Levine, George. "Isabel, Gwendolen, and Dorothea." *English Literary History* 30 (September 1963): 244–57.

————. *The Realistic Imagination*. Chicago: University of Chicago Press, 1981.

Lindsay, Jack. *George Meredith: His Life and Work*. London: The Bodley Head, 1956.

Litz, A. Walton. "The Genre of *Ulysses*." In *The Theory of the Novel: New Essays*, ed. John Halperin. New York: Oxford University Press, 1974.

Lubbock, Percy. *The Craft of Fiction*. New York: Viking Press, 1957.

Lucas, John. "Meredith's Reputation." In *Meredith Now: Some Critical Essays*, ed. Ian Fletcher. London: Routledge & Kegan Paul, 1971.

Lunn, Eugene. *Marxism and Modernism: An Historical Study of Lukács, Brecht, Benjamin, and Adorno*. Berkeley: University of California Press, 1982.

Marcus, Jane. " 'Clio in Calliope': History and Myth in Meredith's *Diana of the Crossways*." In *Art and Anger: Reading Like a Woman*. Columbus: Ohio State University Press, 1988.

Martin, Robert. "Notes Toward a Comic Fiction." In *The Theory of the Novel: New Essays*, ed. John Halperin. New York: Oxford University Press, 1974.

———. *The Triumph of Wit*. Oxford: Oxford University Press, 1974.

McGlamery, Gayla S. " 'The Malady Afflicting England': *One of Our Conquerors* as Cautionary Tale." *Nineteenth-Century Literature* 46 (December 1991): 327–50.

McKeon, Michael. *The Origins of the English Novel, 1600–1740*. Baltimore: The Johns Hopkins University Press, 1987.

———, ed. *Theory of the Novel: A Historical Approach*. Baltimore: The Johns Hopkins University Press, 2000.

McMaster, Graham. "All for Love: the Imperial Moment in *Lord Ormont and His Aminta*." *Shiron* 30 (1991): 35–55.

McWhirter, David. "Imagining a Distance: Feminism and Comedy in Meredith's *The Egoist*." *Genre* 22 (fall 1989): 263–85.

Meredith, George. *The Letters of George Meredith*. 3 vols. Ed. C. L. Cline. Oxford: Clarendon Press, 1970.

———. *The Ordeal of Richard Feverel*. 1859 edition. Ed. Edward Mendelson. London: Penguin Books, 1998.

———. *The Poems of George Meredith*. 2 vols. Ed. Phyllis B. Bartlett. New Haven: Yale University Press, 1978.

———. *The Works of George Meredith*. Memorial Edition. 29 vols. New York: Scribner's Sons, 1910.

Michaut, G. *Les Luttes de Molière*. Paris: Librairie Hachette, 1925.

Mill, John Stuart. *The Subjection of Women*. Arlington Heights: AHM Publishing: 1980.

Miller, Hillis. *Fiction and Repetition*. Cambridge, Mass.: Harvard University Press, 1982.

———. " 'Herself Against Herself': the Clarification of Clara Middleton." In *The Representation of Women in Fiction*, ed. Carolyn G. Heilbrun and Margaret R. Higonnet. Baltimore: Johns Hopkins University Press, 1981.

Millet, Kate. *Sexual Politics*. New York: Doubleday, 1970.

Molière. *La Critique de L'École des femmes*. In *Oeuvres complètes de Molière*. Vol 1. Ed. René Bray and Jacques Scherer. Paris: Le Club du meilleur livre, 1954.

[Molière?]. "Lettre sur la comédie de L'Imposteur." In *Oeuvres complètes de Molière*. Vol 2. Ed. René Bray and Jacques Scherer. Paris: Le Club du meilleur livre, 1954.

Moore, W. G. *Molière: A New Criticism*. London: Oxford University Press, 1964.

Morgan, Susan. *Sisters in Time: Imagining Gender in Nineteenth-Century British Fiction*. Oxford: Oxford University Press, 1989.

Morris, John W. "Inherent Principles of Order in *Richard Feverel.*" *PMLA* 78 (1963): 333–40.

Moses, Joseph. *The Novelist as Comedian: George Meredith and the Ironic Sensibility*. New York: Schocken Books, 1983.

Muendel, Renate. *George Meredith*. Boston: Twayne, 1986.

Murray, Janet Horowitz. *Courtship and the English Novel: Feminist Readings in the Fiction of George Meredith*. New York: Garland, 1987.

Nagel, Thomas. *The View from Nowhere*. New York: Oxford University Press, 1986.

Payne, Susan. *Difficult Discourse: George Meredith's Experimental Fiction*. Pisa: Edizioni ETS, 1995.

Perosa, Sergio. *Henry James and the Experimental Novel*. Charlottesville: University Press of Virginia, 1978.

Plato, *Philebus*. Trans. Seth Benardete. Chicago: University of Chicago Press, 1993.

Poirier, Richard. *The Renewal of Literature*. New York: Random House, 1987.

Polhemus, Robert. *Comic Faith: The Great Tradition from Austen to Joyce*. Chicago: University of Chicago Press, 1980.

Priestly, J. B. *George Meredith*. New York: Macmillan, 1926.

Pykett, Lyn. *Engendering Fictions: The English Novel in the Early Twentieth Century*. London: Edward Arnold, 1995.

Ren, Robert. "Les Commentaires de première main sur les chefs-d'oeuvre de Molière." *Revue des sciences humaines* 81 (1956): 19–49.

Roberts, Neil. *Meredith and the Novel*. New York: St. Martin's Press, 1997.

Said, Edward W. *The World, the Text, and the Critic*. Cambridge, Mass.: Harvard University Press, 1983.

Scholes, Robert, and Robert Kellogg. *The Nature of Narrative*. Oxford University Press, 1966.

Scott, Sir Walter. *Ivanhoe*. Ed. Ian Duncan. Oxford: Oxford University Press, 1996.

———. *Waverley; or, 'Tis Sixty Years Since*. Ed. Claire Lamont. Oxford: Oxford University Press, 1981.

Shaheen, Mohammad. *George Meredith: A Reappraisal of the Novels*. Totowa: Barnes and Noble, 1981.

Sherman, Stuart Pratt. Meredith Obituary. 3 June 1909. *Nation* 88. Reprinted in *Meredith: The Critical Heritage*, ed. Ioan Williams. London: Routledge and Kegan Paul, 1971.

Simon, Richard Keller. *The Labyrinth of the Comic: Theory and Practice from Fielding to Freud*. Tallahassee: Florida State University Press, 1985.

Smirlock, Daniel. "The Models of *Richard Feverel.*" *The Journal of Narrative Technique* 11 (spring 1981): 91–109.

Smith, Jonathan. "'The Cock of Lordly Plume': Sexual Selection and *The Egoist*." *Nineteenth-Century Literature* 50 (June 1995): 57–77.

Spånberg, Sven-Johan. *The Ordeal of Richard Feverel and the Tradition of Realism*. Uppsala: Acta Universitatis Upsaliensis, 1974.

Sprinker, Michael. "'The Intricate Evasions of As': Meredith's Theory of Figure." *Victorian Newsletter* 53 (spring 1978): 9–12.

Stendhal. *La Chartreuse de Parme*. Paris: Le Livre de poche classique, 1972.

———. *Le Rouge et le noir*. Paris: Garnier-Flammarion, 1964.

Stevenson, Lionel. *The Ordeal of George Meredith*. New York: Scribner's Sons, 1953.

Stewart, Maaja A., and Elvira Casal. "Clara Middleton: Wit and Pattern in *The Egoist*." *Studies in the Novel* 12 (1980): 210–27.

Stone, Donald David. "Meredith and Bakhtin: Polyphony and *Bildung*." *Studies in English Literature* 28 (fall 1988): 693–712.

———. *Novelists in a Changing World*. Cambridge, Mass.: Harvard University Press, 1972.

Sundell, Michael C. "The Functions of Flitch in *The Egoist*." *Nineteenth-Century Fiction* 24 (1969): 227–35.

Sutherland, John. "A Revered Corpse." *Times Literary Supplement*, 5 September 1997, 4927:5.

Swaminathan, S. R. "Meredith's Pictures of the Comic Muse and Clara Middleton." *Notes and Queries* 11 (1964): 228–29.

Swanson, Donald R. *Three Conquerors: Character and Method in the Mature Works of George Meredith*. The Hague: Mouton, 1969.

Tarratt, Margaret. "*The Adventures of Harry Richmond*—*Bildungsroman* and Historical Novel." In *Meredith Now: Some Critical Essays*, ed. Ian Fletcher. London: Routledge & Kegan Paul, 1971.

Tolstoy, Leo. ["Woman's work."] Quoted in Sophia Tolstoy's diary. Tran. George Gibian. *Anna Karenina*. New York: Norton Critical Edition, 1970, 751.

Trilling, Lionel. *E. M. Forster*. New York: Harcourt Brace Jovanovich, 1971.

Van Ghent, Dorothy. *The English Novel*. New York: Rinehart, 1953.

Walters, Karla K. "Ladies of Leisure: Idle Womanhood in the Victorian Novel." Ph.D. diss., University of Oregon, 1980.

White, Allon. *The Uses of Obscurity: The Fiction of Early Modernism*. London: Routledge & Kegan Paul, 1981.

Wilkenfeld, Roger B. "Hands Around: Image and Theme in *The Egoist*." *English Literary History* 34 (1967): 367–79.

Williams, Carolyn. "Natural Selection and Narrative Form in *The Egoist*." *Victorian Studies* 27 (autumn 1983): 53–79.

———. "Unbroken Patternes: Gender, Culture, and Voice in *The Egoist*." *Browning Institute Studies* 13 (1985): 45–70.

Williams, I. M. "The Organic Structure of *The Ordeal of Richard Feverel*." *Review of English Studies* 18 (1967): 16–29.

Williams, Ioan, ed. *Meredith: The Critical Heritage*. London: Routledge & Kegan Paul, 1971.

Wilt, Judith. *The Readable People of George Meredith*. Princeton: Princeton University Press, 1975.

Woolf, Virginia. *Mrs. Dalloway*. New York: Harcourt, Brace & World, 1925.

———. "Notes of a Day's Walk." Typescript quoted in *Covert Relations: James Joyce, Virginia Woolf, and Henry James*, by Daniel Mark Fogel. Charlottesville, University of Virginia Press, 1990, 70.

———. "The Novels of George Meredith." In *The Second Common Reader*. New York: Harcourt, 1932.

———. "On Re-reading Meredith." *The Essays of Virginia Woolf: 1912–1918*. Vol. 2. Ed. Andrew McNeillie. London: The Hogarth Press, 1987.

———. "On Re-reading Novels." *The Essays of Virginia Woolf: 1919–1924*. Vol 3. Ed. Andrew McNeillie. New York: Harcourt Brace Jovanovich, 1988.

———. *A Writer's Diary*. Ed. Leonard Woolf. New York: Harcourt Brace Jovanovich, 1973.

Wright, Walter. *Art and Substance in George Meredith*. Lincoln: University of Nebraska Press, 1953.

Zola, Émile. *Le Roman expérimental*. Paris: Garnier-Flammarion, 1971.

Index